T0318902

Rhetoric in financial discourse

Utrecht Studies in Language and Communication

26

Series Editors

Wolfgang Herrlitz
Paul van den Hoven

Rhetoric in financial discourse

A linguistic analysis of ICT-mediated disclosure genres

Belinda Crawford Camiciottoli

Amsterdam - New York, NY 2013

Cover photo: www.morguefile.com

The paper on which this book is printed meets the requirements of "ISO
9706:1994, Information and documentation - Paper for documents -
Requirements for permanence".

ISBN: 978-90-420-3759-5
E-Book ISBN: 978-94-012-1010-2
©Editions Rodopi B.V., Amsterdam – New York, NY 2013
Printed in The Netherlands

Contents

List of tables and figures

Tables

Figures

Acknowledgements

This book was inspired by what I began to perceive as a disconnect between the type of language typically presented in business communication courses and the discourse that is actually found in the financial world. The rapid expansion of ICT-mediated corporate communication has resulted in new genres that have radically changed the ways that companies interact with their stakeholders. However, the teaching of business communication does not seem to adequately reflect these changes. Thanks to a personal contact in the finance profession, I became more aware of important new communicative trends, and decided to undertake this study as a way to help bridge the gap between academia and professional practice.

I would like to acknowledge several people whose support made a significant contribution to this project. First of all, I am very grateful to the finance professional who served as an informant to the study. His advice enabled me to procure the data for the analysis, and his insights that emerged during our interviews proved invaluable in interpreting the findings. I would also like to thank my friends and colleagues Inma Fortanet-Gómez, Miguel Ruiz-Garrido, Juan Carlos Palmer-Silveira, Gina Poncini, Christine Räisänen and Pilar Garcés-Conejos Blitvich, all of whom provided feedback during the various phases of the project. Their helpful comments and constructive criticism helped me to improve the final product considerably.

Finally, a special *thank you* goes to my husband, Adriano Camiciottoli, for his steadfast encouragement in all my endeavours.

Belinda Crawford Camiciottoli
Scandicci, Italy
August 2013

1.1 The rise of financial communication

Communication is an essential element of daily business operations. Whether written or spoken, for internal or external use, it is only through effective communication that a business can ensure that its message is clearly understood, and will thus more likely produce the desired outcomes. For this reason, *business discourse* has become a well-established discipline for the systematic study of how business professionals communicate, leading to an improved understanding of the nature and role of language in corporate settings (cf. Trosborg & Flyvholm Jørgensen, 2005, Bargiela-Chiappini, 2009).

Today financial communication represents one of the most important types of business discourse, specifically in the form of *financial disclosure*, or the periodic reporting and publication of economic data relating to a company's performance in order to inform interested parties of its current financial standing. Although large companies in many countries are legally required to regularly render financial information public, this type of reporting has taken on greater significance following the high-profile accounting scandals that shook the international corporate community in the early 2000s (e.g., Enron, Ahold, Parmalat). The on-going financial difficulties stemming from the global financial crisis that began at the end of 2008 have further accentuated a generalised loss of confidence in the corporate world. As a result, companies are now extremely keen to promote an image of transparency among their various stakeholders which include investors, shareholders, bankers and competitors, as well as the general public (Rogers, 2000; Gunnarsson, 2005). Accordingly, they have begun to look for innovative ways to disclose financial information, which has led to new communicative formats and instruments developed specifically for this purpose.

Advances in information and communication technology (hereinafter ICT) have played a key role in the emergence of new forms of financial disclosure. These technologies have succeeded in dramatically reshaping the communicative practices of businesses. Companies that effectively exploit ICT not only come across as more transparent, but also appear dynamic and innovative. Moreover, the concept of 'audience' for financial communication has taken on a new global meaning as it is now possible to establish essentially unlimited contacts throughout the world at relatively low costs.

For written communication, the Internet has become a valid instrument for diffusing reports and press releases containing earnings data, reaching far beyond traditional printed financial news sources (Strobbe & Jacobs, 2005). For oral communication, in addition to face-to-face live meetings, companies may now rely on teleconferencing which allows their executives to present financial results and interact directly with investors from all over the world in an extremely cost-effective way (Du-Babcock, 2004). This also allows companies to be better equipped to respond to the on-going challenges of globalisation as a critical factor for success in the business world.

Parallel to the growing impact of ICT on corporate financial disclosure, we have also witnessed the rise of English as the *lingua franca* of international business communication. Indeed, it is now beyond question that English has become the dominant language of business transactions (Louhiala-Salminen, 1996; Scollon & Scollon, 2001, Palmer-Silveira et al., 2006), and is used extensively by speakers of other languages as a *lingua franca* to conduct business (Vandermeeren, 1999; Louhiala-Salminen & Charles, 2006). Clearly, this is also the case when communication is of a financial nature.

1.2 The aim of the study

In light of the new trends in financial communication discussed above, the objective of this study is to contrastively analyse two key technology-mediated genres of English-language financial disclosure:[1]

-   *earnings presentations*, i.e., reports of financial results given by company executives via teleconferencing;
-   *earnings releases,* i.e., press releases of financial results published on the Internet.

Both earnings presentations and earnings releases contain information about quarterly economic results and both have the same broad communicative purpose: to bring the investment community up to date on the current financial situation and the future outlook of the company. Although some research has been done to identify and analyse the structural and linguistic features of the more traditional genres of financial disclosure, including annual reports (Thomas, 1997), letters from Chief Executive Officers (CEOs)

---

[1] . The term *genre* will be used in this study to refer to written and spoken texts that can be defined according to their communicative purpose, context of usage, structural patterning and prominent linguistic features (Swales, 1990). The notion of genre will be discussed thoroughly in Chapter 3.

to shareholders (Hyland, 1998), Chairmen's statements (Ruiz-Garrido et al., 2006), corporate press releases (McLaren & Gurău, 2005) and CEOs' live presentations of earnings results (Rogers, 2000), ICT-mediated earnings presentations and earnings releases have not yet been studied in-depth. What is more, because the two genres differ according to mode of delivery (spoken vs. written), they offer the opportunity to carry out comparative analyses on their distinctive structural, linguistic and, especially, rhetorical features.[2] In addition, by looking at two new technology-driven genres, the study will provide insights into the impact of ICT on financial disclosure in today's globalised corporate community.

The analysis of the two genres will be undertaken from a rhetorical perspective, focusing first on their structural features, and then on linguistic expressions of *evaluation*. In recent years, there has been growing interest in evaluation as a major dimension of communication and interpersonal relations. Evaluation broadly refers to how we inject our attitudes, opinions and feelings into what we are talking or writing about. In other words, evaluation is a reflection of how we interpret the world around us and how we share these interpretations with others (Bednarek, 2006). Thus, it is ultimately a manifestation of our values and identities in various spheres of interaction, e.g., social, professional, cultural. Evaluative language also has a *rhetorical* function. According to Martin and White (2005, p. 2):

> Attitudinal evaluations are of interest not only because they reveal speaker's/writer's feelings and values but also because their expression can be related to the speaker's/writer's status or authority as construed by the text, and because they operate *rhetorically* to construct relations of alignment or rapport between the writer/speaker and actual or potential respondents. (my italics)

Not surprisingly, evaluation is an extremely pervasive and multifaceted phenomenon which can be expressed in many different ways, both explicitly when lexical items are by nature evaluative (e.g., *terrible, good*) and implicitly when lexical items are not inherently evaluative, but take on such a meaning in the context of usage (e.g., *to have a real concern* that often has a negative connotation). Fortunately, to deal with this complex construct we can rely on some comprehensive frameworks to describe evaluation both

---

[2]   Throughout this book, the terms *rhetorical* and *rhetoric* are used in the scholarly analytic sense, and not the common non-academic meaning relating to uses of persuasive language that are perceived as lacking in substance and sincerity, with consequent negative connotations.

conceptually and functionally (cf. Biber et al., 1999; Hyland, 1999; Thompson & Hunston, 2000; Martin & White, 2005).

In all forms of corporate communication, the evaluative nuances of messages must be carefully gauged if they are to produce the desired rhetorical effect on stakeholders. Clearly, in spoken and written forms of financial disclosure where companies are keen to convince listeners and readers of their financial soundness and credibility, evaluative language assumes a crucial rhetorical function and is thus a particularly worthwhile aspect of language to study.

Drawing on the above considerations, it is now possible to formulate some broad research questions that will serve to guide this study:

1.   What are the distinguishing structural features of earnings releases vs. earnings presentations?
2.   What are the distinguishing rhetorical features of earnings releases vs. earnings presentations?
3.   How do the structural and rhetorical features of earnings releases and earnings presentations combine into distinct communicative patterns?
4.   How are the structural and rhetorical features of earnings releases and earnings presentations impacted by the roles of their participants and their ICT environments?

To address these questions, I have compiled two corpora containing authentic and naturally-occurring language representative of the two genres that are the focus of this study: earnings presentations and earnings releases. In this way, I hope to gain a better understanding of these two genres which are acquiring an increasingly important status in the international world of finance, but have yet to be adequately studied.

1.3 Target readership

The intended audience of this book comprises several different communities of practice. From a descriptive perspective, because the study contributes to the growing body of empirical linguistic evidence, it will be useful to language scholars and graduate students interested in spoken and written variation in language in general, as well as those who focus on specialised language, i.e., business or financial discourse.

From a methodological perspective, the study can provide insights for linguists who work with small specialised corpora that are especially suitable to computerised textual processing with follow-up qualitative analysis. The volume can also be of interest to academics whose research interests lie more in the area of communication rather than linguistics *per se*, particularly those who teach corporate and organisational communication as frequent core courses of business degree programmes.

From the teaching and learning perspectives, this study offers new input and materials for instructors of financial communication courses. While the more recent textbooks may mention audio/video teleconferencing, they do not provide sufficient information about their distinctive structural, linguistic and rhetorical features, nor do they include activities to help students learn them. The students to whom these courses are addressed can also draw some benefits from this book. Although they will likely not be interested in the theoretical aspects or detailed linguistic analyses, the wealth of examples provided throughout the book can introduce them to the authentic language and rhetorical practices of the financial world.

Finally, the book can be useful to corporate professionals. An understanding of the characteristics of persuasive language used in authentic oral and written financial communications can benefit those who are actually involved in producing such texts. Financial communication professionals may also find that computer-assisted textual analysis is a useful resource to understand and improve oral and written texts addressed to investors and other key stakeholders. Text analysis software is becoming increasingly user-friendly and accessible to those outside the field of language study, and can thus be channelled towards enhancing the effectiveness of financial reporting.

1.4 Overview of the book

Following this introduction designed to set the scene for the study, Chapter 2 situates the upcoming analysis within the discourse community of global finance. I begin by discussing the concept of financial disclosure, its communicative purposes and textual forms, and how it has evolved over the years. Other pertinent issues that come into play here are the use of English as a *lingua franca*, the impact of technology and the role of company leadership in financial communication. The discussion is supported with references to significant research that deepens our understanding of financial disclosure.

Chapter 3 illustrates the fundamental principles and key features of the three analytical approaches that were implemented synergistically in this study: qualitative genre analysis, quantitative methods from the field of corpus linguistics and ethnographically-inspired contacts with an informant from the professional world of finance. This serves as an important backdrop to understand how rhetorical strategies in financial discourse can be identified, analysed and interpreted.

Chapter 4 presents the theoretical framework used to gain insights into rhetorical dimension of financial discourse. I begin with a discussion of the broad notion of *evaluation*, i.e., how speakers and writers inject attitudes, opinions and feelings into discourse, often as a way to persuade their interlocutors. I then focus specifically on *appraisal* (Martin & White, 2005) as the analytical model that was applied to tease out rhetorical features in financial discourse. This model is capable of articulating evaluative language at a highly refined level. More specifically, the appraisal framework distinguishes the linguistic resources used to (1) express emotions and evaluate concrete or abstract entities (*attitude*), (2) align/disalign oneself with others (*engagement*) and (3) upscale or downscale one's evaluations (*graduation*). Clearly, a model of such comprehensive scope can provide important insights into how corporate speakers and writers use language rhetorically to negotiate consensus according to their strategic goals in the context of financial communication. The chapter also includes a review of some significant research on evaluative language in corporate discourse which has particular relevance for this study.

Chapter 5 is dedicated to a description of the data and methodology. First, I illustrate the two corpora on which the study is based, representing two genres of technology-mediated financial disclosure which are widely used today: oral earnings presentations and written earnings releases. This includes a discussion of the issues that were involved in the design and collection of the data and their compilation into two comparable corpora. The chapter continues with a description of the analytical procedure as undertaken in several interconnected phases encompassing: 1) genre analysis to determine the structural features of the two corpora at the macro level, 2) computer-assisted processing to investigate rhetorical features at the micro level, 3) follow-up contextual analysis to better interpret emerging empirical results, and 4) combined macro-micro analysis of key rhetorical features to highlight distinct patterns of usage across the two corpora. In this chapter, I also indicate which rhetorical features have been selected for investigation and how they are mapped onto Martin & White's (2005) appraisal model: evaluative adjectives (attitude), concessive connectives (engagement) and intensifiers/mitigators (graduation). The chapter ends with a discussion of the role of the professional informant from the financial sector who provided numerous insights into the communicative context and possible motives that underlie the rhetorical choices of company leaders, thus allowing for a more informed interpretation of the findings.

Chapter 6 presents the structural analysis of the two corpora. As two relatively unexplored genres, it is important to understand the structural features of earnings presentations and earnings releases which shed light on their rhetorical dimension. I provide schematic illustrations and thorough descriptions of the discursive patterns and rhetorical moves that were identified within each of the two genres, as well as an analysis of their distribution across both corpora. The chapter concludes with a discussion of the similarities and differences found in the two macro-structures and a chapter wrap-up to summarise the most important findings.

The next three chapters (7, 8 and 9) present and discuss the findings of the analysis of the rhetorical features described above. Chapter 7 focuses on *attitude* as expressed by evaluative adjectives, Chapter 8 deals with *engagement* as expressed by concessive connectives and Chapter 9 concentrates on *graduation* as expressed by intensifiers/mitigators. The three chapters are organised largely in the same way. Each one begins with an explanation of the preliminary elaboration and editing of the data that was generated by automatic retrieval procedures using text analysis software. This is followed by a presentation of the quantitative results, integrated with a discussion of similarities and differences found in the frequencies of the rhetorical features across the two corpora. The chapters then continue with various types of qualitative and functional analysis to gain insights into how and why these rhetorical devices are used by corporate speakers and writers. The discussion of the results is further integrated with input from the professional informant. Each of the three chapters contains a section describing the combined macro-micro analysis to determine the key communicative patterns of the two corpora. These chapters also conclude with a summarising chapter wrap-up.

The final chapter of the book highlights the main contributions of the study, reviews the most salient findings and suggests some promising areas for further research. It concludes with practice-oriented discussions of the implications for two important communities of practice: educators who teach financial communication at the university level and professionals working in the area of financial disclosure.

2.1 Defining financial disclosure

As we saw in the previous chapter, financial disclosure is a crucial facet of corporate life. Thus, it is important to understand precisely what it entails, how it fits into the communication activities of companies, and how it has developed and changed over the years.

From a discursive perspective, financial disclosure is a type of financial communication that falls under the broad domain of *financial discourse*. Although there seems to be no clear definition of latter in the literature, taking inspiration from Bargiela-Chiappini and Nickerson (1999), I suggest that financial discourse refers to any type of spoken or written text that is related to the management of assets and liabilities of companies.[3] In this sense, financial discourse includes not only texts used by companies that contain financial information, but also news or journal articles of a financial nature that may be written by external parties, e.g., members of the financial press or academics of finance. In contrast, *financial communication* has been characterised more specifically as company-produced texts that involve the diffusion of financial information or the promotion of the corporate financial image (de Bruin, 1999). Financial communication is therefore closely linked to the information requirements of stakeholders, as well as the company's need to steer perceptions regarding financial issues. Moving towards greater explicitness, Gibbins et al. (1990, p. 196) define *financial disclosure* as:

> [...] any deliberate public release of financial information, whether voluntary or required, numbers or words, formal or informal, at any time during the year.

In this definition, we find additional aspects concerning how, when and why companies communicate financial information and also begin to see the complexities involved in this process. Financial disclosure occupies a large share of a company's activities on two major fronts: (1) the resources needed

---

3   Bargiela-Chiappini and Nickerson (1999, p. 2) define *business discourse* as "talk and writing between individuals whose main work activities and interests are in the domain of business and who come together for the purpose of doing business".

to collect and elaborate the data resulting from commercial transactions and operations and (2) those needed to diffuse the elaborated data using the appropriate forms and instruments.[4] The process of financial disclosure draws on a variety of professional figures including accountants, financial executives, auditors, financial analysts, actuaries, legal advisors, media liaisons, public relations experts and press officers. In a survey of *Fortune* magazine's top 500 US companies carried out by Laskin (2009), preparing documentation for financial disclosure was identified among the most frequent business activities, spanning across several departments, including finance, communication and especially *investor relations* which has been described by Marston (1996, p. 447) as:

> the link between a company and the financial community, providing information to help the financial community and investing public evaluate a company.

According to Argenti (2009), the area of investor relations represents a vital component of strategic corporate communication. More specifically, over the last twenty years or so, it has evolved into an area of crucial importance for the successful management of stakeholder support (Marston, 2004). Financial disclosure now absorbs substantial economic resources and requires specific competencies in the fields of finance, marketing, communications and law, thus constituting a "multi-disciplinary management function" (ibid., p. v).

2.1.1 Mandatory financial disclosure

In the world of finance and investment, public companies (i.e., companies whose shares can be bought or sold on a stock exchange) have legal obligations to disclose financial information. This ensures that all potential investors have equal access to knowledge in order to make informed decisions about whether to buy, sell, or hold the shares of a company. In fact, without timely and reliable financial information, investors would be unable to accurately evaluate risks linked to investment opportunities, which would lead to critical consequences in global financial markets.

In order to avoid such a situation, strong efforts have been made to establish globally acceptable accounting and disclosure standards and principles. In many parts of the world (e.g., the US, the European Union, the Middle East, Hong Kong, Australia, India, Russia, South Africa and

---

[4]   In these contexts, *financial disclosure* is sometimes referred to as *financial reporting*. For the purposes of this study, the two terms are considered to be interchangeable.

Singapore), companies are required to implement policies in which they adopt internationally recognised accounting principles to prepare and to present financial information. In addition, countries with stock exchanges have regulatory authorities to guarantee that financial information is reported systematically, thus constituting what it known as *mandatory* disclosure. For example, in the US the Securities and Exchange Commission (SEC) requires all companies (both US and non-US) that list stocks on American exchanges to periodically render public their financial results through a series of standardised documents, such as quarterly and annual reports.[5] Mandatory financial disclosure has become even more important after some major corporate scandals at the beginning of the millennium that caused a generalised loss of confidence among investors and stockholders.[6] As a response, in 2002 the US Congress passed the Sarbanes-Oxley legislation which introduced important reforms to existing regulations, aiming to increase the amount of financial disclosure, enhance corporate responsibility and combat accounting fraud. Similarly, in 2004 the EU Commission ratified the European Transparency Directive that requires issuers listed on European stock markets to release annual reports produced according to International Financial Reporting Standards (Sheehan, 2005).

2.1.2 Voluntary financial disclosure

As Gibbins et al.'s (1990) definition cited at the beginning of this chapter indicates, financial disclosure may also be *voluntary*. Today companies use a variety of instruments to voluntarily communicate financial information, such as press releases, management forecasts, investment analysts' briefings and conference calls (Brown et al. 2004, Saatchi 2007).[7] Voluntary forms of financial disclosure have been steadily gaining traction as they allow businesses to proactively engage stakeholders in an increasingly competitive environment (Beattie et al., 2008; Tasker, 1998a). In addition, voluntary financial reporting enables companies to exert more control over the message, achieve greater visibility and enhance perceived value (Williams, 2008), while promoting an image of transparency and competence. At the same time, companies can also reap economic benefits from this process.

---

[5] For further information see http://www.sec.gov.

[6] Among the most well-known are Enron, Worldcom and Tyco. However, such scandals are not limited to the American scenario; they have also occurred in other countries, e.g., Barings Bank (UK), Skandia (Sweden), Ahold (The Netherlands) and Parmalat (Italy).

[7] See Ettredge et al., (2002) for a categorisation of voluntary vs. required financial disclosure.

Research in the area of finance has shown that regular voluntary financial disclosure can reduce information asymmetry (i.e., some potential investors having more information than others) which eventually leads to higher costs for companies (Brown et al., 2004).

To wrap up this section dedicated to defining financial disclosure, Figure 2.1 provides a schematic representation that discursively situates this communicative activity.

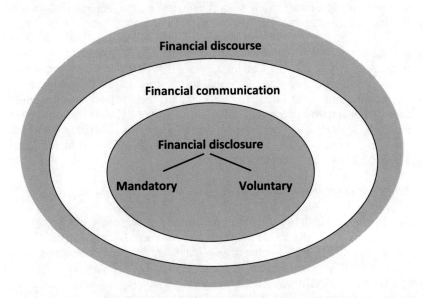

Figure 2.1: Financial disclosure from a discursive perspective

The next section will be dedicated to an overview of the types of texts that companies use to disclose financial information, from the more traditional written forms to the more recent ICT-mediated forms, as well as relevant research that has been carried out on them.

2.2 Genres of financial disclosure

Financial genres can be distinguished from other types of business genres[8] as

---

[8]   Common business genres that have been investigated structurally, linguistically and rhetorically include: sales letters (Zhu, 2000), mission statements (Isaksson, 2005), emails (van Mulken & van der Meer, 2005), business reports (Ruiz-

speech events and written texts that companies use specifically to disseminate financial information (both numerical and verbal) to current and potential investors. These may include annual general meetings of shareholders, live earnings announcements and earnings presentations via teleconferencing, as well as CEOs' letters to shareholders, annual reports, shareholder circulars, and press releases containing financial performance data. Bhatia (2005) refers to annual reports, audit reports and sales reports as examples of *reporting genres* used in business contexts which share the same communicative purpose, i.e., to disclose financial information

Yet research on some of these financial genres has shown that they are actually rather complex and often cannot be categorised as exclusively financial and informative. In a study focusing on the interdiscursive aspects of annual reports produced by 15 companies listed on the Hong Kong stock exchange, Bhatia (2008, p. 167) observed two distinct types of discourse. Most of the annual reports could be characterised as *accounting discourse*, based on the financial data of the company's past performance. However, there was also *public relations discourse*, particularly in the narrative sections of the report and the Chairman's letter, which aims to promote a positive image of the company and instil confidence among stakeholders in the company's future. Although these two types of discourse reflect different corporate practices (i.e., standard and legally required accounting procedures vs. marketing and public relations activities), they were used in conjunction within the same document to achieve favourability and credibility among readers at the same time. Thus, even though genres of financial disclosure exist to report objective data and information, they also reflect an underlying promotional and rhetorical dimension, as will be further illustrated by some of the studies reviewed below.

2.2.1 Traditional financial genres

Companies routinely use a series of conventional and well-established written documents for purposes of financial disclosure. One of the most common is the *annual report, a* lengthy and complex text produced by companies in fulfilment of obligations to disclose their financial results. They are typically divided into numerous sections. Some are mainly technical and numerical, aiming to provide an expert reader with information, while others are more narrative and descriptive, seeking to

---

Garrido, 2001), management meetings (Bargiela-Chiappini & Harris, 1995) and CEO speeches (David, 1999).

emphasise the positive results of the company, and thus persuade readers and potential investors of its worth (Malavasi, 2006).

The language of annual reports has been investigated by a number of researchers. In a study of the discursive strategies of annual reports, Ruiz-Garrido et al. (2005) found that both British and Spanish documents demonstrated a textual structure that could include 16 possible moves,[9] such as *information about the company*, *financial review* and *shareholder information*. Looking instead at linguistic features, Rutherford (2005) carried out a corpus-based study of the lexis of the operating and financial review sections of annual reports, which he classified as a genre of accounting narrative. The analysis revealed a pronounced use of positively-charged lexical items resulting in "the Pollyanna effect" (ibid., p. 349), meaning that everything is slanted towards the positive regardless of reality, and despite recommendations that such texts should contain neutral language. In a study of management messages found at the beginning of annual reports of US companies, notable differences were found in the descriptions of 'good years' vs. 'bad years' (Thomas, 1997). During a year of good performance, messages were framed in positive lexis (e.g., *profitability, best, ability*) that attributed the results to the management. On the other hand, in a year of poorer performance, messages that contain negative lexis (e.g., *setback, disappointing*) were attributed to non-human agents beyond the control of the company.

CEOs' letters and *Chairmen's statements* are written financial genres which are attributed to leading figures of companies. These documents usually accompany or are embedded into the larger annual report, and are also produced under the formal requirements to report financial results. Both CEOs' letters and Chairmen's statements are designed to put the company in a positive light and thus bolster the trust of the reader, according to Nickerson and De Groot (2005). In addition, the different roles and objectives associated with the CEO vs. the Chairman were reflected in an analysis of British and Dutch CEOs' letters and British Chairmen's statements. On the whole, the CEOs' letters were more informational since these writers are more concerned with aspects related to the routine running of the company. The Chairmen's statements instead tended to be more promotional, reflecting their keenness to demonstrate accountability to stockholders. On a structural level, the content of the two genres was articulated into six moves: *context, financial performance past year, financial performance future, operations, strategy* and *credentials*. Although some moves were common to the CEOs' letters and Chairmen's statements, there was also a certain degree of

---

[9]   Swales (2004, p. 228) defines a *move* as "a discoursal or rhetorical unit that performs a coherent communicative function".

flexibility in their usage, which seemed to be linked to the distinct roles and aims mentioned previously. With particular reference to Chairmen's statements, Skulstad (1996) devised a model for their structural organisation that contained three main functional moves which reflected their communicative purpose: *establishing the relationship between the Chairman and the reader, maintaining confidence* and *reinforcing the relationship already established*. Other linguistic elements that play an important role in executive statements are personal pronouns and possessive forms, which contribute to projecting a company's sense of identity through the words of its leaders. In a contrastive study based on Chairmen's Statements embedded in British and Spanish annual reports, Ruiz-Garrido et al. (2006) found that, overall, the British Chairman's statements had higher frequencies of both pronouns and possessive adjectives than their Spanish counterparts, with plural forms being the most prominent, particularly in moves that aimed to promote an image of corporate solidarity. Executive annual letters of European and US multinationals also showed evidence of systematic use of concessive connectives (e.g., *yet, although, however*) that counter a weaker proposition with a stronger one, which seems to have a primarily persuasive purpose (Garzone, 2005a).

Another written financial genre that is of particular relevance to this study is the *corporate press release*. These documents actually fall under the broader press release genre, studied extensively by Jacobs (1999) as texts containing pre-formulated information issued by organisations to journalists who are encouraged to copy them word-for-word into their articles. Corporate press releases are produced by professional writers or by in-house press officers/media liaisons who are employed in special company divisions dedicated to public relations (Sleurs & Jacobs, 2005). Although press releases do not indicate the name (or names) of who actually writes them, the names of press officers or media contacts are often listed on the web pages of companies (IBM España S.A., 2005).

Companies produce and distribute press releases for a number of reasons, which may be summarised as follows (McLaren & Gurău, 2005, p. 12):

> [...] to shape their corporate image, to show how well they are doing and to persuade potential investors that the company is worth investing in, as well as reassuring existing investors that their choice is still a good one.

In addition to providing financial information, corporate press releases may also communicate other news, such as the opening of new facilities, expansion into new markets, acquisitions and mergers, and the outcome of product trials and tests. In McLaren and Gurău's (2005) study, corporate press releases were described as a rather stable genre, with a consistent structural patterning of *announcement, elaboration, CEO comments, contact details* and *editor's note*. However, they found that the linguistic features are often contrasting in nature. On the one hand, positive evaluative lexis is used to accentuate the company's merits. On the other hand, hedging (e.g., *The company should achieve good results, Sales are expected*) is used to 'safeguard' the company from unforeseen events. Tench (2003) applied the genre analysis model to company press releases that contain announcements of new policies and decisions. Six different functional moves were identified, which can be articulated as follows: *introducing the business decision, providing credentials to support the decision, stating the impact and benefits of the decision, clarifying the value of the offer, soliciting response/feedback* and *offering further information*.

Investigating corporate press releases on the micro-level, McLaren-Hankin (2007) found that they are characterised by a marked use of overtly positive self-evaluation through lexical choices such as *innovative, high-value* and *ideally*, but often make use of the third person, seeking to 'objectify' the news at the same time in a somewhat paradoxical way. Similarly, Jacobs' (1999) observed some distinctive metapragmatic features used by the writers of press releases, including third-person self-reference (e.g., *The company*), performative verbs (e.g., *announce, remark*) and self or pseudo-quotation, where the organisation 'quotes' itself through text that is attributed to some high-ranking member, but actually produced by a press officer or other professional writer. According to Jacobs (ibid.), although these metapragmatic features are designed to give an impression of objectivity and authority, they are nonetheless signals of the rhetorical goals of press releases that attempt to convince readers of a given position and the sender's trustworthiness. Thus, it appears that self-evaluation and persuasion are, in effect, more important than objectivity. This seemingly inconsistent nature of press releases is also reflected in Lassen's (2006) study, which highlighted their fuzziness in terms of communicative purpose. Indeed, she even questioned the generic status of press releases, preferring the term *disembedded genre* due to their potential to convey different purposes, depending on the views and aims of the senders. Her study showed how value-laden lexical phrases (e.g., *significantly expanded, hope to encourage*) and logico-semantic conjunctions (e.g., *although, therefore*) were frequently used rhetorically to construct the argument of the sender.

In a study with an intertextual slant, Catenaccio (2006) showed how the content of corporate press releases can be changed as they move through the chain of distribution. She traced the information from the press releases issued by the Enron company during the initial phase of their financial crisis to the final articles that appeared in financial newspapers, showing how it was successively transformed by journalists. In fact, they used distancing strategies (e.g., reporting verbs) when re-writing the information for publication in more neutral sources, thereby thwarting the Enron company's attempts to persuade and manipulate readers.

Less work has been done on traditional spoken financial genres. This is likely due to the considerable difficulties encountered by language researchers when trying to gain access these events. Business organisations are very concerned about safeguarding their confidentiality and are often reluctant to open their doors to 'outsiders' (Bargiela-Chiappini & Harris, 1997; Fox, 1999; Warren, 2004). They also want to know "what's in it for us" (Bargiela-Chiappini, 2009, p. 11). As a consequence, research on spoken financial communication has been quite limited. Rogers (2000) studied CEOs' *live presentations* in conjunction with earnings announcements to an audience of investment analysts. These were characterised as "a key genre of voluntary financial reporting" (ibid., p. 427). Although presentations of earnings data could be considered as mainly informative in nature (Nickerson and De Groot, 2005), Rogers (2000) viewed them as both informational and relational, suggesting a desire on the part of the CEOs to exploit face-to-face interaction to enhance their relations with investment analysts. Rogers' (2000) study suggests that executive financial presentations might be more accurately positioned within the burgeoning category of mixed genres which have more than one communicative purpose (Bhatia, 2004). Indeed, they can be seen as the hybridisation of two discourse colonies: the reporting and the promotional. They ostensibly report information on the financial performance, business operations and future outlook of the company over a certain time period to an audience of largely professional investors. Yet given the nature of the publicly quoted company that depends crucially on investors and the volatility of stock markets, their purpose is not only to inform, but also to promote the firm and persuade the audience that the company merits their trust.

2.2.2 ICT, multimodality and new financial genres

The term ICT refers to communicative instruments that incorporate some form of technology. This includes radio, television, cellular phones, computers and networks, hardware and software, and satellite systems, in addition to the services and applications that may be linked to them, such as videoconferencing and distance learning. The acronym ICT tends to be used in European contexts, while IT (Information Technology) is found more often in US contexts where it is defined as "the study, design, development, implementation, support or management of computer-based information systems".[10]

ICT has progressively transformed how spoken and written texts are produced and distributed not only in the corporate community, but in all domains of human communication (Lassota Bauman, 1999; Shortis, 2001; Fairclough, 2001; Crystal 2006). In modern society, the benefits of ICT go beyond the inherent technology-driven assets, allowing us to access increasingly sophisticated and wide-ranging sources of information and channels of communication. According to Fairclough (2003), new communication technologies have had a major impact on the development of mediated forms of communication that are much more far-reaching than the traditional media channels of print, radio, television. Indeed, ICT now plays a key role in many fields outside of media, such as education, health care and business where it is essential to produce, process and communicate large amounts of information on a regular basis. Moreover, ICT is now an integral part of the daily lives of many people, particularly the younger generation that uses it not only for communication, but also for entertainment (e.g., video games, MP3 devices, YouTube and social media platforms).

ICT communicative environments typically exploit semiotic resources that go beyond the verbal message by routinely integrating graphical, auditory and kinetic elements (Shortis, 2001). For this reason, discourse that is associated with ICT is often characterised as *multimodal*. More specifically, Thibault (2000, p. 311) affirms that multimodal texts

> [...] combine and integrate the meaning-making resources of more than one semiotic modality – for example language, gesture, movement, visual images, sound and so on – in order to produce a text-specific meaning.

In traditional discourse studies, the term *mode* has been used to refer to the channel by which verbal language is conveyed, i.e., by speech or by writing. For example, in systemic functional linguistics (Halliday, 1989), *mode* is a variable that classifies discourse according to one of only two modes: spoken or written. However, when we speak of *multimodality*, we must take a broader perspective where the spoken and written modes represent only two of many semiotic resources available for meaning-making, going beyond verbal language to include visual images, music, sounds, gaze, gestures and rhythms (Baldry, 2000). Taking this idea a step further, Kress and van Leeuwen (2001) maintain that speech and writing are not actually modes in

---

[10]   http://searchcio-midmarket.techtarget.com.

themselves, but simply different *media* through which the mode of *language* is realised.

Because the term *multimodal* typically brings to mind high-tech instruments and applications, it is important to distinguish between the concepts of *multimodality* and *multimediality*. The former refers to the integration of semiotic resources used to produce texts, i.e., *mode*, while the latter refers to the integration of technologies used to distribute or transmit texts, i.e., *medium* (Kress & van Leeuwen, 2001). In reality, however, new communicative instruments often reflect an overlapping of multimodality and multimediality. For example, during a webcast financial presentation, different modes are being used to produce the discourse (e.g., speech, gestures, visual supports) and different media are being used to transmit the discourse (e.g., audio, visual and Internet technologies).

The Internet has provided a particularly fertile environment for multimodal ICT-mediated communication. According to Lassota Bauman (1999), this is due primarily to three fundamental attributes of Internet texts. First of all, they are ubiquitous and available in unlimited copies. Anyone in any part of the world with a computer can access them. Secondly, Internet texts are not subject to temporal or spatial constraints in either their production or their reception. They can be immediately accessed regardless of time differences or distances between interlocutors. Finally, they can be collaboratively and progressively shaped (e.g., Wikipedia), whereas speech and writing are produced by one or a fixed group of persons. This has led to the emergence of new genres that are found only on the Internet, such as commercial, institutional and personal websites, as well as discussion lists, chat-rooms and blogs.

Another important property that characterises many Internet texts is intertextuality (Mitra & Cohen, 1999), which is seen in the use of hypertext links that allow readers to freely navigate through series of embedded texts. In such cases, a given text is no longer an isolated instrument of communication, but exists only in relation to other texts to which it gives access or through which it is accessed. Internet texts can also be immaterial (Askehave & Ellerup Nielsen, 2004), since there may be no physical print counterpart. This feature renders them quite dynamic as they can be easily changed, updated and improved, but also removed from the Internet, and therefore vanish at any moment in time.

The new options provided by ICT have had an enormous impact of how companies communicate with their stakeholders. Reinsch and Turner (2006) discuss the capacity of new technologies to reshape the discursive practices and rhetorical objectives of the corporate community, particularly in terms of image-building. In the era of the Internet, businesses can address their message to a vastly larger audience than in the past, given the virtually unlimited contacts that are now possible and often at very low costs. This has led not only to the transferal of traditional print genres to the web (e.g., e-advertisements, e-newsletters), but also to the emergence of new genres to take advantage of this possibility (e.g., staff chat-rooms, FAQs, and blogs maintained by expert employees to communicate with customers). In this way, companies succeed in satisfying the public's ever-growing demand for sophisticated and multimodal communicative experiences, which brings the added benefit of creating a favourable impression of the companies themselves. On this point, Garzone et al. (2007, p. 12) observe:

> The fast-changing nature of technological development, combined with a heightened demand for multimodal contexts and the transformation of communication conventions, is bound to foster a proliferation of genres (both through genre migration and through the birth of novel genres) [...]

In the context of financial communication, ICT has led to the transformation of traditional print written financial genres into their virtual counterparts found on the Internet. These texts are typically found on increasingly prevalent *investor relations* webpages linked to company websites where Internet users can find financial information. A study by Deller et al. carried out in 1999 found that high percentages of major companies in the US, UK and Germany had dedicated investor relations webpages: 91 per cent in the US, 72 per cent in the UK and 71 per cent in Germany. Although already quite high, those percentages are likely to have increased considerably today.

This shift from 'physical' to 'virtual' has not only significantly broadened the intended audience of these documents, but has also led to some interesting changes in their features thanks to multimodal digital platforms. For example, annual reports are now often posted on company websites where they have evolved from the "rather dull financial document" (Beattie et al., 2008, p. 181) to an attractively designed text that is full of colourful images and sophisticated graphics. Such 'revitalised' annual reports can be freely accessed and downloaded, and thus play a key role in impression management (Clatworthy & Jones, 2003), i.e., companies' efforts to put themselves in the best light possible. From a discursive perspective, Nickerson and DeGroot (2005) suggest that the migration of CEOs' letters and Chairmen's statements to the Internet reinforces their status as distinct genres from the annual reports in which they are embedded as they can often be accessed independently as separate documents on company websites.

Alongside the conventional hard-copy press releases sent by companies to journalists who then incorporate them into articles, we now have *e-releases*, i.e., "press releases on the Internet" (Strobbe & Jacobs, 2005), which can be accessed by a vastly wider audience. This new trend is bringing some interesting linguistic changes to the genre; we find more direct forms of discourse (e.g., second person pronouns, imperatives), as well as superlatives and emphatic capitalised lettering. Such features are instead normally absent in print press releases. Catenaccio (2007) explored the effect of the migration of financial press releases to the Internet by contrastively analysing a print press release and a web-mediated press release, both dealing with the Enron crisis. She concluded that the growing presence of hypertext links and multimodal features of ICT-mediated releases not only opens them up to a much wider potential audience, but also to an audience that can become active participants in the unfolding of the text, and no longer passive recipients.

ICT has had a particularly strong impact on spoken financial communication, playing a crucial role in both the production and distribution of financial information by oral channels. The production of financial data is now greatly facilitated by digital technology. For example, computer software programs such as Powerpoint can be used to display data which are also easily transmitted electronically to interested parties or posted on websites for consultation and downloading. With reference to distribution, ICT has allowed companies to develop new oral financial genres. In the past, oral financial presentations were given during face-to-face meetings to a restricted number of invited investment analysts (Rogers, 2000). However, in recent years the increasing pressures of global competition have encouraged businesses to take advantage of new technologies that allow them to interact with many more stakeholders. One widely-used method is teleconferencing, defined by Rogan and Simmons (1984, p. 1) as "interactive group communication (three or more people in two or more locations) through an electronic medium". Teleconferencing may use primarily the audio channel via telephone, or it may integrate video or Internet technology, as in the case of videoconferencing or webcasting, which in turn may be broadcast either live or in deferred mode.

Today companies make routine use of a particular form of teleconferencing known as a *conference call*. Essentially, this is a business meeting conducted via telephone and organised through a teleconferencing service. Indeed, conference calls have been described as "the business meetings of the 21st century" (Garcés-Conejos Blitvich, 2007, p. 57). In the context of financial disclosure, a particular type of conference call is organised, often referred to as an *earnings call* between the executive management of a company and investment analysts operating in that particular business sector. During these multi-party calls, the executives first give a presentation of their financial results. Then, participating analysts have the opportunity to interact directly with the speakers in lengthy question and answer sessions which are moderated by the teleconference operator. While such audio-only interaction may deprive business interlocutors of some of the interpersonal benefits of face-to-face meetings (Drolet & Morris, 2000), it is undoubtedly more cost-effective, flexible and far-reaching (Du-Babcock, 2004), and is thus a highly attractive solution for modern business organisations that also want to portray themselves as "tech-savvy" (Radner, 2003, p. 1). In fact, earnings calls have now largely replaced the traditional live meetings that companies used to organise to present their results to investors face-to-face (Rogers, 2000).

Earnings calls are technically a form of voluntary financial disclosure in that companies are not required to release financial information specifically in this way (Ettredge et al., 2002). However, many companies, particularly those that operate on an international scale, now make such regular use of earnings calls that they have become expected events (Ryan & Jacobs, 2005), and a sudden discontinuation would likely raise suspicion among financial operators. Thus, in practice, earnings calls may actually resist classification according to the mandatory/voluntary dichotomy.

Since the late 1990s, earning calls have been recognised as the main channel through which company management communicates directly with financial analysts and investment portfolio managers (Tasker, 1998a). Over the years, thanks also to continuing advances in technology, they have undergone a progressive expansion in scope. Most companies listed on stock exchanges now routinely conduct what are known as *open calls* that are webcast and accessible not only to professional financial analysts, but also to an unlimited number of individual investors among the public at large (Roelofsen, 2010; Skinner, 2003). To illustrate the dramatic scope of this change, Jorgensen & Wingender (2004) determined that in 1999 approximately two-thirds of companies that organised earnings calls allowed only professional financial operators to participate. By 2002, more than 90 per cent had opened the calls also to private individuals, as well as members of the media. To facilitate the investment community, companies also produce verbatim transcripts of the speech of all earnings calls participants. Such transcripts are typically available only to professionals and at relatively high costs. Nevertheless, in the last few years, it has become possible to find some posted on company websites or financial news websites, albeit quite sporadically.

From the above, it is clear that earnings calls have become a standard venue for financial reporting that involves vast numbers of participants, all of whom are engaged in strategic communication. On the one hand, the corporate executives that present financial results are keen to convince the audience that their company is sound and worthy of investment. On the other hand, the audience wants to glean information that will allow them to write accurate forecasts and determine ratings (in the case of professional analysts), or to make good investments (in the case of private individual investors). Figure 2.2 illustrates the chronological and social evolution on the earnings call as a key channel for financial reporting.

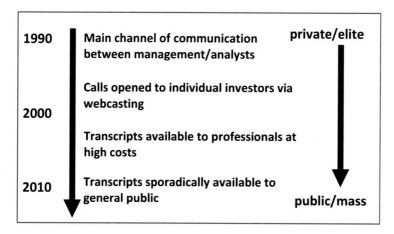

Figure 2.2: The evolution of earnings calls

Some research has investigated earnings calls from the perspective of informational content and company performance. Tasker (1998b) found that firms with less informative written financial statements were more likely to hold earnings calls than those with more informative statements. Frankel et al. (1999) measured volatility and trading volume during earnings calls to conclude that they provide more information to market participants than what is found in the written earnings releases that typically accompany the calls. Bushee et al. (2003) found that companies that opt for *open* earnings conference calls appear to generate higher levels of trading activity in comparison with companies that conduct *closed* calls, in which only a select group of investment professionals are invited to participate.

Other studies dealing with earnings calls have taken a discourse analytic approach to learn more about their discursive and linguistic features. This was accomplished by procuring the earnings calls transcripts in order to analyse the actual speech of the participants. Matsumoto et al. (2006) investigated the relationship between the length of earnings calls (measured in terms of transcript word counts) and market performance. They found that both management presentations and the following Q&A sessions with financial analysts tended to be longer when earnings and stock market performance were poor. This was attributed to management's choice to provide lengthier explanations about poor performance. Focusing exclusively on the dialogic Q&A sessions of earnings calls, Larcker and Zakolyukina (2010) devised a model to predict deceptive reporting by company executives during these unrehearsed parts of earnings calls. By comparing the Q&A sessions to written financial restatements issued later by the same companies, they found that 'deceptive' Q&A sessions contained fewer self-references, more impersonal pronouns, fewer negative and more positive emotion words, fewer expressions of both certainty and hesitation, and made less mention of shareholder value and value creation than 'truthful' ones. Crawford Camiciottoli (2009) used text analysis software to analyse patterns of analyst questions' during earnings calls. She found that indirect requests for information (e.g., *I'd love to hear more about...*) were twice as frequent as direct requests (e.g., *What are the...?*), even if the latter would seem entirely appropriate in such routine informative events. Follow-up interpretive analysis suggested that the motivation behind this usage was linked to the ICT-constrained conference call setting where analysts aim to hold the floor as long as possible in order to extract maximum information from the executives. The usefulness of discourse-oriented research on financial disclosure has recently been noted by finance and accounting scholars. They have become more attuned to the role of language in financial disclosure and have called for more of this type of interdisciplinary work (Beyer *et al.*, 2010; Berger, 2011).

The conference call format may also be used for communicative events of a financial nature other than periodic reports on earnings. Palmieri (2008) looked at Mergers and Acquisitions (M&A) conference calls in which managers present financial analysts and investors with information relating to a proposed financial transaction. Using a case study approach to analyse the transcript of an M&A conference call, he determined that that this type of event is not limited to simply providing and collecting information, but is instead highly argumentative and even confrontational when managers seek to defend and justify their proposed actions in the face of pressing questions from analysts.

2.2.3 Earnings presentations and earnings releases

Expanding on the insights from the studies discussed above, I am now in a position to clearly define the two ICT-mediated financial disclosure genres that are the object of this study.

Earnings presentations are oral reports of periodic financial results delivered by members of executive management to a group of investment analysts via audio teleconferencing.[11] Typically, companies use an external teleconferencing service that provides the necessary technological platform and logistical organisation. However, some companies may have their own in-house teleconferencing facilities.

---

[11]   Earnings presentations are actually only one component of complete earnings calls described above that also contain lengthy Q&A sessions between executives and investment analysts. These will not be dealt with in this study.

In the executive team, there are usually several presenters representing company leadership and symbolic 'figureheads', among whom may be the CEO, the CFO (Chief Financial Officer), Senior Vice President, Treasurer and Director of Investor Relations. Den Hartog and Verburg (1997, p. 355) note the following:

> CEOs play an important part in crafting and dispersing organizational values and visions to both organization members and the external environment [...]

For these reasons, earnings presentations have become vital channels for shaping the corporate image and identity, and great care is taken in their preparation (Larcker & Zakolyukina, 2010).

The audience of earnings presentations depends on whether the earnings call is *closed* or *open*, as discussed earlier. In closed calls, the audience is limited to professional investment analysts who are expressly invited by management to participate. The number of investment analysts who are connected via telephone may vary. However, because most earnings calls are restricted to about an hour, the number of participating analysts is necessarily conditioned to a certain extent by how many can feasibly have the opportunity to ask questions in the allotted time.[12] In open calls, in addition to the invited analysts, any interested party who registers on the company's investor relations website may access the webcast call, but in listen-only mode without the possibility of direct interaction with the executives during the Q&A sessions that follow the presentations. Thus, the presence of a potentially unknown audience introduces a complicating factor for executive presenters. As pointed out by Huhtinen (2008), while earnings presentations are targeted primarily towards the participating finance professionals, the speakers must also be aware of this 'secondary' audience. At any rate, the audience of earnings presentations can be described as a "rhetorical audience", i.e., "only those persons who are capable of being influenced by discourse and of being mediators of change" (Bitzer, 1968, p. 8). In fact, from a rhetorical perspective, the purpose of financial presentations is to influence the audience's thoughts and actions in the realm of investing.

The content of earnings presentations centres mainly on the financial results of a given quarterly period and outlook for future performance. The investment analysts are normally able to refer to accompanying tables of data in the form of electronic files made available to them prior to the call, or via the company website during the call itself in the case of simultaneous

---

[12]   In my experience with earnings calls, this number has ranged from a minimum of three to a maximum of 21.

webcasting. While the authorship of the verbal message contained in the presentations is not known (i.e., whether they are authored by the executives who deliver them or by other company staff), it is highly likely that they are actually multi-authored. The professional informant with extensive experience as a participant of earnings calls who I interviewed for this study suggested that earnings presentations pass through various departments before arriving in the hands of the executive presenters. This probably includes the investor relations department that prepares the oral text based on a template used for quarterly earnings calls and the legal department that verifies its compliance with laws and regulations. The professional informant also shed light on the extent to which earnings presentations are either delivered spontaneously by executives or 'canned', i.e., simply read from a prepared text. He believes that there is likely to be a combination of both, with executives usually adding some commentary to avoid an overly 'canned' effect. However, he made the following interesting comment: "*The older, wiser and most respected CEOs will not read verbatim. They would consider that to be in poor taste or beneath them*".

Earnings releases are documents containing periodic financial results that are distributed by companies either in print form to journalists or published on the Internet where they are available to a generally wider audience. Like other types of press releases that are issued by companies, earnings releases are also written by professionals and often in-house press officers, who are usually on a lower hierarchical level of the company structure in comparison with the person (or persons) who actually provide the information to be transmitted to the public (Scollon & Scollon, 2001). Therefore, the addresser-addressee relationship is more complicated and much less direct than what is found in earnings presentations. In effect, there is an implied writer who suppresses his/her own individual persona and writes the earnings release from the viewpoint of the company. Similarly, the implied readers are assumed to be people who have some level of interest in the performance of the company (e.g., business partners, shareholders, investors, customers and competitors), although there is no certainty as to whether or not earnings releases will actually be read, or by whom.

It is important to distinguish earnings releases from other types of press releases that companies often issue, e.g., to announce new products or changes in company structure or personnel. These have in fact been labelled with the more generic term *corporate press releases* by McLaren and Gurău (2005), as discussed in section 2.2.1. In comparison to these non-specific corporate press releases, earnings releases have a much more focused content. They contain primarily financial information (verbal narrative and/or numerical data typically in tabular form) about the economic results of the company during a given quarterly period, as well as forecasts for performance in the future. Thus, earnings releases could be considered a special type of corporate press release with a more specific content and purpose and, I would argue, constitute an important sub-genre within the overall press release genre, which has not yet been clearly defined.

In terms of communicative purpose, earnings presentations and earnings releases can be seen as comparable genres having the same aims. They seek to inform various stakeholders of the current financial status and future outlook of the company, thereby constituting a type of "reporting genre" (Bhatia, 2004, p. 83), but also to convince them of the company's soundness and thus also a "persuasive genre" (ibid., p. 133). For this reason, both earnings presentations and earnings releases may also be seen as instances of "hybrid, embedded and mixed forms" (Bhatia, 2002, p. 30), where more than one purpose is served within the same text. These have become increasingly common in the dynamic discourses of the professional world (Bhatia, 2004).

Both earnings presentations and earnings releases are part of a "genre chain" (Swales, 2004, p. 18) or succession of related genres, but also belong to a "system of genres" (Bazerman, 1994, p. 97), where each genre has intertextual links to other genres within the system (Bhatia, 2005). As illustrated in Figure 2.3, the financial disclosure process typically starts with an earnings call announcement (1). This is a brief written text that announces the date and time of an upcoming conference call that will report financial earnings, along with technical information about how to access the earnings call and usually a few sentences summarising the company's main activities. Earnings call announcements are published on the company's website or in other sources of financial information. The earnings call itself (2) then takes place, following the publication of the corresponding written earnings release issued by the company at some time prior to the call. In fact, during the presentation part of the earnings call, the speaker may instruct the audience to refer to the earnings release that has just been made available through financial newswires. Information from the earnings call and releases is then later incorporated into mandatory filings (3), e.g., quarterly and annual reports. Thus, we also see evidence of intertextuality, or more specifically, "manifest intertextuality" (Fairclough, 1992, p. 271), where texts have explicit reference or links to previous texts.

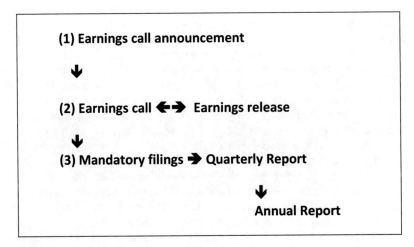

Figure 2.3: The genre chain of financial disclosure

The role of ICT in the whole process of financial disclosure has also benefited companies in terms of a new flexibility in managing the timing of their reporting. Garcia (2007) describes an episode in which a company released its quarterly earnings figures on its website 10 minutes *before* transmitting them to the traditional business newswires. The company subsequently came under criticism as financial information is normally sent out to various channels of disclosure simultaneously in order to avoid giving an unfair advantage to any given receiver. However, the company's CEO defended the anticipated disclosure claiming that it would result in greater transparency and facilitate access to information. Thus, it appears that ICT is destined to bring changes, and perhaps controversial ones, to how companies disclose financial information.

As a speech event that is not readily accessible to most language researchers, there is a paucity of work specifically on earnings presentations. In a study focusing on the structural features of complete earnings calls, Crawford Camiciottoli (2010) observed that the presentation component appeared to be quite regular with recurring categories of content (e.g., disclaimers, overall results, financial details, final summary) and also demonstrated a high level of intertextuality (i.e., cross-references to other spoken and written financial texts), reflecting a cohesive professional community that has shaped and consolidated its own distinctive communication practices. In an exploratory study that looked at how companies deal with having to report poor performance, Crawford Camiciottoli (2011) identified some lexical items (e.g., *continue, maintain, strong, solid, disciplined*) that appeared to be aimed at bolstering the corporate image in terms of reliability and ethical practices. These results suggested the need for additional in-depth and comprehensive research on rhetorical strategies in oral financial communication.

On the written front, although some recent studies have investigated corporate press releases on a general level (McLaren & Gurău, 2005; Maat, 2007), none have looked specifically at earnings releases as a unique instrument used by companies to maintain and enhance their vitally important investor relations function. This study attempts to fill this gap, with the added benefit of contrastive insights (spoken vs. written) about new technology-mediated communicative instruments that are destined to play an important role in the fast-paced world of international finance.

Because financial disclosure is an activity that is becoming increasingly global in nature involving people of diverse cultural backgrounds, also thanks to the possibilities offered by ICT, in the next section I discuss an important related issue: the use of English as the language of choice for financial disclosure among internationally-oriented companies.

2.3 English as the *lingua franca* of financial disclosure

According to House (2003, p. 557), the term *lingua franca* can be traced back to the Arabic expression 'lisan-al-farang' which was considered an intermediary language used by Arabs to speak to Western Europeans who travelled to their countries. However, it is now commonly used with reference to English as the language used by speakers of diverse languages in global communicative situations such as business, commerce, education and tourism. A useful definition of English as a *lingua franca* that captures this broader meaning has been formulated as follows:

> [...] a contact language between persons who share neither a common native tongue nor a common national culture, and for whom English is the chosen foreign language of communication. (Firth, 1996, p. 240)

Graddol (2006) pointed out that, on a general level, non-native speakers using English outnumber native speakers by about four to one. In other words, English is no longer the exclusive property of native speakers in an age where international contacts are the norm in everyday life. This is strongly linked to the concept of *global English* (Crystal, 1997), referring to English that has been used all over the world since the 1950s and which encompasses a range of local varieties (or 'world Englishes') that do not necessarily conform to the more Anglo-centric varieties of English (e.g., British, American, Australian).

The rise of English as a *lingua franca* has led to some broad concerns about the risk of linguistic imperialism (Canagarajah, 1999), which poses a threat to the ideals of multiculturalism and plurilingualism. However, other scholars have rejected this idea. For example, House (2003, p. 566) made the distinction between the use of a language for "identification" vs. "communication", seeing the latter as an instance of English as a *lingua franca* for utilitarian purposes which allows users to achieve their goals. Similarly, Seidlhofer (2000) underlined the pragmatic incentive for using English as a *lingua franca* by non-native speakers, who tend to see it as an instrument for facilitating cross-border communication and who are concerned primarily with language efficiency rather than ideological issues. Moreover, a study by House (2003) showed that the widespread use of English lexical items in German texts did not influence their typically German orientation in terms of information content and presentation. This led to the conclusion that English is, in effect, not threatening German as the national language. In sum, it would seem that the benefits of communicating in English as a *lingua franca* outweigh the possible negative implications for other languages, at least in the eyes of those who actually use English in this way.

2.3.1 English in the corporate world

In international business transactions, it is now widely recognised that English has become the dominant *lingua franca* (Bilbow, 1997; Scollon & Scollon, 2001, Palmer-Silveira et al., 2006). This trend is strongly linked to globalisation which allows for a growing number of contacts between people of different cultures, a trend that is destined to continue well into the future (Gotti, 2005). It has been estimated that up to 80 per cent of business communication involves speakers whose native language is not English (Louhiala-Salminen & Charles, 2006), and who thus use English as a *lingua franca*.

When choosing a language through which to operate internationally, companies typically take a very pragmatic view and tend to select the one that best suits their purposes, albeit different from their own national language (Rogerson-Revell, 2007). As Graddol (2006, p. 92) noted:

> In practice, within many large companies, and even in parts of the European governmental institutions, English has become a common working language.

Taking this idea a step further, an acronym has been coined for the use of English in business contexts: BELF (Business English Lingua Franca). According to Louhiala-Salminen et al. (2005, pp. 403-404), BELF is used for conducting business within the global business discourse community, whose members are BELF users and communicators in their own right – not 'non-native speakers' or 'learners'.

Some scholars have looked at various communicative contexts in which companies rely on a *lingua franca*. According to Feely and Harzing (2003), multinational companies now engage in what is known as *language management*, i.e., the crafting of policies regarding which language to use in order to effectively coordinate international activities and manage communication, particularly in the presence of language barriers. For example, during multicultural business meetings, English as a *lingua franca* may be used to shape business relationships and respective roles, particularly in situations when it is important to facilitate active participation among all members (Poncini, 2002). English also tends to be used as a *lingua franca* in companies based in non-English speaking countries more for external communications than for internal ones (Nickerson, 1999), and also when the company is large and/or operates in high-tech sectors (Vandermeeren, 1999). Because financial disclosure is a form of external communication, in the next section I discuss how English is used as a *lingua franca* specifically in this context.

2.3.2 English for financial communication

The companies that systematically produce and distribute financial disclosure documentation in English are usually large multinationals that may be based in different countries around the world. Simply browsing the websites of well-known European or Asian multinationals serves to confirm that many maintain bilingual websites where financial information is posted in both the native language and in English, typically on an *investor relations* webpage. Thus, English-language financial information is available to interested parties around the world, also through a series of hypertext links to both mandatory (e.g., SEC filings in the US) and voluntary (e.g., earnings releases, webcast conference calls) forms.

Very few studies have actually addressed the use of English as a *lingua franca* in financial disclosure, and have done so mainly from a strategic perspective rather than a linguistic or rhetorical one. Jeanjean et al. (2010) examined the annual reports of nearly 4,000 companies in 27 non-English speaking countries. They found that the motivation to issue annual reports in English is linked to greater visibility and an expansion in the number of investors that become aware of the company. Roughly half of the companies they looked at issued annual reports in English. This decision was driven by some particular factors, including size of the firm, level of foreign sales achieved and the status of the native language, i.e., to what degree it is understood internationally and may constitute a barrier for global communication. The fact that an increasing number of companies in non-English speaking countries are producing annual reports in English was also highlighted by Tarca (2004), who was able to procure large numbers of English language annual reports from German, French and Japanese companies for her investigation of international accounting practices. With particular reference to web-based financial reporting, Boubaker et al. (2012), found that 85 per cent of a sample of 529 French firms maintained English language webpages in order to provide financial information to foreign investors.

The use of English as the *lingua franca* in the international financial community also has implications concerning the language competence of the non-native speakers who must produce and receive written and oral financial texts in English. In a study based on the communication practices of the various subsidiaries of a Finnish multinational, Marschan Piekkari et al. (1999) found that both reading and writing financial reports in English presented significant challenges for some members of staff who were not native speakers. With reference to the Q&A sessions of earnings calls whose participants were Korean executives and native English-speaking financial analysts, Cho and Yoon (2013) found that poor speaking skills and lack of generic/pragmatic awareness of the type of language typical of these events led to break-downs in communication. Thus, the ability of non-native speakers involved in financial communications to use English effectively is an important skill to ensure the accuracy and success of financial disclosure.

2.4 The role of corporate leadership in financial disclosure

Although a great deal has been written over the years about corporate leadership (cf. Vance, 1983; Den Hartog & Verburg, 1997; Bragg, 2011), Barrett (2010) notes that there is still not a strong consensus among researchers as to what it actually entails. However, a series of statements proposed by this author can perhaps shed light on some qualities that we can agree upon to describe people who are viewed as leaders in corporate settings (ibid., 2010, p. 3):

> They are men and women who influence others in an organization or in a community. They command others' attention. They persuade others to follow them or pursue goals they define. They control situations. They improve the performance of groups and organizations. They connect with others, and they get results.

Clearly, an effective corporate leader can actually achieve these goals only through effective communication. As Barrett (2010, p. 5) aptly notes:

"Without effective communication, leaders accomplish little. Without effective communication, a leader is not a leader".

2.4.1 Leadership communication, language and rhetoric

From the discussion above, it is evident that there is a strong link between leadership, communication and language. Some research in the area of management leadership has begun to recognise the crucial role of language in the successful running of a business. A recent study by Clifton (2012, p. 149) highlights a discursive approach to leadership, pointing out that "leadership is a language game in which meaning is managed". The analysis of an extract of a monthly staff meeting revealed discursive techniques used by the chairman and other participants in positions of authority to frame, assess and challenge decisions that were being made. Relying on methods inspired by Conversation Analysis, Svennevig (2011) examined interactions between managers and subordinates in feedback sessions. He found that managers' leadership styles emerged from the sequencing of their responses to subordinates which tended to centre on assessment, diagnosis and directions for future actions. With particular reference to executive leadership (e.g., CEOs), the communications they engage in are often highly strategic in nature, aiming to establish, reinforce and maintain positive attitudes towards the company among key stakeholders (Johnson & Scholes, 1999). As pointed out by Argenti and Forman (2002, p. 110):

> [...] the CEO who stands at the helm of an organization can project *through his or her person alone* a company's commitment to goals, a commitment that would be less credible if voiced by anyone else (original italics)

There is also strong link between leadership and *rhetoric*. As we know, at the crux of the concept of rhetoric is *persuasion*. In fact, the Oxford Dictionary defines *rhetoric* as "the art of effective or persuasive speaking or writing" and "language that is designed to have a persuasive or impressive effect". In corporate contexts, persuading people with words has been characterised as a key "managerial activity", along with "interpreting situations, creating meanings and building identities" (Bonet et al., 2011, p. 7). With particular reference to executive managers, these figures are often highly influential not only among internal and external stakeholders of the company, but also among the general public, often participating actively in conversations about important social issues of the day (Amernic & Craig, 2006).[13] Thus, it stands

---

[13]   We need only think of such iconic leaders as Bill Gates (Microsoft), Jack Welch

to reason that the discourse of executive management tends to be highly persuasive in order to tell "the version of the story that the company wants heard" (Amernic & Craig, 2006, p. 49). In their book *CEO-speak: The language of corporate leadership*, Amernic and Craig (2006, p. x) analyse the persuasive language found in the written communication of famous CEOs. Like Clifton (2012), they interpret this language to be a component of a "language game", aiming to shape perceptions and create ideologies.

Company leaders are intensely involved in financial communication. A study by Marston (1996) found that executives spend an average of 36.5 days annually working on investor relations activities. According to Argenti et al. (2005), CEOs and CFOs represent the main channel for financial communication. The fact that executive management is so engaged in financial disclosure suggests their key role in this particular communicative activity not only on an informative level, but also on a rhetorical one.

It may seem somewhat odd that financial information, normally construed to be primarily factual and numbers-oriented, can also have a strong rhetorical dimension. However, in an entry to the New Palgrave Dictionary of Money and Finance, entitled "The Rhetoric of Finance", the well-known economist Deirdre McCloskey (1992, p. 350) writes "the jargon of the financial market is of course ripe for rhetorical study". This claim is supported in the ensuing discussion of some rhetorical features of financial language (e.g., metaphor, figures of speech, story-telling) whose origins can be traced back to Aristotle's masterpiece *Rhetoric*. On a general level, classical rhetorical analysis of language typically refers to the three modes of persuasion described by Aristotle in *Rhetoric* (Book I, Chapter II): *logos* (appeals to reason), *ethos* (appeals to good character) and *pathos* (appeals to emotions). More specifically, Aristotle defines logos as the speaker's "power of proving a truth, or an apparent truth, by means of persuasive arguments, ethos as "the speaker's power of evincing a personal character which will make his speech credible, and pathos as "his power of stirring the emotions of his hearers".[14]

2.4.2 Executive financial communication

In the context of financial disclosure, some research has applied the classical framework described above to gain insights into rhetorical strategies in

---

[14]   (GE) and the late Steve Jobs (Apple).
From the online version of *Rhetoric* available at http://rhetoric.eserver.org/aristotle/index.html, based on the translation of the classical scholar W. Rhys Roberts, and made available electronically by Lee Honeycutt.

written documentation attributed to top management, namely the executive letters that typically accompany annual reports. It should be noted that we cannot be entirely sure of the actual authorship of these documents: they may be penned by the executive who signs them, represent a joint effort of more than one executive (Geisler, 2001) or even be "ghost-written" by professional writers acting as company spokespeople (Hyland, 2005, p. 74). At any rate, they are always attributed to executive management and are intended to be construed as such.

Hyland (2005) found that CEOs' letters to shareholders embedded in annual reports of companies listed on the Hong Kong stock exchange contained a range of rhetorical features that could be interpreted as expressions of logos, ethos and pathos. For example, executive writers expertly used logical connectives (e.g., *therefore, nevertheless*) in order to appeal to readers' sense of rationality and therefore steer their interpretation of the message in the desired direction. Such connecting devices also create a sort of 'dialogue' that tells readers how ideas should be connected and thus understood, encouraging the reader to accept the writer's position. The presence of phrases such as *we strongly believe* and *our duty* serve to foster ethos, i.e., a perception of the writer's (and consequently the company's) credibility and reliability. Pathos is communicated through language that conveys emotions (e.g., *pleased, confident, concerned*), as well as first and second person pronouns that establish an interpersonal connection and solidarity with readers.

Strikingly similar rhetorical appeals were also identified by Chakorn (2008) in a corpus of Chairman's messages incorporated into Thai companies' annual reports. Interestingly, expressions of pathos (e.g., words linked to thanking and conveying solidarity) were usually found at the end of the messages, perhaps in an effort to leave readers with a favourable impression. In a case study dealing with a large international firm based in France, Chanal and Tannery (2011) analysed CEOs' oral financial communications to investors during roadshows,[15] finding a prominent use of logos in highly sophisticated argumentation patterns, with less evidence of ethos and particularly pathos.

A recent study by Marais (2012) perhaps sheds some light on underlying motivations of CEOs' rhetorical strategies in financial communication. A content analysis was carried out to identify types of rhetoric used by CEOs of French firms in written and oral communications with investors and shareholders in the context of corporate social responsibility. In these cases, the CEOs' frequently engaged in what the

---

[15]   A financial roadshow is a series of meetings across different cities in which top executives meet and interact with current or potential investors.

author called "instrumental rhetoric" (ibid., p. 227) to "develop pragmatic legitimacy", i.e., the perception among stakeholders that they will in some way benefit if they opt to support the company.

In this chapter, the concept of financial disclosure, its instruments and important issues related to the use of English and corporate leadership have been discussed to bring into focus the two genres that will be investigated in this study: earnings presentations and earnings releases. In the next chapter, we will shift our attention to the methodological approach that will be applied to analyse these genres.

Chapter 3
The three-pronged analytical approach

3.1 Discourse analysis: a top-down method

Discourse analysis can be defined as the study of authentic types of text and talk, with particular attention to how they are organised above the sentence level or and how they are influenced by the social setting in which they take place (Stubbs, 1983). It is the emphasis on the contextual aspects of communication that go beyond mere words and phrases (hence the term *top-down*) that makes discourse analysis a particularly suitable method for this study that focuses on speech and writing used by professionals for purposes of financial disclosure.[16]

According to van Dijk (1997), there are three fundamental criteria that come into play when analysing discourse: 1) *language use* (how it is used, by whom, when, where and why), 2) the *communication of beliefs* (within the context of an event or situation) and 3) *interaction* (among the participants of the social setting). By considering all three dimensions, discourse analysis offers not only systematic descriptions of language, but also explanations of its usage. In addition, there are also several principles that should guide discourse analysts (ibid.), which as can be summarised in the following points:

- Text and talk to be analysed should be naturally occurring and unedited;
- Discourse should be studied as an integral part of its local, global, social and cultural context;
- Both written and spoken forms of discourse should be studied and construed as forms of social practice;
- All levels or structural units of texts should be described and interpreted relative to the preceding ones;
- Discourse analysts should seek to understand not only meanings (what or how), but also motivations for given usages (why);
- Discourse analysts should seek to uncover challenges to rule-governed language use and reveal strategies of speakers and writers;
- Discourse   analysts   should   consider   the   shared   socio-cultural

---

[16]   An excellent explanation of the terms *top-down* vs. *bottom-up* from the linguistic perspective is provided by Brown and Yule (1983, p. 234), who describe them as "world knowledge" vs. "words on a page", respectively.

representations (e.g., knowledge, attitudes, ideologies) of language users when describing and explaining their language.

In addition to formulating these principles, van Dijk (1977) also developed the important concept of the *macro-structure* of a text, meaning the global description of the content of a text based on the hierarchical sequencing of its parts. More specifically, understanding how the content of a text unfolds helps us understand what speakers and writers aim to accomplish.

3.1.1 From discourse to genres

While *discourse analysis* highlights the relationship between texts and the social context in which they are used, *genre analysis* goes a step further by describing texts according to their textual and lexico-grammatical features which reflect the needs and purposes of a given community of practice. Referring to genres and genre analysis, Hyland (2013, p. 1) states

> Genres are the recurrent uses of more-or-less conventionalised forms through which individuals develop relationships, establish communities, and get things done using language. As a result, genre analysis sees texts as representative of wider rhetorical practices and so has the potential to offer descriptions and explanations of both texts and the communities that use them.

The modern concept of *genre* can be traced back to Bakhtin, whose essay *The Problem of Speech Genres* (1986) first introduced the idea of language as a product of social relations and not of isolated minds. According to Bakhtin (1986, p. 78), *speech genres* are

> determined by the specific nature of the given sphere of communication, semantic (thematic) considerations, the concrete situation of the speech communication, the personal composition of its participants, and so on.

Speech genres are further classified as *primary speech genres* used for daily communication (e.g., conversation) and *secondary speech genres* which take place in a sphere of communication that is relatively formal and culturally-organised (e.g., discourse in institutions or professions). This socially-oriented theory of genre, as opposed to the traditional literary-oriented view[17], provides important insights into the nature of both spoken and written

---

[17]   Literature genres are exemplified by the novel, the poem or the play (Steen, 1999).

discourse in specific communicative settings because it highlights the relationships among participants, as well as how they exploit text types to achieve their aims.

Beginning in the 1990s, the Bakhtinian concept of genre has seen significant expansion into the area of language for specific purposes. Genre analysis has become a widely used method to study specialised spoken and written texts in terms of their recurring structural patterns that are articulated into series of rhetorical moves (Swales, 1990), which can be determined by the communicative purpose of the discourse participants within a given interactional context. The Swalesian method of genre analysis was originally developed for the study of academic research articles, but has since been applied in numerous other domains, including law (cf. Bhatia, 1993), politics (cf. Trosborg, 2000) and media (cf. Scollon, 2000). Genre analysis has also been widely applied to the study of business discourse, offering key insights into the language of corporate settings on both the descriptive and interpretive levels (cf. Bargiela-Chiappini & Harris, 1995; Ruiz-Garrido, 2001; Zhu, 2005).

3.1.2 New trends in genre analysis

In light of the vast number of genre-based studies that have emerged over the last three decades, it is not surprising that this approach has been elaborated and expanded to incorporate new perspectives and challenges. In fact, there has been a 'revisitation' of the concept of genre (Swales, 2004), stemming from research suggesting that the fundamental criterion of *communicative purpose* to distinguish a particular genre is often not as straightforward as it may seem. Genres may have "complex, multiple and evasive" social purposes and functions (ibid., p. 69), and indeed may need to become "repurposed" (ibid., p. 72) on the basis of new insights, but also according to changing social trends. A case in point is the company annual report. What was previously a rather sober fact-oriented genre addressed to a relatively small number of stakeholders has become a dynamic, graphically attractive and somewhat promotionally-oriented genre available to a much wider audience thanks to the Internet.

Another aspect of genre-based language study that has come to the forefront in recent years concerns how different genres are related to one another. Bhatia (2004) described these relationships in terms of the position of genres either *within* or *across* professional discourse domains. In the case of genres within domains, we may find *genre sets*, which refer to a variety of text types that a specific discourse community produces in the course of daily work routines, e.g., various kinds of letters serving different purposes used by companies to communicate with clients. He also explained the broader concept of *genre systems*, citing Bazerman (1994), which also includes the genres produced by all discourse participants involved in the interaction (e.g., both companies and their clients). To explore how genres are used across domains, Bhatia (2004) introduced the concept of *genre colonies*, representing groups of genres that have essentially the same communicative purpose, but are used by different communities of practice. For example, promotional genres can be found in academics (e.g., book reviews), business (e.g., advertisements) and public administration (e.g., informative campaigns).

However, there are other types of relationships that can exist between genres. Räisänen (1999) and Swales (2004) have described *genre chains* as chronological successions of genres linked to a series of events, where one is a necessary requisite for the other. In Chapter 2, we saw a clear example in the genre chain of financial disclosure. Genres may also form a *genre network* (Swales, 2004, p. 22), which includes all the genres that are available for use in a particular sector in any given moment in time. In the same way, Fairclough (2003, p. 69) used the term "situated genres" to refer to those used for "particular networks of practices". An interesting feature of the genres that comprise a genre network is that they can be *recontexualised* (Linell (1998, p. 154), which involves

> [...] the extrication of some part or aspect of a text or discourse, or from a genre of texts or discourses, and the fitting of this part or aspect into another context, i.e., another text or discourse [...].

This is often found in professional settings, where texts are re-elaborated or re-compiled from other texts (e.g., company annual report derived from previously elaborated financial statements).

It is also possible to analyse individual genres 'from within' in order to reveal their links to other genres. Bhatia (2004) described instances of *genre mixing*, where we find two or more genres embedded within the same text type (e.g., a letter or interview embedded within an advertisement), and *genre bending*, where the features of one genre are appropriated into another in such a way as to create conflicting interpretations. This is particularly characteristic of texts used for persuasive purposes. For example, texts that are similar to book reviews are often used by commercial enterprises to promote their products (i.e., advertorials). However, they focus exclusively on the positive attributes rather than providing the kind of balanced evaluation that is typically associated with the original genre.

In the above discussion of genres and their interrelationships, there are two important underlying concepts that help us to understand these phenomena better. The notion of *intertextuality* was inspired by Bakhtin's (1986, p. 69) affirmation that "any utterance is a link in a very complexly organised chain of other utterances". Genres display intertextuality when they explicitly or implicitly incorporate texts from other sources (Candlin & Maley, 1997). Fairclough (1992, p. 271) makes a distinction between *manifest* intertextuality, where a given text contains an explicit reference to another specific text (e.g., references to previous correspondence in letters or previous events during meetings), and *constitutive* intertextuality, where a given text is formulated according to the conventionalised practices of other types of texts (e.g., an advertisement formulated as an interview). The latter type of intertextuality actually has much in common with what others have called *interdiscursivity*, where genres incorporate features of other discourses and practices (Bhatia, 2010), e.g., a financial presentation that incorporates accounting discourse and promotional discourse. As pointed out by Bargiela-Chiappini and Nickerson (1999), both intertextuality and interdiscursivity are very useful analytical constructs for investigating the communicative practices of large organisations that produce multiple types of texts for various purposes within a complex structure of internal and external relations.

In sum, it is clear that genre analysis is a powerful tool capable of shedding light on the complex and dynamic processes involved in the production and interpretation of discourse found in professional contexts.

3.1.3 Genre analysis and rhetoric

The connection between genre analysis and the rhetorical dimension of communication was suggested by Hyland's (2013) quote found at the beginning of this chapter which describes genre analysis in terms of rhetorical practices. This perspective also surfaces from the work of scholars of new rhetoric genre theory who focus on the situational context in which genres occur, with particular attention to the social actions or purposes that genres aim to achieve (Miller, 1984, Freedman & Medway, 1994).[18] Indeed, Miller (1984, p. 151) affirms:

> a rhetorically sound definition of genre must be centered not on the substance or the form of discourse but on the action it is used to accomplish

Similarly, Heuboeck (2009, p.38) views rhetoric in discourse as "intentional

---

[18]   New rhetoric studies focus on the capacity of discourse to trigger actions, whereas classical rhetoric in the Aristotelian tradition is more interested in the formal and aesthetic characteristics of persuasive speech and writing (Enos, 1996).

(purpose-driven) and instrumental (designed to fulfil that purpose)". These interpretations of rhetoric strongly reflect the *purpose* of communication, and thus are closely aligned with the key feature necessary to distinguish a genre, i.e., its communicative purpose.[19] In particular, genre analysis determines the schematic structure texts in terms of functional moves which sheds light on the communicative purposes of speakers and writers, as well as the rhetorical organisation of texts, i.e., how they are structured in order to achieve a desired outcome.

Structural analyses of genres can also be undertaken within the framework of argumentation theory which is closely aligned with rhetoric (cf. van Eemeren et al., 1996). In particular, argumentative genres (e.g., editorials, reviews, essays) can be articulated into different parts, such as the *claim-data-warrant* pattern described in Toulmin's (1958) model for analysing arguments. Here the claim is that statement that is to be accepted, the data is the backing for the claim and the warrant is the link between claim and data, which together constitute a rhetorical strategy based on logic.

From the above discussion, it is clear that a full understanding of a genre necessarily encompasses its rhetorical dimension. Andrus (2013) discusses the notion of *rhetorical discourse analysis* as the intersection between the field of *rhetoric* and *discourse analysis*. I would like to extend this framework to also comprise *genre analysis* in order to account for the specificity of texts associated with particular discourse communities and their purposes, as illustrated in Figure 3.1.

---

[19]   In his seminal work, Swales (1990, p. 58) defines genres as communicative events whose members "share some set of communicative purposes" and describes discourse communities as "socio-rhetorical networks that form in order to work towards sets of common goals" (ibid., p. 9).

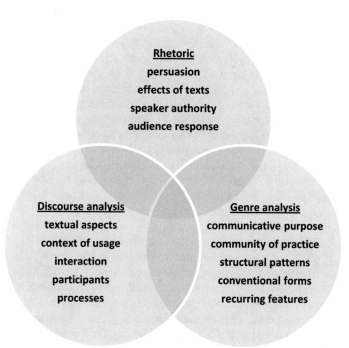

Figure 3.1: Rhetoric, discourse analysis and genre analysis

3.1.4 Analysing spoken vs. written genres

In this section, I discuss speech vs. writing as the two main modes of communication that come into play in the investigation of oral earnings presentations and written earnings releases. As we have seen in Chapter 2, communication mode is an important aspect of financial disclosure which ultimately reflects the strategic choices of companies. Therefore, it is important to have a thorough understanding of key differences between speech and writing that may influence these choices.

The first studies of variation across spoken and written genres distinguished a series of characteristics considered typical of spoken vs. written language (Chafe, 1985). In speech, the face-to-face and real-time nature of the interaction is encoded by features of involvement and fragmentation, such as first and second person pronouns, simple coordinating conjunctions (e.g., *and*, *so*), flow-monitoring devices (e.g., *well*, *now*), dysfluencies and ellipsis.[20] In writing, both the remoteness from readers and editing possibilities inherent to written language are reflected in features of detachment and integration (e.g., nominalisation, attributive or pre-posed adjectives, participle forms). Another difference between speech and writing is how attitudes are expressed, particularly with regard to *evidentiality* (ibid., p. 118), or how reliable knowledge is judged to be. The remote production of written language leads writers to be more concerned about the accurateness and reliability of propositions in comparison to speakers who engage in direct and 'on-the-spot' interaction with others. The real-time vs. remote production factor was also underscored by Ochs (1979) who observed that unplanned spoken discourse tends to contain more demonstratives, active voice and present tense in comparison with planned written discourse.

Halliday (1989) explained variation in speech and writing in terms of process vs. product, where spoken language is a dynamic process with a structure based on verb clauses, while written language is a static product with high lexical content that privileges nominal groups. Brown and Yule (1983) maintain that spoken language is primarily interactional (i.e., used to establish social relations and express attitudes), while written language is primarily transactional (i.e., used to explain and transmit information). Similarly, Tannen (1993) described spoken discourse as having a focus on interpersonal involvement and internal evaluation. This is reflected in language where there is more speaker intrusion (i.e., self-references), as well as greater subjectivity, emotivity and ambiguity. On the other hand, written language focuses on the content of the message, characterised by detachment from the text and external evaluation, and tends to be more objective, logical and precise.

However, both Chafe (1985) and Halliday (1989) caution against a rigid polarisation of spoken vs. written language. For example, some forms of speech (e.g., news broadcasts, prepared formal addresses) may completely lack features that are normally associated with spoken discourse, such as dysfluencies and ellipsis, while including such features as formal linking adverbials (e.g., *however, as a consequence*) found more frequently in carefully planned written language. On the other hand, some written texts (e.g., novels, letters) may purposely assume a conversational style by using contractions, emphatic particles and marked use of evaluative expressions. Indeed, such hybridisation is likely to become more pronounced in light of the constantly evolving technologies that will lead to new modes of

---

[20]   Dysfluencies are false starts, repetitions and pause fillers (e.g., *uh, erm*), while ellipsis refers to the omission of lexico-grammatical elements of sentence of clause structure that can be recovered from the linguistic or situational context (e.g., *Any questions?* vs. *Do you have any questions?*) (Biber et al., 1999)

communication which exhibit a blending of attributes of spoken and written discourse. A good example is the email where we find numerous features of spoken language embedded in a written text. These involve both linguistic properties, such as informal expressions, marked ellipsis, lack of punctuation (Louhiala-Salminen, 2002; Argondizzo & Plastina 2004), but also content that is emotionally-charged and encourages the personal disclosure of writers (Baron, 1998). Fairclough (2001, p. 23) points out the growing influence of visual communication in modern society as witnessed in the mass media and affirms that "the traditional opposition between spoken and written language has been overtaken by events".

The notion of blurred boundaries between spoken and written language was also discussed by Gunnarsson (1998) who emphasised the need to look at text and speech in an integral way. Speech and writing are frequently not separate events, but instead constitute components of a process that combines them into an intertextual chain. For example, an oral business presentation may be derived from previously written notes, but also incorporate other types of written texts (e.g., printed documents or Powerpoint slides). In addition, technological features have also changed traditional associations of spoken language with real time face-to-face interaction and written language with remote interaction and lack of temporal constraints. In fact, oral communications that utilise telephony and, more recently, Internet technologies are in real time but interlocutors are not physically face-to-face.

3.2 Corpus linguistics: a bottom-up method

Corpus linguistics refers to the study of language using a relatively large amount of machine-readable text, known as a *corpus* (*corpora* in the plural form). A useful extended definition of the term *corpus* that captures both its essence and usage is found in *The Oxford Companion to the English Language*, (McArthur [Ed.] 1992, p. 266):

> In linguistics and lexicography, a body of texts, utterances, or other specimens considered more or less representative of a language, and usually stored as an electronic database. Currently, computer corpora may store many millions of running words, whose features can be analysed by means of tagging (the addition of identifying and classifying tags to words and other formations) and the use of concordancing programs. Corpus linguistics studies data in any such corpus.

A more concise and practice-oriented definition was provided by John Sinclair, the leading figure behind the dramatic rise of corpus linguistics in recent years as "a collection of naturally occurring language text, chosen to characterise a state or variety of a language" (Sinclair 1991, p. 171). The important feature of representativeness is further highlighted in McEnery and Wilson's (1996, p. 177) description of a corpus as a "finite collection of a machine-readable text, sampled to be maximally representative of a language or variety".

Corpus-based studies use rigorously authentic language. This is not in itself a new approach. As we have seen at the beginning of this chapter, traditional discourse analysis also makes use of authentic texts. However, corpus linguistics differs in its use of data in electronic form which can be analysed systematically by means of automatic and large-scale retrieval of items of interest. In fact, corpus linguistics has developed considerably in recent years thanks to the possibility of elaborating large quantities of text in order to generate empirical evidence of particular features of language usage. Thus, just as discourse analysis is considered to be a relatively new approach to the study of language in use (van Dijk, 1990), corpus linguistics can be seen as a 'newcomer' to textual analysis, due to its reliance on increasingly sophisticated computer technology. Yet corpus linguistics is quite distinct from discourse analysis in its focus on lexico-grammatical features at the micro level, which can be described as "bottom-up" from the text, rather than "top-down" from the context (Brown & Yule, 1983).

However, it is important to recognise that corpus linguistics involves much more than simply collecting and automatically processing texts. In fact, the task of the corpus linguist is not only to find texts and transform them into analysable format, but also to interpret the results. On this point, Fairclough (2003, p. 6) offered the following somewhat critical comment about excessive emphasis on automated analyses:

> Such findings are of value, but their value is limited, and they need to be complemented by more intensive and detailed qualitative textual analysis.

In other words, it is crucial to integrate the 'bottom-up' information derived from the computerised study of individual words or phrases (e.g., word frequency counts and distributions, co-occurrences and patterning, keyword analysis) with the 'top-down' knowledge derived from the broader textual context and situational aspects of usage.

Various types of corpora have been developed over the years by language researchers for a range of different purposes, including linguistic analysis, lexicography and natural language processing applications, such as speech recognition devices and machine translation systems. Corpora have also been effectively exploited in the area of language teaching. McCarthy (2004) discusses "corpus-informed" approaches where corpus research findings and corpus data itself can be used to design educational curricula and materials.

The initial development of corpora for language applications dates back to the early 1960s, corresponding to what Kennedy (1998, p. 23) has called "first generation corpora". The first major electronic corpus was The Brown Corpus, made available in 1961, consisting of one million words of written American English. In the same year, the LOB (Lancaster-Oslo-Bergen) corpus was designed to contain one million words of British written English to complement the Brown corpus. These early corpora are now considered to be *sample corpora* since they contain fragments of texts rather than complete texts, now the recommended procedure in corpus collection (Sinclair, 1991). The LLC London-Lund corpus was the first spoken corpus (435,000 words) and was based on transcriptions of recordings of speech.

In the years that followed into the 1980s and 1990s, it became clear that for certain types of research (e.g., large-scale lexicographical projects and studies of regional language variation), it was necessary to have much larger corpora. This led to the development of "second generation megacorpora" (Kennedy 1998, p. 45) that contained many millions of words of both spoken and written English. These large scale projects have contributed to the growing body of language that is now available to researchers, and to advancing the field of corpus linguistics, not only to improve its analytical techniques, but also to expand on its theoretical issues. For example, Tognini-Bonelli (2001, p. 2) considers corpus linguistics to be an approach that "operates within the framework of contextual and functional theory of meaning". She articulated two distinct approaches to the use of corpora. One is *corpus-based*, which uses corpus evidence to test or support pre-existing notions (i.e., deductive), while the other is *corpus-driven*, which uses corpus data itself as the primary source of evidence from which new theories can be developed (i.e., inductive).

3.2.1 Corpus design

There are many criteria that need to be considered when designing a corpus, such as size, variety of language (both national and dialectal), characteristics of the producers of the texts (e.g., age, language background), mode of transmission, period of time covered, and texts types and genres to be included (Pearson, 1998; Luzón et al., 2007). These decisions are ultimately governed by the type of corpus one is aiming to create and especially how it will be used. If a corpus is being designed for general purposes, then it will be as large as possible and incorporate many different types of language. Following Sinclair (1991), a *general corpus* is compiled from a large variety of sources so that the individuality of any one source becomes obscured. This type of corpus has also been characterised as *heterogeneric* (Partington 2003, p. 4). Examples are mega-corpora such as the Bank of English, the British National Corpus (BNC) and the Longman Corpus Spoken and Written

English, which have been developed to be representative of language in general for the benefit of the scientific community at large. They are especially suitable for the production of grammars and dictionaries, but also serve the important function of benchmarks for other language studies.

However, because more and more linguists have begun to use corpus-inspired methods, there is now a growing tendency to design smaller corpora with specific research goals in mind. Such corpora are typically much more restricted in scope, perhaps targeting only written or spoken language, or a particular historical period, or even specific varieties of language that occur only in certain contexts. These corpora have been described as *specialised* (Partington 2004, p. 13) or *monogeneric* (Partington 2003, p. 4) in terms of both the type of language they contain and their purpose. Pearson (1998, p. 48) made a more fine-tuned distinction, using the term "special purpose corpora" to refer to specialised corpora as described above, while reserving the term "special corpora" for those that contain language that in some way deviates from the norm (e.g., the language of very small children).

Because specialised corpora are more restricted in scope and have fewer language variables, they naturally tend to be smaller in size than general corpora. Yet it is vital that they are carefully designed according to well thought-out criteria. Towards this aim, following Pearson (1998, p. 52-53), we can make a distinction between "external" criteria, referring to mode, genre, origins, participants and aims, from "internal" criteria, which instead involve topic and style. Attention to both types of criteria is important if a specialised corpus is to achieve the purpose for which it was created.

When compiling a specialised written corpus, the selection of appropriate materials is greatly facilitated by the pre-existing nature of print itself, e.g., books, articles, essays. Written corpora usually require only minor adjustments to be transformed into an analysable format. On the other hand, when compiling a spoken corpus, it is often necessary to access a live speech event and arrange to record it. This entails a number of potentially complicating issues, such as costs, availability of recording equipment, permission to record, as well as unforeseen 'glitches' that may include technical equipment break-downs, disturbances and last-minute changes involving the agenda or speakers. These can render data incomplete, inconsistent in quality or, at worst, unusable. Such difficulties in the assembly of spoken corpora can lead to what McCarthy (1998, p. 8) described as an "opportunistic" design, whereby compilers tend to 'throw in' whatever data they have been able to access and collect.

The above difficulties can be attenuated by using 'pre-collected' spoken data from other sources. Nowadays, the Internet is becoming an increasingly rich source of audio files of recorded speech and even corresponding transcripts that can be downloaded directly for research purposes. While this drastically reduces many of the difficulties involved in accessing live speech and generally increases the availability of data for linguistic analysis, the fact that the researcher is completely removed from the recording and transcription process can also be a disadvantage. Biber et al. (2002) note that not being able to participate and observe interactions can result in the loss of key information about the setting, unless it can be recuperated in some other way, for example by contacting the participants involved in the speech event or utilising other reliable sources of information. Thus, decisions concerning the source of data for spoken corpora must be weighed with careful consideration to the financial and logistical issues involved in the project, the type of corpus to be collected and the research aims.

3.2.2 Corpus techniques

As we have seen above, the distinguishing feature of *corpus linguistics* is its reliance on computer-assisted methods to study language stored in electronic form, making it possible to systematically analyse large amounts of authentic speech and writing. This is achieved by processing the text with computer software applications that generate quantitative profiles of linguistic features.[21] For example, a particular item can be searched and retrieved automatically, along with empirical data on its frequency and distribution in the corpus, something which would not be feasible with traditional manual discourse analysis, unless one is working with very limited amounts of text.

According to Scott (2008), corpus software allows us to understand "how words behave in texts". This is accomplished through a series of specific functions and tools provided by text analysis software. With the wordlist tool, all the words in a text can be processed in both alphabetical and frequency order. The software also provides key statistical information, such as type (number of different words)/token (number of running words) ratio, number of sentences and number of paragraphs. The concordancer tool produces vertical lists of a searched item, along with some co-text to the right. This is useful for understanding important types of patterning, including collocates (items that tend to co-occur), colligates (items that tend to occur in certain grammatical patterns), and whether an item tends to be used in positive or negative contexts of meaning. Searched items can also be lemmatised, so that a search for the lemma *go* will retrieve all it morpho-syntactic variations (i.e., *goes, going, gone* and *went*).

In addition, corpus software programs can produce graphical images of the distribution of particular items from the beginning to the end of a text, i.e., whether they tend to occur at certain positions, or whether they are

---

[21]   Some widely-used ones are *Wordsmith Tools* (Scott, 2008), *MonoConc* (Barlow, 2004) and *Sketch Engine* (Kilgarriff et al., 2004).

uniformly distributed across the text or the speech event. Information about how words combine together can also be accessed. *Clusters* are multi-word units which are found repeatedly together in a given text, representing a closer relationship than collocates (Scott, 2008). These have also been called *lexical bundles* (Biber et al. 1999, p. 994) and more recently *n-grams*, defined by Stubbs (2007, p. 90) as "recurrent strings of uninterrupted word forms". In the case of two- or three-word units, we may also refer to *bigrams* or *trigrams*. It is also possible with some corpus tools to identify *concgrams*, i.e., recurring associations of two are more words that are not necessarily contiguous (Cheng et al., 2006).

Another important feature of corpus-based analyses is the possibility to annotate texts with various types of additional information (often called *mark-up*) that is useful to integrate into the raw text of an electronic corpus. At the most basic level, corpora can be marked up with structural annotation (e.g., page and paragraph breaks), but also with identifying and contextual annotation (e.g., title, source, author, speaker, date, register or genre), also called *metadata*, i.e., 'data about data' (Wynne, 2004). Particularly for spoken corpora, it can be useful to annotate other types of contextual information that can help researchers better interpret utterances, such as indications of laughter, silence, or accompanying physical gestures. This type of annotation is typically done by means of well-established standards that indicate how corpora should be marked up. For example, the Text Encoding Initiative (TEI) mark-up system provides guidelines to facilitate accessibility and comprehensibility of corpus resources among the community of language researchers. For example, TEI mark-up distinguishes various types of extra-textual information within the characters "<....>", which can then be excluded from computerised analytical procedures. In this way, valuable structural or contextual information is still available to researchers, but does not interfere with automatic searches and search item processing.

The degree to which mark-up is necessary or useful depends on various factors: 1) whether the corpus was compiled/transcribed by researchers or whether texts/transcripts were procured 'ready-made' from other sources, 2) whether the corpus was originally compiled/transcribed specifically for linguistic research or not, and 3) which types of discourse and linguistic features are to be investigated within the framework of the research. For instance, in the case of dialogic discourse containing overlapping speaker turns with research targeting prosodic features, mark-up will need to be extensive. On the other hand, in the case of monologic discourse with research that focuses on certain linguistic or contextual features, mark-up can be minimal.

Linguistic annotation instead adds information that is useful on the analytical level. Part-of-speech (POS) tagging assigns a code to each lexical unit indicating its part of speech. It is perhaps the most basic form of linguistic annotation and provides an important foundation for further types of analysis. Moreover, by performing a search on a particular category of tag (e.g., general adjectives) rather than only certain lemmas, it is possible to carry out exhaustive analyses on entire word classes. Part-of-speech taggers now achieve a high level of accuracy. According to the website of the CLAWS part-of-speech tagger developed by UCREL (University Centre for Computer Corpus Research on Language) at Lancaster University, the accuracy rate of their POS tagger is 96-97 per cent. Semantic tagging is another tool that assigns all lexical items in a corpus to pre-established semantic domains, and labels each accordingly. A semantically tagged corpus can provide insights into salient themes and values associated with a particular type of discourse and the community that uses it.

Other more advanced types of corpus annotation involve marking the text with discursive or pragmatic tags, such as dialogue turns or speech acts (Leech, 2005). On an even higher level of annotation, we find *parsing*, which entails not only the grammatical category, but also the function of each word in a group or phrase, e.g., subject, object or verb complement (Kennedy, 1998).

3.2.3 Comparability of corpora

According to Sinclair (2001), one of the main reasons for carrying out corpus-based language study is to make comparisons between different varieties of language. In fact, the distinguishing features of one type of text only come to the forefront when contrasted to another type of text. Going a step further, Partington (1998, p. 146) commented:

> By and large, we are not methodologically justified in interpreting the significance of a particular linguistic event unless we can compare it with other similar events.

One of the major applications of comparative corpus-based research has been in the field of translation and contrastive studies (Aijmer & Altenberg, 1996). The general premise of contrastive studies is that the entities that are compared differ in some respect, but also present some degree of sameness, i.e., the concept of *tertium comparationis*, which can refer to various levels of discourse comprising macrostructure, lexis, syntax and phonological features (Connor & Moreno, 2005). It is now quite common to investigate language from a multilingual perspective through the collection of *parallel* or *comparable* corpora. Although there is some discrepancy as to how these two terms have been used in the literature (Pearson, 1998), the general consensus is that *parallel* corpora contain source texts and their translations in two or more languages (e.g., laws and statutes of the European Union translated into different languages), while *comparable* corpora contain texts with a similar content or composition in two or more languages (e.g., collections of articles published on certain topics in the newspapers of different countries).

Although the term *comparable* is often used with reference to multilingual corpus study, the idea of corpus comparability is not restricted only to this area. Indeed, monolingual corpora can also be considered comparable when they are matched according to certain parameters of particular interest to the research, such as genre, register, mode of delivery, domain, topic, period, and characteristics of participants. As pointed out by Ädel (2006), it is important that two corpora are comparable in some respect in order to justify the research, e.g., corpora representing certain genres, but within the same discourse domain. At the same time (and for the same reason), there must be some clear differential that constitutes the focus of the research, e.g., corpora representing speakers of different language backgrounds or different modes of communication. These criteria for corpus comparability are reflected in the present study. In fact, the two corpora under investigation are similar because they represent parallel financial genres. Yet they are also different in terms of their communicative mode (spoken vs. written), which constitutes the key contrastive dimension of the study.

So far, I have discussed the key issues involved in the 'top down' approach of discourse analysis which begins by looking at a text from a global standpoint and the 'bottom up' perspective of corpus linguistics that focuses on individual words and phrases. This two-pronged approach has also been described by Biber (2008) as applying a theoretical framework to a text (top-down) and then analysing its patterns with corpus linguistics (bottom-up). The combination of these approaches is gaining ground among language researchers, particularly when dealing with genres and that are used in specific contexts and with particular discourse communities. However, in this case, to accurately interpret findings, it is important to integrate this dual-focused approach with a third approach that is able to provide contextual insights into the community of practice in question. This issue will be addressed in the next section.

3.3 Professional contacts: an ethnographically-inspired method

When linguistic research deals with discourse used in a particular domain with which language researchers may be unfamiliar, it is important to find ways to integrate vital contextual knowledge in order to more accurately interpret findings. One ethnographically-inspired method is to interview professional informants whose pertinent real-life experience can confirm and further illuminate research results (Swales, 1998; Hyland, 2000; Flowerdew,

2002), or gain insights into "how the speech events/texts under investigation fit into the overall communicative context" (Garcés-Conejos & Fortanet-Gómez, 2009, p. 72).

Agar (1996, p. 58) states that research carried out from an ethnographic perspective involves "the long-term association with some group, to some extent in their own territory, with the purpose of learning from them their ways of doing things and viewing reality". The ability to procure this type of external knowledge is particularly useful in the presence of a "rich point" (Agar 1996, p. 30), i.e., a phenomenon which the researcher is unable to clearly interpret due to the gap between the world of the researcher and the world being studied. Similarly, with such knowledge, researchers are able to construct 'thick' or explanatory descriptions that consider the social processes involved in the research context, as opposed to 'thin' descriptions based only on factual information that emerges from an analysis (Geertz, 1973, p. 12).

In an effort to fill in contextual gaps, I established contact with a professional working in the field of finance and investment. Over the course of the research, I corresponded with him via email and also conducted a face-to-face interview. This professional has vast experience with the earnings call as a communicative event and has participated in as many as 200 earnings calls per year. As an investment analyst, he represents the audience to which both earnings presentations and earnings releases are directed. In fact, because this informant was on the receiving end of the discourse, the focus of our discussions was mainly on contextual issues, participant relationships and the social dynamics underlying the communicative event, rather than on the specific language choices of the speakers and writers themselves. Thus, the data collected from these contacts served to provide important background about the context of communication of interest to this study that could not be otherwise ascertained.

Chapter 4
Evaluation as a rhetorical strategy

4.1 Evaluation in discourse

According to *The Cambridge International Dictionary of English*, the verb *evaluate* means "to judge or calculate the quality, importance, amount or value" Although this definition refers to general English usage,[22] it nonetheless shares a common core of meaning with *evaluation* as a linguistic phenomenon. In language research, *evaluation* can be broadly defined as how writers and speakers express attitudes, opinions and judgments (Thompson & Hunston, 2000). Evaluation in this sense has received an increasing amount of attention from linguists who are particularly interested in the interactional, interpersonal and rhetorical dimensions of communication, and no longer strictly concerned with the idea of language as an expression of propositions or ideas (Aijmer, 2005).

The underlying concept of evaluation is actually not a new one and has been addressed in the literature by a number of scholars. However, quite different terminology has been used to describe the various facets of this phenomenon: *connotation* (Lyons, 1977), *modality* and *modalisation* (Halliday, 1985), *evidentiality* (Chafe, 1986), *commentary markers* (Fraser, 1996), *stance* (Biber & Finegan, 1988; Biber et al., 1999; Hyland, 1999), *evaluation* (Thompson & Hunston 2000; Hunston, 2011) and *appraisal* (Martin, 2000; Martin & White, 2005). While these various descriptions are all oriented towards attitudinal meanings, they are not necessarily interchangeable as each has its own focus and patterns of articulation. Throughout this study, I use the term *evaluation* to refer to the superordinate concept, unless when discussing a particular framework associated with one of the above-mentioned linguists.

Evaluation can be expressed by speakers and writers in a myriad of different ways. It can be encoded linguistically through the choice of certain adjectives, adverbs, nouns, verbs, but also grammatically through the use of modals, tense or aspect. Evaluation may also function at the textual level depending on its position in a text. For example, it is often found at particular discourse boundaries, such as the end of a paragraph, or it may signal clause relations within a paragraph (Thompson & Hunston, 2000). Moreover,

---

[22] It is worth noting that in general usage *evaluate* also means *assess*, especially in academic and professional settings.

evaluation can be expressed paralinguistically (e.g., intonation, laughter, silence) and even extra-linguistically (e.g., gaze, gestures, body posturing). Thus, we are undoubtedly dealing with a very complex phenomenon that can permeate all types of language from diverse directions. Testimony to this are the numerous lengthy publications dedicated to evaluation that have appeared in recent years (see Table 4.1). It is interesting to note the trend of acceleration seen in the table after Hunston and Thompson's milestone volume published in 2000. Another indication of the growing importance of evaluation as a linguistic construct is the development of a website dedicated to *appraisal* which contains useful resources and a discussion forum for all those interested in this aspect of communication.[23]

---

[23]   The Language of Attitude, Arguability and Interpersonal Positioning - www.grammatics.com/Appraisal

Title	Format	Author/Editor/Year
Evaluation in text: Authorial stance and the construction of discourse	Book	Hunston & Thompson (Eds.), 2000
Evaluation in academic discourse (*Journal of English for Academic Purposes*)	Special Issue 2 (4)	Bondi & Mauranen (Eds.), 2003
Negotiating heteroglossia: Social perspectives on evaluation (*Text*)	Special Issue 23 (2)	Macken-Horarik & Martin (Eds.), 2003
Academic discourse. New insights into evaluation	Book	Del Lungo Camiciotti & Tognini Bonelli (Eds.), 2004
Evaluation in oral and written academic discourse	Book	Anderson & Bamford (Eds.), 2004
The language of evaluation. Appraisal in English	Book	Martin & White, 2005
Evaluation in media discourse. An analysis of a newspaper corpus	Book	Bednarek, 2006
(R)evolutions in evaluation (*Textus*)	Special Issue XX (1)	Dossena & Jucker (Eds.), 2007
Stance-taking in discourse	Book	Englebretson (Ed.), 2007
Evaluation and text types (*Functions of Language*)	Special Issue 15 (1)	Bednarek (Ed.), 2008
Appraising research: evaluation in academic writing	Book	Hood, 2010
Corpus approaches to evaluation. phraseology and evaluative language	Book	Hunston, 2011
Evaluative uses of language: The appraisal framework (*Revista Canaria de Estudios Ingleses*)	Special Issue 52 (Nov 2012)	Hernández Hernández & González Rodríguez (Eds.), 2012
Stance and voice in written academic genres	Book	Hyland & Sancho Guinda, 2012
Evaluation in context	Book	Thompson & Alba-Juez (Eds.), forthcoming

Table 4.1: Survey of publications dedicated to the concept of evaluation

4.2 An overview of evaluation in linguistic research

Labov (1972) was one of the first linguists to use the term *evaluation* in relation to the narrative structure of a text, where it refers to the main point of the story and why it was recounted. He identified four main evaluative devices that are used to enrich the narrative: *intensifiers* to strengthen and emphasise statements, *comparators* to evaluate events by offsetting them against others, *correlatives* to highlight similarities with other events and *explicatives* to explain why or how an event happens. Shifting to the micro-level of words and phrases, Lyons (1977) recognised that words can have emotive or affective components of meaning in addition to their central meaning, a phenomenon which he called *connotation*.

Within the framework of systemic functional linguistics, the expression of attitudes and opinions fall under the sphere of *interpersonal* meaning. According to Halliday (1978), this type of meaning is used to establish and maintain personal relations, and entails the status of the participants, degree of familiarity, as well as affect, i.e., the emotional component of the communication or the viewpoint or attitude towards the topic. Speakers and writers also use *modality* subjectively to grade their propositions (e.g., *I think*, *perhaps*) (Halliday, 1985). Modality can be further articulated into *modalisation* (relating to probability or usuality) and *modulisation* (relating to obligation and inclination). Chafe (1986, p. 262) similarly described the concept of *evidentiality*, or "attitudes towards knowledge". He categorised *evidentials* into three main types: degree of reliability (e.g., *probably*), indications of knowledge based on belief (e.g., *I believe*) and indications of reasoning (e.g., *apparently*). Thus, Chafe tended to view the expression of attitudes and opinions more in terms of likelihood (what is also referred to as *epistemic modality* - Palmer 1979) and less in terms of positive vs. negative assessments. This perspective began to broaden with Biber and Finegan's (1988) study of adverbials of stance which revealed several other functions beyond probability, most notably attitude (e.g., *sadly*) to evaluate some entity positively or negatively.

In a more recent study, Linde (1997) looked at evaluation from the perspective of its role in social interaction. She investigated the use of evaluative language in professional settings as a way to understand aspects of group identities and values, and how these are established, maintained and shared. In particular, she focused on how evaluation is used among professionals who are working with new communication technology. She showed how one speaker's explicit evaluations of the technology are in turn negotiated with other speakers until satisfactory closure on the matter is reached. In addition, evaluation served the functions of marking the end of a discourse segment and filling in gaps of silence that occur when using technological devices. Therefore, evaluation is not only an expression of social values, but also an important structural instrument of discourse. Indeed, evaluation is described as standing "at the cross-roads of linguistic and social structure" (ibid., p. 170).

Given the complexities involved in how speakers and writers convey evaluation, in recent years, several linguists have developed important theoretical frameworks and analytical models to help us better understand its semantic and functional features. Indeed, we now have the option of choosing among some very comprehensive models that delve much deeper into the concept of evaluation than the earlier studies and provide a greater articulation of its various facets. In the following sub-sections, I review some particularly broad-spectrum models that have been widely applied to the study of evaluation in different types of discourse.

4.2.1 Biber, Johansson, Leech, Conrad and Finegan

In Biber et al.'s (1999) highly influential work the *Longman Grammar of Spoken and Written English*, the concept of evaluation is referred to as *stance*, i.e., how speakers and writers express their attitudes, opinions and judgments. According to Biber et al.'s (ibid.) model, stance markers can be classified into three principal types: *epistemic, attitudinal* and *style of speaking*. Epistemic stance refers to the level of commitment that speakers and writers make to the truth value or reliability of their propositions. Typical examples are *probably, I think, without a doubt*, as well as hedges such as *sort of* and *kind of*. Indications of the source or perspective of information (e.g., *according to the government*) are also put into this category. Attitudinal stance has to do with the expression of personal feelings or emotions (e.g., *love, afraid*), or attitudes (*interestingly, ironic*). Style of speaking stance (e.g., *honestly, with all due respect*) refers to speakers' and writers' commentary on the unfolding communication itself, or what other linguists have referred to as *reflexivity* (Mauranen, 2001) or *metadiscourse* (Ädel, 2006; Hyland, 2005). On this particular point, there is actually a certain amount of disagreement as to the distinction between *stance* and *metadiscourse*. Taking a broad perspective, Hyland (ibid.) considers attitude markers that convey stance to be a sub-category of interactional metadiscourse. On the other hand, Mauranen (2002) and Ädel (2006) take a narrow perspective and consider metadiscourse to be only elements that refer to the text itself and exclude any attitudinal devices.

Using the corpus compiled for the *Longman Grammar of Spoken and Written English*, Biber et al. (1999) have tested their model of stance. They have shown that the attribution of stance can be explicit (e.g., *I hope, it seems to me*) or implicit without specific referents (e.g., *it could be that, typically*). Moreover, the corpus findings indicated that, overall, stance markers are considerably more frequent in conversation in comparison with written registers. In particular, some of the most common evaluative adjectives and adverbs of stance (e.g., *good, nice, really*) are more prominent in conversation as compared to written academic prose. The fact that this model of stance has been applied to a large corpus and has yielded rigorous empirical data that serves as a benchmark for language researchers worldwide is a clear demonstration of its value.

4.2.2 Hyland

Another important model was developed by Hyland (1999) who also used the term *stance*, originally with reference to written discourse and, in particular, to research writing. In Hyland's (ibid., p. 101) words,

> Stance refers to the ways that writers project themselves into their texts to communicate their integrity, credibility, involvement and a relationship to their subject matter and their readers. It therefore expresses a writer's socially defined persona [...]

Hyland proposed a taxonomy of stance markers articulated into five different categories (1999, p. 103-104):

1. hedges: to indicate a lack of complete commitment (e.g., *perhaps, might, generally*);
2. emphatics: to signal certainty and force (e.g., *it is obvious, of course*);
3. attitude markers: to express affective attitude (e.g., *unfortunately, remarkable*);
4. relational markers: to address readers explicitly (second person pronouns, question forms, imperatives);
5. person markers: to present propositional material (first person pronouns).

In a later study, he referred to stance as the "attitudinal dimension" of written discourse (Hyland, 2004:15), in which we can find both attitudinal and epistemic meanings realised by four types of devices: boosters, hedges, attitude markers and self-mention (ibid., p. 16).

Hyland's model of stance has proved to be a valid framework, especially in terms of understanding aspects of a given discourse community's practices and values, and how stance devices are used rhetorically to promote solidarity and persuade others.

4.2.3 Thompson and Hunston

A landmark contribution to understanding how speakers and writers express attitudes and opinions is certainly represented by the volume *Evaluation in Text*, edited by Hunston and Thompson (2000), which contains a collection of articles written by leading linguists who have dealt with this notion. In the introductory chapter to the volume, Thompson and Hunston (2000, p. 5) define *evaluation* (the term they prefer) as:

> the broad cover term for the expression of the speaker or writer's attitude or stance towards, viewpoint on, or feeling about entities or

propositions that he or she is talking about. That attitude may relate to certainty or obligation or desirability or any number of different values.

Thus, their conception of evaluation comprises epistemic, deontic and positive/negative attitudinal meanings. Their framework is articulated into three fundamental functions of evaluation. First and foremost, it is used to *express opinions and attitudes*. This refers to an underlying system of values that can be described along four parameters: positive-negative, certainty, expectedness and importance. Second, evaluation is used to *establish and maintain relations*. By means of devices such as mitigation and politeness, speakers and writers are able to manipulate language as they see fit. Finally, evaluation is used to *organise discourse*. By imposing a particular structure on an unfolding text, speakers and writers constantly monitor and comment on the text itself. Yet the authors point out that these three functions are not mutually exclusive. Evaluative resources may perform more than one function at the same time, which further contributes to the pervasiveness of evaluation in language. Parallel to the three functions of evaluation are specific categories of linguistic and discursive devices by which it can be expressed:

1. expressing opinions and attitudes: lexical items including adjectives, adverbs, nouns and verbs that encode a positive or negative value (e.g., *beautiful, terribly, success, fail*);
2. establishing and maintaining relations: lexico-grammatical devices including modal verbs and adverbs, hedges and emphatics that express various degrees of certainty or politeness (e.g., *could, may, possibly, sort of, really*);
3. organising discourse: textual devices referring to discourse structuring patterns that encode evaluation due to the positioning in the text (e.g., *and that is the upshot of what happened* in the final position in a narrative passage.

The far-reaching conceptualisation of evaluation provided by this model is further reinforced by its correspondence to the three metafunctions of language at the basis of Hallidayan systemic functional linguistics: *ideational* (expressing opinions), *interpersonal* (maintaining relations) and *textual* (organising discourse).

4.3 Martin & White's appraisal model

The most recent comprehensive framework for the study of evaluative language was developed by Martin and White (2005) and introduced in their book *The Language of Evaluation. Appraisal in English*. These authors use the term *appraisal* to refer to "the way language is used to evaluate, to adopt stances, to construct textual personas and to manage interpersonal positionings".[24] From this description, we can see that the strong interpersonal focus of this model renders it particularly well suited to an investigation of the rhetorical dimension of communication to shed light on how interlocutors assume positions with the aim of influencing others. For this reason, among the various theoretical frameworks described above, for this study I have opted to utilise the appraisal model.

In an earlier paper, Martin (2000) described appraisal as a system for categorising linguistic resources used to express emotions, moral assessment and evaluations, which corresponded to the sub-categories of *affect, judgment* and *appreciation*. According to this model, *affect* refers to how emotions are construed (e.g., *fear, happy*), *judgment* to how moral evaluations of behaviour are construed (e.g., *ethical, brave*) and *appreciation* to how aesthetic quality is construed (e.g., *innovative, desirable*). This model was later greatly expanded in Martin and White (2005). Appraisal is now described as having three major dimensions, among which features of *affect, judgment* and *evaluation* are subsumed into the first (*attitude*). There are two new dimensions: *engagement* that involves interpersonal positioning with respect to others, and *graduation* that calibrates the strength of evaluation. The new model is illustrated schematically in Figure 4.1 and will be further explained in the following subsections.

---

[24]   www.grammatics.com/Appraisal

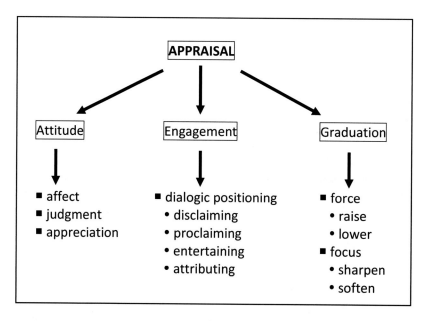

Figure 4.1: The appraisal model (adapted from Martin & White 2005)

4.3.1 Attitude

As can be seen in the figure, *attitude* (feelings, judgments of behaviour and evaluations of things) is still articulated into the three sub-categories of *affect, judgment* and *appreciation* as in the earlier version of the appraisal framework (Martin, 2000). However, in the new model, *affect* is reserved for the expression of feelings and emotions attributed to the self or other participants, while *appreciation* involves the evaluation of things, that can be concrete, abstract or semiotic. *Judgment* refers to attitudes towards behaviours that can be criticised or praised. The new model also makes provisions for borderline cases and recognises a certain degree of overlapping among the three sub-categories. For example, the same attitudinal lexis can be used to judge the behaviour of a person (e.g., *It was honest of him to come*) and to appreciate a thing (e.g., *I consider it to be an honest book*). Similarly, *affect, appreciation* and *judgment* can all merge in a negatively-charged word like *disgust*, where a person can feel disgusted (*affect*), find something *disgusting* (appreciation) and be disgusted with someone's actions (*judgment*). Attitude can be further described as *inscribed* when it is encoded explicitly with inherently evaluative lexis, but also as *invoked* when it invites an attitudinal interpretation. For instance, in the phrase *we were packed in like sardines*, the negative attitude is found in the ideational meaning of the phrase rather than in any inherently negative lexis.

4.3.2 Engagement

Engagement is concerned with the interplay between different voices in discourse, i.e., whether and how speakers/writers position their own ideas and opinions dialogically with those of others. In other words, engagement has to do with how speakers and writers acknowledge what others have previously expressed, what they assume others may believe or how they expect others to respond. This is achieved through lexico-grammatical items that convey alignment/disalignment (or agreement/disagreement) in relation to attitudes, beliefs, situations or events. Resources for engagement are categorised as follows:

- Disclaiming: denying (negation) or countering (e.g., *although, however*);
- Proclaiming: concurring (e.g., *of course*), pronouncing (e.g., *I contend*), endorsing (e.g., *he has shown*);
- Entertaining: recognising alternatives (e.g., *apparently, perhaps*);
- Attributing: acknowledging (e.g., *he believes*) or distancing (e.g., *he claims*).

With this strongly dialogic perspective of engagement, Martin and White (2005) draw on the Bakhtinian notions of heteroglossia vs. monoglossia to conceptualise engagement and systematically account for utterances that allow for dialogistic options (heteroglossic), as opposed to simple assertions that do not (monoglossic). For example, the bare statement *He was wrong* is monoglossic in nature. On the other hand, by proclaiming a position in *I would argue that he was wrong*, the speaker acknowledges the possibility of an alternative view, and therefore the statement is heteroglossic in nature.

In another example of engagement, the use of *although* has a disclaiming function in the statement *Although she was the best qualified, she did not get the job*. It expresses the speaker's alignment which is at odds with a certain turn of events. At the same time, it signals an expectation that the interlocutor will interpret the statement in the same way.

4.3.3 Graduation

The third major dimension of the model, *graduation*, refers to the gradability of evaluation, i.e., the adjustment of the degree of evaluation in terms of how strong or weak it is. In other words, it has to do with the upscaling or downscaling of evaluation. According to Martin and White (2005), graduation is actually a somewhat fuzzy category. It overlaps into *attitude* because it can reflect greater or lesser degrees of positivity or negativity, but it also coincides with *engagement* because it can serve to vary the degree of speakers' and writers' alignment with others. However, for purposes of clarity, graduation is described within the appraisal model in two ways:

-    as the *force* of attitudes that can be *raised* or *lowered* through devices of intensification or quantification (e.g., *extremely*, *small*);
-    as the *focus* of boundaries of attitudes that can be sharpened or softened (e.g., *absolutely*, *sort of*).

From the above description of the appraisal model, we can see that it is firmly grounded in systemic functional linguistic theory, referring especially to the interpersonal metafunction. However, it adds new depth to this concept by placing greater emphasis on feelings and attitudes, which expands the traditional focus on interactional features (e.g., mood and modality) in the Hallidayan framework. Thus, with the appraisal model, we are able to achieve a fuller understanding of interpersonal meaning in discourse. In Martin and White's words (2005, p. 1), we can understand

> how writers/speakers construe for themselves particular authorial identities or personae, with how they align or disalign themselves with actual or potential respondents, and with how they construct for their texts an intended or ideal audience.

To summarise this section, it is clear that an analytical framework of such a comprehensive scope can provide important insights into the rhetorical aims of speakers and writers. It can enable us to see how evaluative language is used in various ways and from different angles in order to negotiate meaning according to strategic communicative goals.

4.4 Previous research on evaluation in financial discourse

The theoretical frameworks of evaluation, stance and appraisal described in the previous sections have inspired numerous studies in various discourse domains, including academic (e.g., Fortanet-Gómez, 2008; Hood, 2010), media (e.g., Murphy, 2004; Bednarek, 2006) and politics (e.g., Miller, 2004; Ponton, 2011). Relatively few studies have investigated financial discourse from this standpoint and have been largely restricted to written forms of financial disclosure. These will be reviewed in the following paragraphs.

Referring to Thompson and Hunston's (2000) framework, Malavasi (2006) analysed evaluative adjectives and verbs across four sections of banks' annual reports (Chairman's Statement, Chief Executive's Report, Bank and Business Description, and Corporate Governance Description), concluding that they are used to convey a positive image of competitiveness, international importance and innovativeness. Similarly, Piotti (2006) found a marked presence of positive evaluative lexis (e.g., *excellent, important, preferred*) in both CEOs' letters and Chairmen's statements produced by executive managers of US and UK companies. These items were frequent in passages that emphasised the notions of *relevance* and *reliability*, in an attempt to persuade readers of the quality of the information. Also applying Thompson and Hunston's (2000) evaluation framework, Poncini and Hiris (2012) analysed CEOs' letters of US securities firms in a period of financial crisis and determined that both explicit/implicit evaluative lexis were used strategically to orient perceptions in challenging times.

With reference to Hyland's (1999) conceptualisation of stance, Piotti (2009) analysed hedging strategies in the annual reports of European-based multinational companies. She found that hedges such as *generally* and *typically* often functioned as vagueness markers in contexts in which writers aimed to steer readers' perceptions towards overall performance and away from precise outcomes.

The appraisal framework was implemented in Maat's (2007) study of corporate press releases to classify promotional elements in the form of evaluative lexis (e.g., *leading, terrific*) in terms of attitude (appreciation), and intensifying adjectives (e.g., *important, extensive*) in terms of graduation. Interestingly, these appeared not only in the news-oriented segments of the press releases, but also in the informative segments that reported financial results. The author also noted a strong discrepancy between what he found in reality and what is typically recommended in press release style manuals, i.e., to "avoid excessive use of adjectives" (ibid., p. 62). In a recent study that distinguishes itself by dealing with computer-mediated financial discourse, Sokól (2011) used the appraisal framework to analyse attitudinal positioning among participants in an Internet forum dedicated to investing in the Polish stock exchange. Her analysis highlighted the linguistic construction of participant identities through positioning strategies that differentiate 'insiders' from 'outsiders' within the discussion community.

As the studies reviewed in this section have shown, the application of theoretical frameworks to analyse evaluation in language can provide important insights into the rhetorical aims of professionals who engage in communication for financial purposes.

5.1 The corpora

This study is based on a contrastive analysis of two small specialised corpora of financial discourse: spoken earnings presentations (hereinafter EP) and written earnings releases (hereinafter ER). The corpora were specially designed and collected within the framework of this analysis. As discussed in Chapter 3, there are several factors to consider when designing a corpus, such as size, variety of language, mode of transmission and period of time covered. These decisions are influenced by the type of corpus envisaged and its foreseen use. For example, if a corpus is designed with a specific research goal in mind, then it is likely to be more restricted in scope, perhaps targeting a particular domain of language and thus considered to be a "specialised" corpus (Partington, 2004, p. 13). When designing and collecting corpora of discourse used in professional environments (particularly corporate settings), accessibility becomes an extremely important issue. In fact, because business organisations are very concerned about safeguarding their confidentiality, we cannot assume that they will 'open their doors' to language researchers in the same way that academic institutions usually do. Testimony to this attitude, Warren (2004) found that compiling the business sub-corpus of the *Hong Kong Corpus of Spoken English* proved to be the most challenging of all the discourse domains that are represented.

In compiling the two corpora for the study, the issues mentioned above emerged at various levels. With reference to corpus design, because the research aim entails spoken and written variation in financial discourse, the two corpora were created to reflect these features. Although they are both genres that report financial information, one uses the spoken channel, while the other uses the written channel. However, the overall content of the two corpora is substantially equivalent; both the companies and the reported financial periods to which the corpora refer have been strictly matched. In this way, any significant variation can be more accurately attributed to the spoken vs. written mode, without being influenced by substantial differences in content. With reference to accessibility, in order to collect the spoken data that make up the EP corpus, it was necessary to procure special permission, which was fortunately granted, albeit with some conditions that will be explained in the following sub-section.

5.1.1 The Earnings Presentations (EP) corpus

The EP corpus consists of the transcripts of 25 earnings presentations (approximately 101,000 words) given by executives of multinational corporations to investment analysts via teleconferencing, i.e., a multi-party telephone call organised and moderated through an external teleconferencing service. As anticipated above, it was compiled thanks to the special authorisation of an Internet-based firm that provides information services for the global financial community. These include teleconferencing services that allow companies to organise events in which they can interact with investors and other stakeholders by means of technology-mediated communication systems. The firm produces and distributes financial documentation for interested parties, such as written briefs and transcripts of the spoken events conducted via teleconferencing. Access to these services is normally available to carefully screened business professionals and on payment only. However, after contacting the Internet firm and explaining my research interests, I was granted complimentary access to their website for a period of 30 days during which I was able to download the transcripts of a series of earnings presentations that were given during conference calls between corporate executives and professional investment analysts.[25] The 25 earnings presentations utilised for this study were, in fact, extracted from a larger corpus of complete conference calls (approximately 300,000 words), which also includes extended question and answer sessions between the executive presenters and the investment analysts participating via telephone. These will not be dealt with in the present study. On the whole, I believe that the collection of this corpus reflects a valid compromise to reconcile the problematic issues of data accessibility in private corporate settings and "opportunistic" corpus design (McCarthy, 2004, p.8 – see Chapter 3) that necessarily came into play here.

According to the Internet firm, all conference calls are transcribed by experienced professional transcribers and the transcriptions represent a verbatim report of the call. The final versions of the transcripts have been listened to a second time by a team of professional editors to confirm that the content of the call has been transcribed accurately. The final transcripts have also been approved by the companies hosting the events.

All of the earnings presentations exploited the audio mode via telephone without accompanying video facilities. However, one call was also scheduled to coincide with a live earnings meeting so that some investment analysts

---

[25]   I am grateful to the Academic Program of CCBN Street Events (now Thomson Street Events) for granting me permission to access their transcripts for my research purposes.

were connected via telephone while others were physically present. Five of the 24 audio-only earnings presentations were webcast simultaneously from the companies' websites. Unfortunately, I was not granted access to the audio files of the earnings presentations for reasons of corporate confidentiality. Nevertheless, because this study does not focus on language features that would be crucially influenced by paralinguistic phenomena, I believe that the possibility of accessing spoken discourse from a relatively large number of sensitive business environments to which linguists rarely have access amply compensates for not having the corresponding audio files.

Table 5.1 provides an overview of the EP corpus. As can be seen, it covers a wide range of business sectors – from information technology, to manufacturing industries, to service-oriented companies. Most of the companies were headquartered in the US and therefore most of the presenters were native speakers of American English. This is because the majority of the companies that were available during the limited access period happened to be US-based. However, in an attempt to offer a realistic picture of today's globalised business activities which are increasingly conducted among speakers of diverse language backgrounds using English as a *lingua franca*, an effort was made to include as many international firms as possible. Among the presenters there was one speaker of British English and several who were native speakers of other languages: German, Finnish, Korean, Spanish and Hindi.[26] The financial periods that were reported on during the presentations ranged from the third and fourth quarters of 2003 to the first quarter of 2004. The number of speakers from the executive management team ranged from one to six, with an average of three. Also evident from the table is the rather wide variation in the word counts of the transcripts, from approximately 1,000 to 7,000 words, with an average of 4,178 words. Thus, some presentations were relatively brief events, while others were much longer and elaborate in terms of content.

---

[26]   Because the transcripts include the names of all speakers, I was able to verify language backgrounds from the corresponding biographical sketches of the top management available on corporate websites.

Comp	Business sector	Headquarters	N. speakers	N. words
C1	Information technology/IT	US	3	6,803
C2	Insurance	Germany	2	5,314
C3	Internet retail	US	3	2,422
C4	Consumer Finance	US	2	3,461
C5	Computers	US	6	1,398
C6	Banking	US	3	4,451
C7	Restaurants	US	4	2,838
C8	Food products	US	3	5,654
C9	Chemicals	US	2	4,826
C10	Internet retail	US	3	3,672
C11	Digital technology	US	4	1,872
C12	Pharmaceuticals	US	2	3,863
C13	Energy	US	4	6,248
C14	Biotechnology	US	3	7,169
C15	Semiconductors	US	3	3,804
C16	Banking	US	4	3,098
C17	Chemicals	US	4	4,096
C18	Electronic products	Finland	3	3,071
C19	Foods and staples	US	3	3,357
C20	Oil and gas	Netherlands	1	2,641
C21	Electronic products	Korea	6	3,974
C22	Electronic products	US	2	2,310
C23	Media	US	4	5,627
C24	Electronic equipment	US	2	3,120
C25	Internet services	US	4	6,304
			TOTAL	101,393

Table 5.1: The EP corpus

5.1.2 The Earnings Releases (ER) corpus

The ER corpus (approximately 47,000 words) consists of 25 earnings releases also downloaded from the Internet. Unlike the transcripts of earnings presentations, earnings releases are freely accessible to any Internet user, typically from the investor relations page of the websites of major companies. According to IBM España (2005), among 170 of the largest companies that they surveyed from all over the world, the vast majority maintains websites with links to areas that contain both financial and non-financial news. These are known alternatively as the press room, press area, media relations or media centre, where various types of press releases are posted and archived for several years. In these archives, the companies normally classify press releases according to their content: those containing primarily financial information (i.e., *earnings releases* based on quarterly financial periods) and those reporting non-financial news about various company activities and initiatives, often called *news releases*.

An overview of the ER corpus is shown in Table 5.2. As can be seen, the companies, business sectors and headquarters correspond exactly to those listed in Table 5.1. In fact, the ER corpus was designed to be strictly comparable to the EP corpus. When downloading texts to compile this corpus, the companies and financial periods (comprising the third and fourth quarters of 2003 and the first quarter of 2004) could be matched exactly to those of the EP corpus by searching for the corresponding earnings releases on the companies' websites. In this way, the overall content of the two corpora is largely equivalent. Most of the earnings releases (17 out of 25) contain both verbal text and accompanying tables of data (e.g., consolidated earnings information, statement of operations, cash flow statement, balance sheet, net sales and business outlook).

Company	Business sector	Headquarters	Format	N. words
C1	Information technology/IT	US	Text/tables	2,199
C2	Insurance	Germany	Text/link	1,927
C3	Internet retail	US	Text/tables	1,617
C4	Consumer Finance	US	Text/tables	2,925
C5	Computers	US	Text/link	727
C6	Banking	US	Text/tables	2,466
C7	Restaurants	US	Text/tables	1,017
C8	Food products	US	Text/tables	1,829
C9	Chemicals	US	Text/tables	1,549
C10	Internet retail	US	Text/tables	2,218
C11	Digital technology	US	Text	748
C12	Pharmaceuticals	US	Text/tables	2,860
C13	Energy	US	Text/tables	1,839
C14	Biotechnology	US	Text/tables	2,314
C15	Semiconductors	US	Text/tables	2,619
C16	Banking	US	Text/tables	1,168
C17	Chemicals	US	Text/tables	1,843
C18	Electronic products	Finland	Text	797
C19	Foods and staples	US	Text/tables	2,412
C20	Oil and gas	Netherlands	Text/link	2,776
C21	Electronic products	Korea	Text	630
C22	Electronic products	US	Text/tables	3,985
C23	Media	US	Text	780
C24	Electronic equipment	US	Text	1,042
C25	Internet services	US	Text/tables	2,427
			TOTAL	46,715

Table 5.2: The ER Corpus

As can be deduced from the word counts, earnings releases tend to be much shorter texts with respect to the earnings presentations. Indeed, while 25 earnings presentations total about 101,000 words, the same number of earnings releases totals only about 47,000 words. This is probably influenced by the pre-formulated nature of such releases (Jacobs, 1999) where the authors can streamline information into more concise formats, unlike the transcribers of earnings presentations who must produce a verbatim record of the oral speech of the executive presenters. Yet there is noticeable variation in the word counts of the individual earnings releases, ranging from less than 1,000 to close to 4,000, with an average of 1,868 words. Therefore, some companies issued much more detailed earnings releases than others. It should be noted that the word counts here refer to the verbal text only. Because these electronic files were then prepared for elaboration with *WordSmith Tools* (Scott, 2008) which processes data only in textual format, all tables of data were removed. However, the original files complete with tables that had been downloaded from the Internet in html or pdf format were conserved for other types of analysis, as will be discussed in the next section.

To conclude this section, in line with the research aims and the characteristics of the two corpora under investigation, both were prepared for elaboration with *WordSmith Tools* (Scott, 2008) using a very limited amount of TEI mark-up (see Chapter 3) to distinguish individual transcript/text files and their key structural components, e.g., speaker turns, titles, subtitles.

5.2 The analysis

Concerning small corpora, Sinclair writes:

> A small corpus is seen as a body of relevant and reliable evidence, and is either small enough to be analysed manually, or is processed by a computer in a preliminary fashion [...]; thereafter the evidence is interpreted by the scholar directly. (2001, p. :xi)

The methodology used in this study reflects this dual-focused approach, drawing on quantitative methods from corpus linguistics and qualitative discourse analysis (see Chapter 3), thus combining electronic text elaboration with the in-depth reading of the printed transcripts (EP corpus) and text files (ER corpus). This approach is especially appropriate when, as in this case, research focuses on complex phenomena such as evaluation and rhetoric. Indeed, because such phenomenon tend to focus on meaning rather than linguistic form, they are often difficult to investigate with a single methodological approach, be it quantitative or qualitative (Hunston, 2004).

According to Henry and Roseberry (2001), in addition to yielding empirical data obtained via computerised processing, small corpora can offer other important insights since they can also be analysed from a global perspective. Therefore, as an initial step, a *structural analysis* was performed on the two corpora in order to identify differences and similarities in their macro-structures (van Dijk, 1977; Swales, 1990; Bargiela-Chiappini & Harris, 1995; McLaren & Gurău, 2005). Given the relative newness and lack of previous research on the two genres in question, it seemed important to first familiarise readers with them by providing a broad overview of their content and organisation. The structural analysis was carried out by means of a careful study of the earnings presentations transcripts and the original html or pdf files of the earnings releases, in order to identify recurring moves, as meaningful units of discourse linked to communicative and rhetorical purposes, as well as their patterning in the texts.

5.3 Analysing rhetorical features with the appraisal model

Discrete rhetorical features of the two corpora were investigated through the application of Martin and White's (2005) appraisal model, which was thoroughly illustrated and discussed in Chapter 4. In order to identify which types of rhetorical features were particularly prominent in the two corpora and therefore worthy of further analysis, I first carried out a preliminary manual overview of the EP corpus transcripts and the ER corpus text files. This process revealed what seemed to be a marked use of evaluative adjectives (e.g., *excellent, fantastic*), formal concessive connectives (e.g., *although, however, despite*), and intensifiers and mitigators, i.e., lexical items that serve to strengthen or weaken the force of an evaluative meaning (e.g., *very, slightly*).

To complement the initial perusal of the printed versions of the two corpora, the corresponding electronic versions were then submitted to processing with *WMatrix* (Rayson, 2008), a powerful corpus tool that is able to classify and tag each word according to its semantic domain. The software automatically assigns each word in a corpus to a pre-established semantic field based on 21 over-arching semantic domains (e.g., *Money & commerce, World & environment* and *Emotional actions, states & processes*), which are then further articulated into over 200 specific semantic tags. According to the developer of the software, the semantic tagger has an accuracy rate of 92%. The tool then generates a graphic image in the form of a cloud of items to illustrate which semantic fields have a statistically significant higher frequency in the corpus in question when compared to a larger normative corpus, i.e., the BNC Sampler of Spoken English (982,712 words) for the EP corpus and the BNC Sampler of Written English (968,267 words) for the ER corpus.[27] The purpose of this procedure was to corroborate my initial impression of the most salient rhetorical features in the two corpora. Indeed, if semantic fields that encompassed evaluative adjectives, concessive connectives and intensifiers/mitigators turned out to have significantly high frequencies, this would strengthen the case for their selection as features for the rhetorical analysis.

The key semantic domain clouds produced for the EP corpus and the ER corpus with the procedure described above are shown in Figures 5.1 and 5.2, respectively.

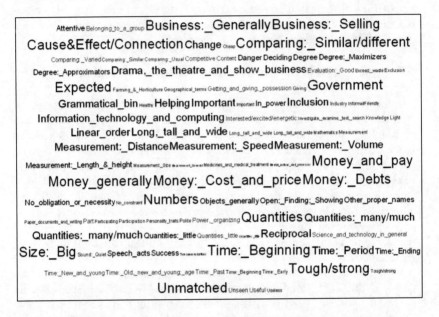

Figure 5.1: EP corpus key semantic domain cloud (Source: *WMatrix*)

---

[27]   The software calculates statistically significant differences at a level of confidence of $p < 0.01$ (99th percentile) when comparing a given dataset to a standard normative text using the log-likelihood method. Items that appear with significantly higher frequencies are then given a keyness score.

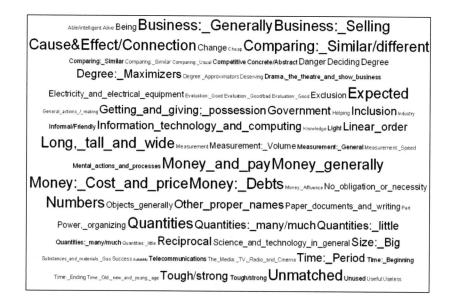

Figure 5.2: ER corpus key semantic domain cloud (Source: *WMatrix*)

Although all the domains present in the two clouds have statistically significant frequencies, those that appear in the larger fonts have the highest keyness scores and are thus the most outstanding in this communicative context. To be considered key, a domain must have a keyness score of 6.63 or higher. The keyness scores of the top 100 key semantic domains of the 216 found in the EP corpus and the 79 domains returned as key for the ER corpus are reported in Appendices 1 and 2, respectively.

A quick comparison of the two clouds and lists of domains in Appendices 1 and 2 highlights a striking similarity, with limited variation in terms of which semantic fields are present and which are particularly strong as shown in the larger fonts. This is not surprising considering that the two corpora were designed to have parallel content (i.e., matching companies and financial periods), and the highly similar clouds indicate that this objective was achieved.

Each domain shown in the clouds could then be further elaborated to produce lists of all the items that are contained within it. For example, within the domain *Evaluation_good*, we find items such as *great* and *outstanding, top-line*, within *Grammatical_bin* items such as *while* and *although*, and within *Degree* items such as *fairly* and *relatively*. This procedure allowed me to identify key semantic domains that largely correspond to the three rhetorical features previously hypothesised, as shown in Table 5.3.

Rhetorical features	Semantic domain tags
Evaluative adjectives	- Evaluation_good/bad - Tough/strong - Success - Interested/excited/energetic
Concessive connectives	Grammatical_bin (contains all grammatical conjunctions and discourse connectives)
Intensifiers/mitigators	- Degree - Degree_maximiser - Degree_approximator

Table 5.3: Rhetorical features and corresponding semantic domain tags

Once the three rhetorical features selected for analysis had been validated through the above-described process, they were then mapped onto the appraisal model as follows:

Evaluative adjectives   → attitude
Concessive connectives → engagement
Intensifiers/mitigators   → graduation

Speakers and writers use evaluative adjectives rhetorically to convey their positive/negative   feelings,   approving/disapproving   judgments   and appreciation/lack of appreciation towards some entity. For this reason, evaluative adjectives are revealing of *attitude*. In the appraisal model, *attitude* embodies the most direct and overt form of evaluation.

Concessive connectives are used to link two propositions when one is admitted (or conceded) and the other is "presented as more valid than the first and somehow goes against the expectations elicited by it" (Garzone, 2005a, p. 132).[28] These devices have also been referred to as conjunctions of concessive relations (Halliday & Hasan, 1976), which may be internal (i.e., derived directly from the content of the propositions in question) or external (i.e., requiring a reasoning process that is less direct, going beyond the propositions themselves), as shown in the following invented examples:

---

[28]   According to Vergaro (2008, p. 98), the word *concessive* "belongs to the terminology developed within traditional grammar to classify adverbials and adverbial clauses. Izutsu (2008) notes that there is a lack of consensus on a clear distinction between *concessive* and *contrastive* meanings. For the purposes of this study, *concessive* meanings entail the countering of conceded weaker propositions with stronger ones within an argumentative context.

(5.1) *Although* we were very tired, we continued to work for several more hours. (internal concessive relation)

(5.2) The current situation is not positive. *However*, we are confident that it will improve in the future. (external concessive relation)

As can be seen from the above examples, concessive connectives may take the form of adverbials (e.g., *although, even if, while, whereas*) or prepositions (*despite, in spite of, notwithstanding*) used to introduce a subordinate clause within a hypotactic construction, where the subordinating clause expresses the protasis and the main clause contains the apodosis (Crystal, 2003, p. 28). Alternatively, concessive connectives can be syntactically free-standing devices used before a main clause, such as the conjunctions *however, nevertheless, even so, still,* and *yet.*

In the appraisal model, concessive connectives are considered to be resources of *engagement*. More specifically, they allow speakers and writers to observe a given reality, and then intrude to express their own stance towards it, thereby anticipating potentially challenging reactions. In example 5.2, after conceding a negative situation, the writer uses *however* to counter-react with a positive evaluation, thus pre-empting the reader's entirely negative assessment. Concessive connectives are thus dialogically-oriented evaluative devices through which speakers and writers communicate their own stance in such a way as to anticipate and influence the stance of their interlocutors. According to Martin and White (2005), as devices of dialogical positioning, concessive connectives have a *disclaiming* function whereby speakers and writers counter or are in some way at odds with a given position.

Intensifiers and mitigators are instead part of the *graduation* component of the appraisal model in that they serve to adjust the *force* of evaluation, i.e., how strong or weak it is. This adjustment can refer to qualities (e.g., *very* nice), processes (e.g., we were *slightly* late) and modalities (e.g., it is *quite* possible). Other linguists have studied the same type of evaluative devices, but have each formulated their own terms of reference: *hedges* and *boosters* (Hyland 2000), *amplifiers, downtoners* and *degree modifiers* (Biber et al., 1999) and *evidentials* (Chafe, 1986).

5.3.1 Attitude: evaluative adjectives

After the EP transcripts and the ER text files were compiled into two separate electronic corpora, part-of-speech tagged versions of each were created with the CLAWS tagger (see Chapter 3). This software attaches a tag to every lexical unit throughout the entire corpus that indicates its grammatical category. For this procedure, the CLAWS7 tagset was applied. It has over

160 tags, representing an extremely rich articulation of all English parts-of-speech.[29]

The two tagged corpora were then queried with the text analysis software suite *WordSmith Tools* (Scott, 2008). In each corpus, a search was performed on the general adjective tag (JJ) in order to generate concordance lines (i.e., vertical lists of the searched item with some co-text to the right and to the left) for all potentially evaluative adjectives. The adjectives were then examined manually and classified as evaluative or not according to Martin and White's (2005) construct of *attitude*, referring to positive or negative evaluations. It is important to point out that when dealing with an open grammatical category such as adjectives in relatively large samples of text, the automatic tagging procedure is the only viable way to carry out a sufficiently exhaustive analysis. In addition, to render follow-up qualitative analysis practicable, only adjectives which are considered to be the "canonical realisation of attitude" (Martin & White 2005, p. 58) were searched. Other types of evaluative lexis in the form of adverbs, nouns and verbs that can also encode positive/negative attitudes were not dealt with here.

5.3.2 Engagement: concessive connectives

The concessive connectives to be investigated were selected on the basis of the results of the manual preliminary overview and the semantic domain analysis of the two corpora, as well as inventories of such items that had been identified in previous work in this area (Eggins, 1994; Biber et al., 1999; Garzone, 2005a; Martin & White, 2005). This resulted in the identification of a closed set of 15 different items: *however, although, though, even though, even if, even so, despite, in spite of, nevertheless, notwithstanding, yet, while, whereas, still* and sentence-initial *but*. With reference to the last item, it was decided to restrict the analysis of *but* only to instances that were found in this position (exclusively in the spoken EP corpus). This was because the overall frequencies of *but* were too high to permit the manual inspection that would be necessary to distinguish simple syntactical coordination from the more concessive meanings of interest to this study, as exemplified below.

(5.3)   We were very tired, but we continued to work for several more hours. (simple syntactic coordination)

(5.4)   This has been a difficult year. But in the near future the situation will surely improve. (concessive meaning)

---

[29]   See http://www.comp.lancs.ac.uk/ucrel/claws7tags.html.

It is important to recognise that in spoken discourse the attribution of sentence-initial status can be somewhat problematic as it depends largely on the transcriber's perceptions. However, following Bell (2007) there were presumably some prosodic cues that induced transcription in this position, which would suggest a more forcefully evaluative meaning beyond simple syntactic coordination. For this reason, I have opted to include these items in the analysis.

WordSmith Tools (Scott, 2008) was then used to produce quantitative profiles of the 15 concessive connectives across the two corpora. These included frequency counts, concordance lines and cluster analysis (i.e., the identification of relatively frequent multi-word items containing the searched item). For two items, the empirical output had to be extensively edited to remove unwanted functions and meanings. Instances of *yet* as an adverb (e.g., *Have you finished your work yet?*) were eliminated, as were instances of *while* and *still* having a temporal rather than concessive meaning (e.g., *While she was waiting for the bus, it started to rain*). The emerging quantitative data served as a catalyst for further qualitative study of items in their surrounding text in order to gain a fuller understanding of how the concessive connectives were used rhetorically in earnings presentations and earnings releases.

5.3.3 Graduation: intensifiers and mitigators

The analysis of intensifiers and mitigators was based on a set of lexical items that serve to adjust the force of evaluation in terms of its intensity according to a strong-weak cline (Martin & White, 2005). However, while these authors use the term of *intensification* (ibid., p. 140) to encompass both the upscaling and downscaling of evaluations, I prefer to use the two distinct labels for these phenomena: *intensifiers* to strengthen evaluation and *mitigators* to weaken evaluation, following Labov (1972). The choice of lexical items for analysis was based on lists compiled by Martin and White (2005), which were integrated with other items that emerged during both the preliminary overviews of the transcripts and automatic searches on the tags of general adverbs (RR) and degree adverbs (RG). This combination of procedures resulted in a set of 15 lexical items articulated as follows:

Intensifiers:	*quite, very, really, extremely, simply, tremendously*
Mitigators:	*slightly, somewhat, pretty, a bit, rather, reasonably, fairly, relatively, just*

In the literature, intensifiers have been called *amplifiers* (Biber et al., 1999) and *maximisers* (Quirk et al., 1985) when they express the highest possible intensity (e.g., *absolutely, totally*). Mitigators have also been referred to as *hedges* (Lakoff, 1973; Channell, 1994; Hyland, 2000), i.e., words or expressions that encode a weakened degree of commitment to what follows. Therefore, on a semantic level, these devices share common ground with devices of *epistemic modality* (Palmer, 1979).

As with concessive connectives, the above intensifiers and mitigators were analysed across the EP corpus and the ER corpus with *WordSmith Tools* (Scott, 2008) to generate various types of empirical data. This was also integrated with qualitative analysis within the context of usage in order to shed light on the underlying reasons for certain linguistic choices.

5.4 Combined macro-micro analysis

The importance of combining qualitative and quantitative methods to study evaluation in discourse has been underlined by Drew (2004, p. 228), who states that:

> [...] a fuller, truer picture of evaluative uses or functions of linguistic constructions can only emerge from integrating quantitative with qualitative approaches. A purely quantitative approach based on some 'obvious' dimensions of similarity of the constructions to be quantified can obscure patterns of (evaluative) meaning, and all patterns of differences in meaning, which can only be identified through close textual and interactional analysis of the occurrence of linguistic constructions in their natural habitats of discourse, in the context in which they were selected by writers or speakers. (original scare quotes and parentheses)

Following this recommendation, each of the three types of rhetorical features (i.e., evaluative adjectives, concessive connectives and intensifiers/mitigators) was studied within the various moves of the macro-structures of the two genres under investigation. This was accomplished by a performing distribution analysis of the features, both on a quantitative level via the dispersion plot function of *WordSmith Tools* (Scott, 2008) and a qualitative level via manual inspection of the EP transcripts and ER text files. The purpose of this combined macro-micro analysis was to understand whether evaluative adjectives, concessive connectives and intensifiers/mitigators tended to be associated with specific moves, in an attempt to acquire a deeper understanding of the rhetorical function of evaluative language in earnings presentations and earnings releases.

5.5 The professional informant

When linguistic research deals with discourse that refers to a particular academic or professional domain and thus is impacted by contextual factors with which language researchers may be unfamiliar, it is important to find ways to more accurately interpret the findings. One ethnographically-inspired method is to interview professional informants whose extensive real-life experience can confirm and further illuminate research results (Swales, 1998; Hyland, 2000; Flowerdew, 2002), or "to understand how the speech events/texts under investigation fit into the overall communicative context" (Garcés-Conejos & Fortanet-Gómez, 2009, p. 72). Agar (1996, p. 58) characterises ethnographic research as involving the

> long-term association with some group, to some extent in their own territory, with the purpose of learning from them their ways of doing things and viewing reality.

According to Agar (1996, p. 30), this type of external knowledge is particularly useful in the presence of a "rich point", i.e., a phenomenon which the researcher is unable to clearly interpret due to the gap between the world of the researcher and the world being studied.

In an effort to attenuate this problem, I established contact with a professional working in the field of finance and investment and conducted interviews with him. This professional has participated extensively in earnings calls (approximately 200 per year) and, as an investment analyst, represents the audience to which both earnings presentations and earnings releases are directed. Because this informant was on the receiving end of the discourse, the focus of the interviews was on contextual issues, participant relationships and the social dynamics underlying the communicative event, rather than on the specific language choices of the speakers and writers themselves. Moreover, it did not seem particularly helpful to question a non-linguist about specific lexico-grammatical features. Thus, the data collected from these interviews should be seen mainly as providing supporting information that could enable a fuller understanding of the results.

After having illustrated the methodological approach in this chapter, in the next four chapters, I present the results of the contrastive analysis of the two corpora. As a preliminary step, in Chapter 6 their macro-structures (van Dijk, 1977) are described and compared. Then, the quantitative analysis of the three rhetorical features under investigation (i.e., evaluative adjectives, concessive connectives and intensifiers/mitigators) is presented in Chapters 7, 8 and 9. These results are discussed to highlight the most interesting quantitative trends and are further integrated with qualitative analysis of the various features within their context of usage. This discussion is followed by the combined macro-micro analysis to show how the rhetorical features are embedded within the structural moves of the corpora. Throughout the analytical chapters, the findings are interpreted with reference to previous significant research, as well as some insights from the professional informant that have been integrated when appropriate.

Chapter 6

Structural analysis

6.1 The macro-structure of earnings presentations

The analysis of the macro-structure of the earnings presentations revealed essentially five main moves: a preliminary move (by the teleconference operator) and four additional moves (by the various speakers giving the presentation), typically in the following order:

1. *Opening*: a welcome to participants by the teleconference operator who provides technical instructions for the multi-party call procedures, and then introduces and passes the floor to the first of the corporate speakers.

2. *Introduction*: a welcome to all participants by the first executive speaker who then introduces the co-speakers and gives a preview of the presentation agenda (i.e., who will be presenting what). This move also comprises what is known as a *Safe Harbour Statement*, or a mandatory disclaimer against potentially different outcomes of any forward-looking statements presented.[30] It is either read aloud in a presumably pre-printed format or concisely summarised by the speaker, who may also refer listeners to other related texts for additional detail.

3. *Financial overview*: a review of the most important results and trends during the financial period in question. These are often compared with previous periods and articulated into business units, brands or geographical regions. The speaker may also mention new products or services in the pipeline, as well as other important upcoming events (e.g., the opening of new facilities, pending legal issues).

4. *Financial details*: a report containing greater details about performance, in which the speaker often walks listeners through various financial statements (e.g., statement of operations, cash flow statement, balance sheet), explaining trends and variations in listed items. In this move, there are often numerous references to visual supports, such as the

---

[30] In the US, Safe Harbour Statements became obligatory for companies reporting financial data under the Private Securities Litigation Reform Act of 1995.

previously issued earnings release or supporting Powerpoint files which are coordinated with the talk and from which listeners can follow along on their computer screens after logging into the webcast earnings calls.[31] This move also indicates expectations of future financial performance, which are often referred to specifically as *outlook* or *guidance*. Information about products and other important events sometimes appears in this move instead of the previous one.

5.   *Wrap-up*: the conclusion of the presentation when the final speaker thanks the listeners and opens up the floor to the question and answer sessions (not considered in this study as previously indicated).

Figure 6.1 shows a schematic representation of the macro-structure of the earnings presentations as described above, while Table 6.1 provides an analysis of the distribution of these moves across the entire EP corpus.

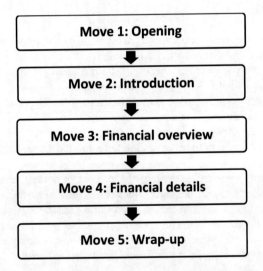

Figure 6.1: The macro-structure of the earnings presentations

---

[31]   This was confirmed by the professional informant with whom I conducted interviews.

Com-pany	Opening	Introduction	Financial overview	Financial details	Wrap-up
C1	✓	✓	✓	✓	✓
C2	✓	✓ (- SH)	-	✓	✓
C3	✓	✓	-	✓	✓
C4	✓	✓	✓	✓	✓
C5	✓	✓	✓	-	✓
C6	✓	✓ (- SH)	✓	✓	✓
C7	✓	✓	✓	✓	✓
C8	✓	✓	✓	✓	✓
C9	✓	✓	✓	✓	✓
C10	✓	✓	✓	✓	✓
C11	✓	✓	✓	-	✓
C12	✓	✓	✓	✓	✓
C13	✓	✓	✓	✓	✓
C14	✓	✓	✓	✓	✓
C15	✓	✓	✓	✓	✓
C16	✓ (+ SH)	✓ (- SH)	✓	✓	✓
C17	✓	✓	✓	✓	✓
C18	✓	✓	✓	✓	✓
C19	✓	✓ (-SH)	✓	✓	✓ (+ SH)
C20	✓	✓	✓	✓	✓
C21	✓	✓ (- SH)	✓	✓	✓
C22	✓	✓	✓	✓	✓
C23	-	✓	✓	✓	✓
C24	✓	✓ (- SH)	✓	✓	✓
C25	✓	✓	✓	✓	✓

Table 6.1: Distribution of moves in the EP corpus

As can be seen from the table, the majority of the 25 earnings presentations contain all five identified moves whose presence is signalled by "✓", which also appear in the same chronological order illustrated in Figure 6.1. With regard to the *Opening*, only one earnings presentation (C23) is not opened by a teleconference operator, but is instead hosted directly by the Vice President of Investor Relations. Apparently, this particular company had in-house teleconferencing facilities. The transcript of this earnings presentation also makes reference to a live audience of investment analysts. Therefore, in this special case, the teleconference earnings presentation coincided with a live presentation at the company's headquarters.

The *Introduction* move is present in all of the calls. In most cases, this is given by the Director or Vice President of Investor Relations who also states the Safe Harbour disclaimer (SH) to alert listeners to forward-looking statements that may be subject to change in the future. The table shows that the SH disclaimer does not appear in the *Introduction* move (- SH) in only six earnings presentations. However, in one case it is instead given by the teleconference operator during the *Opening* move (C16), while in another it appears in the *Wrap-up* move (C19).

Most of the calls contain separate moves for *Financial overview* and *Financial details*. The *Financial overview* is typically presented by the CEO, who then passes the floor to the CFO to report the *Financial details*. Other executives (e.g., Senior Vice President, Chief Accounting Officer, Treasurer) sometimes speak during these moves, especially when the CEO or CFO is not present. However, in some of the earnings presentations, especially those that are briefer and have fewer presenters, these two moves are less distinct and sometimes merge together. For example, in C2 and C3 the speakers embark immediately on quite lengthy and detailed monologues without a clearly distinct overview. In C5 and C11, there is essentially only a financial overview, without going into specific details of economic results. Like the *Introduction*, the *Wrap-up* is obligatory and appears in all 25 calls. It is delivered by the last of the corporate speakers, often being the CEO who takes the floor again to thank the listeners and announces the team's intention to open up the floor to questions.

Table 6.2 shows how this macro-structure can actually be traced in the text of an authentic earnings presentation. The illustration is based on a typical example (C1), containing all five of the potential moves. For reasons of space, only the most essential portions of the presentation transcript have been provided in order to give a general 'feel' for the content. In the *Introduction* move, we clearly see the speaker's announcement of the Safe Harbour disclaimer (in italics). Also quite interesting is the Financial Overview move where the speaker refers the listeners to a copy of the corresponding written news release with earnings data (in italics). This is a reflection of *manifest intertextuality* (Fairclough, 1992, p. 271), where within a given text explicit references are made to other texts.

Move/Speaker	Earnings Presentation Sample (C1)
Opening/Teleconference Operator	Ladies and gentlemen, thank you for standing by. Welcome to the [C1/IT] fiscal '04 earnings conference call. […] if you wish to ask a question, please press the star followed by one on your touchtone phone.[…] I'd like to turn the conference over to […] managing partner at investor relations. Please go ahead.
Introduction/Speaker 1 (Managing Partner, Investor Relations)	Thank you, operator, and thanks, everyone, for joining us today. With me are […] [C1/IT's] Chairman and CEO and […], our CFO. And we're pleased that all of you are joining us for our FY '04 first-quarter earnings announcement. […] On today's call, [FIRST NAME] will begin by providing comments […] and [FIRST NAME] will speak to the detailed numbers and we'll save some time at the end for questions. *As a reminder […] some of the matters we will discuss on this call are forward-looking and I would like to advise you that these forward-looking statements are subject to known and unknown risks and uncertainties that could cause actual results to differ materially from those expressed or implied by such statements.*
Financial overview/Speaker 2 (Chairman and CEO)	Thank you, [FIRST NAME]. Good morning and happy new year to all of you and thank you for joining us. I am going to begin with some commentary on our first-quarter results […]. On Q1 results, *by now, you've seen our news release with the results for the quarter.* We're pleased that revenue grew 11 percent in U.S. dollars and 4 percent in local currency over the first quarter of last year. […] With that, let me hand it over to [FIRST NAME] to go through our first-quarter results in detail.
Financial details/ Speaker 3 (CFO)	Thank you, [FIRST NAME]. Net revenue for first-quarter of fiscal year 2004 was 3.26 billion, an increase of 11 percent in US dollars and 4 percent in local currency compared with the first quarter of last year. […] Let me turn it back to [FIRST NAME] for some final comments.
Wrap-up/Corporate Speaker 1 (Chairman and CEO)	So in closing I want to reiterate that we're confident […] With that, we would be happy to take your questions.

Table 6.2: The macro-structure of earnings presentations with sample

By and large, the structural composition of earnings presentations appears to be quite regular, which is in line with Bargiela-Chiappini and Harris' (1995) analysis of another spoken business genre, i.e., management meetings.

Indeed, there even appear to be some structural similarities, i.e., the *opening phase* and *closing phase* of these business meetings would seem to broadly correspond to the *Introduction* and *Wrap-up* moves of the earnings presentations, respectively. Thus, we have some evidence of *interdiscursivity*, i.e., the use of elements in one discourse practice that carry meanings from other discourse practices (Candlin & Maley, 1997). More specifically, the introductory and closing elements of the teleconference earnings presentations have shared meanings with those of live management meetings. However, because the structural features of presentational genres in business contexts have not been studied, I relied on my professional informant for further confirmation as to what appeared to be overall regularity of structure. He explained that these events have a very routine nature and that information is presented with a high degree of uniformity. In his words, *"There is a well-established protocol and the procedure is formal and regimented, which allows a lot to be accomplished in a limited time frame"*.

The earnings presentations also appear to be very smoothly managed by the team of presenters, who take great efforts to organise the content by carefully and frequently signposting for listeners who will be talking about particular topics. Indeed, in some cases, the speakers even alert listeners to the length of their contributions, as can be deduced by their own comments shown in the example below.

> (6.1)   My remarks should run about 20 minutes and then, as [FIRST NAME] said, we'll be happy to deal with questions. *(EP/C23)*

6.2 The macro-structure of earnings releases

The analysis of the macro-structure of the earnings releases identified nine moves, usually in the following order:

1.   *Title:* the name of the company and the period of earnings reported.

2.   *Subtitle:* one or more brief statements, usually in bold or bullet-listed, reporting the most noteworthy trends.

3.   *Summary:* the initial segment that typically begins with the location and/or date of the release and then continues with a concise description of the financial results. This move often includes embedded quotes attributed to a representative of executive management, such as the CEO or CFO.

4.   *Financial details*: additional information about the financial period in question. It is often signalled with the heading *Financial Highlights* and

the text may be further structured with other sub-headings that report information focusing on specific financial parameters, company divisions or products.

5. *Business outlook*: expectations for the next financial period. This move is sometimes referred to as *Expectations* or *Guidance*, in alternative to *Outlook* and often presented under a separate heading.

6. *Conference call*: information about the date and time of the corresponding conference call during which the same earnings results will be presented by the executive management of the company via teleconferencing, also indicating if it will be audio webcast. Hypertext links to related web pages may be included.

7. *Company info*: a brief statement that describes the company in terms of the products/services it provides and its scale of operations, often presented under a heading "About us/name of the company".

8. *Safe Harbour disclaimer*: text that contains the Safe Harbour statement, although its wording and length may vary considerably.

9. *Contacts*: the names and contact information of the investor relations or media liaisons, usually with corresponding hypertext links to websites and email addresses.

As illustrated in Table 5.2, many of the releases incorporate tables of data, thus corroborating Ruiz-Garrido et al.'s 2005 study that found such visual devices to be highly characteristic of both British and Spanish annual reports, especially in sections about financial information. These usually appear at the end of the text, but in three cases a summarising table is positioned at the beginning of the release after the title and before the body text. Figure 6.2 illustrates the macro-structure of the textual component of the earnings releases schematically.

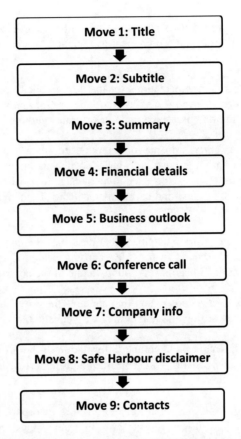

Figure 6.2: The macro-structure of the earnings releases

Table 6.3 presents the distribution of the nine moves across all the earnings releases in the entire ER corpus. As can be seen, not all the earnings releases contain all nine moves. In fact, they present much less structural regularity than the earnings presentations. In addition, although most follow the order presented in Figure 6.2, there is a certain degree of positional variation, particularly with reference to the *Conference call* (CC), *Company info* (Info) and *Safe harbour disclaimer* (SH) moves.

Com-pany	Title	Sub-title	Sum-mary	Details	Out-look	CC	Info	SH	Con-tact
C1	✓	-	✓	✓	✓	✓	✓	✓	✓
C2	✓	✓	✓	✓	-	✓	-	✓	✓
C3	✓	-	✓	✓	✓	✓	-	✓	✓
C4	✓	✓	✓	✓	-	-	✓	✓	-
C5	✓	✓	✓	-	-	✓	✓	✓	✓
C6	✓	✓	✓	✓	✓	✓	✓	✓	✓
C7	✓	-	✓	✓	-	-	-	✓	✓
C8	✓	-	✓	✓	✓	✓	✓	✓	✓
C9	✓	-	✓	✓	✓	-	-	✓	LINK
C10	✓	✓	✓	✓	✓	-	-	✓	✓
C11	✓	✓	✓ (-Q)	-	-	✓	✓	✓	✓
C12	✓	✓	✓	✓	✓	✓	✓	✓	-
C13	✓	-	✓	✓	✓	✓	✓	✓	✓
C14	✓	✓	✓	✓	-	✓	✓	✓	-
C15	✓	✓	✓	✓	✓	✓	✓	✓	-
C16	✓	-	✓	-	-	-	-	✓	✓
C17	✓	-	✓	✓	✓	-	-	✓	-
C18	✓	✓	✓	-	-	-	-	✓	✓
C19	✓	✓	✓	✓	✓	-	-	✓	-
C20	✓	-	✓ (-Q)	✓	-	-	-	✓	LINK
C21	✓	✓	✓ (-Q)	-	-	-	-	-	-
C22	✓	✓	✓	✓	✓	✓	✓	✓	-
C23	-	-	✓	-	-	-	-	-	-
C24	✓	✓	✓	-	-	-	-	✓	✓
C25	✓	✓	✓	✓	LINK	✓	✓	✓	✓

Table 6.3: Distribution of moves in the ER corpus

From the table, it is evident that two moves are obligatory: the *Title* and the *Summary,* with the latter also presenting embedded quotes attributed to company executives in all but three cases: C11, C20 and C21 which indicate (-Q). The *Safe Harbour disclaimer* move (SH) is also a rather regular feature, found in 23 out of 25 earnings releases. In contrast, other moves appear less consistently. The *Subtitle* and *Contacts* moves occur in a little over half of the releases (15 and 14 out of 25, respectively). The presence of the *Financial details* and *Business outlook* moves appears to be linked to the overall length of the earnings release, with the former appearing in all but seven relatively short releases and the latter appearing in twelve relatively long releases. Only 13 out of 25 earnings releases contain the *Conference call* (CC) move, likely due to the fact that companies may issue a separate earnings call announcement (see Figure 2.3). Similarly, the *Company info* move (Info) is optional, occurring in only 12 of the earnings releases. In one case (C25), the *Business outlook* section could be accessed as a separate text through a hypertext link. In the same way, in two cases (C9 and C20) hypertext links are provided to the email addresses of media relations personnel in the *Contacts* move. Such hypertext links to other texts represent a form of *manifest intertextuality* (Fairclough, 1992, p. 271) adapted to the ICT communicative environment.

It was interesting to see that the three companies having the most irregularity in the structural composition of their earnings releases (i.e., missing moves and no embedded quotes) are not US-based: C18 (Finland), C20 (Netherlands) and C21 (Korea). It could be that the styles and protocols of written earnings releases may vary from one country to another. However, it would be necessary to carry out a targeted contrastive analysis to further investigate this possibility.

Table 6.4 exemplifies how the macro-structure described above emerges from the text of an authentic earnings release (C6), which was selected because it presents all nine of the potential moves identified. Again, for reasons of space only the most significant portions of text have been provided here. From the table, we may especially note the use of embedded quotes (in italics) in the *Summary* move, as well as the typographically distinct sub-headings (also in italics) in the *Financial details* (here labelled "Financial Highlights") *Business outlook* and *Conference call* moves.

Move	Earnings Release Sample (C6)
Title	[C6/Banking] Corporation Q4 2003 Financial Results
Subtitle	• 2003 Diluted Earnings Per Share Increase to $2.21, Up 30% From 2002 • 2003 Net Income $135.2 Million, Up 12% From 2002 • Board of Directors Declares Dividend of $0.30 Per Share
Summary	[C6/Banking] Corporation (NYSE:C6) today reported diluted earnings per share for 2003 of $2.21, up $0.51 or 30.0 percent from diluted earnings per share of $1.70 in 2002. […] *"Our positive financial results for 2003 reflect the hard work and focus of our employees, and I'm proud of their accomplishments," said [...] Chairman and CEO.* […] The return on average equity was 18.59 percent during the quarter, up from 16.69 percent in the third quarter of 2003 and up significantly from the same quarter last year.
Financial details	*Financial Highlights* Net interest income for the fourth quarter of 2003 was $93.4 million, up $2.3 million from net interest income of $91.1 million in the third quarter of 2003 and up $3.2 million from $90.2 million in the same quarter last year. The increase in net interest income from the previous quarter was largely due to […]
Business outlook	*Business and Earnings Outlook - Plan for 2004 to 2006* In 2001, the Company announced a three-year plan designed to refocus on maximizing shareholder value over time, which continues to be our governing objective. That plan was successfully completed in 2003. […]
Conference call	*Conference Call* The Company will review its 2003 financial results and discuss the new 2004-2006 plan today at 8:00 a.m. [Geographical location] Time (1:00 p.m. Eastern Time). The presentation will be accessible via teleconference and via the Investor Relations link of [C6] Corporation's web site
Company info	[C6/Banking] Corporation is a regional financial services company serving businesses, consumers and governments in [Geographical locations]. The Company's principal subsidiary, [C6/Banking], was founded in 1897 […]
Safe harbour	This news release contains forward-looking statements concerning, among other things, the economic environment in our service area […] We believe the assumptions underlying our forward-looking statements are reasonable. However, any of the assumptions could prove to be inaccurate and actual results may differ […]
Contact	CONTACT: [C6/Banking] Corporation [FULL NAME],[Telephone number] (Media), [Telephone number] [FULL NAME]@C6.com […]

Table 6.4: The macro-structure of earnings releases with sample

Unlike the macro-structure of the earnings presentations which has no precedent in the literature, the analysis of the earnings releases can be informed by similar work that has been done on other types of press releases. On the whole, the move structure of the earnings releases is quite similar to what McLaren and Gurău (2005) found in generic corporate press releases, which they describe as a relatively stable genre. Moreover, the content and function of several of the moves that they identified largely overlap with mine, even if I have used somewhat different labels:

Corporate press releases (McLaren & Gurău. 2005)		Earnings releases (This study)
Announcement	=	Summary
Elaboration	=	Financial details
CEO comments	=	Summary (with embedded quotes)
Contact details	=	Contacts
Editor's note	=	Company info

Thus, this overlapping reflects a high level of *constitutive intertextuality* (Fairclough, 1992, p. 272) as the earnings releases are largely formulated according to the conventionalised practices of other genres, in this case generic corporate releases (McLaren & Gurău, 2005). Moreover, in the *Summary* move, the date/location of the release and short description of the main results is reminiscent of the *lead* component of the news report genre at the base of journalism, which typically contains a summary based on the five journalists' questions: when, where, who, what and why (Bell, 1991).

In addition, the earnings releases present some features described by Strobbe & Jacobs (2005) as characteristic of 'e-releases', such as emphatic capitalised lettering and superlative forms. Although this study does not specifically target these features, it is interesting to note their usage as illustrated in the following examples:

(6.2)   **[C3] ANNOUNCES RECORD FREE CASH FLOW FUELED BY LOWER PRICES AND YEAR-ROUND FREE SHIPPING** *(ER/C3 title)*[32]

(6.3)   Notably, [C12] has *the best* new product flow in the industry with three launches in 2003 and four launches expected for 2004. *(ER/C12)*

---

[32]   For reasons of confidentiality, all company names have been replaced by the corresponding codes found in Tables 6.1 and 6.3. In addition, all surnames, product names and other private information have been removed.

(6.4)   New bookings for the first quarter were $5.05 billion, our *third-highest quarter ever*, with outsourcing new bookings of $2.98 billion and consulting new bookings of $2.07 billion. *(ER/C1)*

6.3 Structural similarities and differences

A comparison of the macro-structures of the earnings presentations and the earnings releases showed that some of their moves have largely corresponding content:

Introduction in EP	= *Safe Harbour* in ER
Financial overview in EP	= *Summary* in ER
Financial details in EP	= *Financial details* in ER

This overlapping of content reflects Fairclough's (2003, p. 220) notion of an "order of discourse" in that we find discourse being structured according to particular patterns which reflect a "network of social practices" (ibid.) across genres. Indeed, from this perspective, earnings presentations and earnings releases seem to represent a highly consistent order of discourse.

Between the two genres, we also find some evidence of intertextuality in the form of references to each other or to other texts (Candlin & Maley, 1997). For example, the *Conference call* move in earnings releases is an explicit reference to the entire parallel genre of earnings presentations. Moreover, the embedded quotes attributed to company executives that are frequently found in the *Summary* move of earnings releases are ostensibly directly lifted from the earnings presentation itself or from moments of spoken interaction (the phenomenon of embedded quotes will be discussed in more detail below).

However, there are some structural differences between the two genres that seem to depend on several factors. The *Opening* by the teleconference operator and the *Wrap-up* before the question and answer session exclusive to the earnings presentations are clearly impacted by the spoken mode, by the telephone medium and by the presence of the audience of investment analysts, as shown in examples 6.5 and 6.6, respectively.

(6.5)   Good afternoon. My name is [FIRST NAME]. I will be your conference facilitator today. At this time, I'd like to welcome everyone […] *(EP/C11)*

(6.6)   With that, [FIRST NAME] and I will take your questions. Operator, first caller please. *(EP/C12)*

The moves that are exclusive to the earnings releases are similarly influenced by the written mode, the Internet medium and the wider intended audience beyond selected investment analysts. For example, the earnings releases make frequent use of titles (example 6.7), subtitles (example 6.8) and separate section headings (example 6.9), all features that are typical of written texts to organise content and predict upcoming information (Bondi, 1999; Hyland, 2000). By contrast, in the earnings presentations this is accomplished by utterances that signal a shift in speaker and/or topic (example 6.10).

(6.7)   [C5] Reports First Quarter Results (*ER/C5*)

(6.8)   Operating Income of $296 Million *(ER/C25)*

(6.9)   Business Outlook
        The following statements are based on current expectations. Revenue in the first quarter is expected to be [...] *(ER/C15)*

(6.10) With that, let me hand it over to [FIRST NAME] to go through our first quarter results in detail. *(EP/C1)*

The moves that contain hypertext links (*Conference call*, *Contacts*) were clearly determined by the fact that these earnings releases are published on the Internet (example 6.11). The *Company Info* move (example 6.12) is an indication that the earnings releases are addressed to a wider audience, rather than to a limited number of investment analysts, who are presumably already very familiar with the companies that they follow regularly.

(6.11) Contacts:
        [C3] Investor Relations
        [FULL NAME], [Telephone number], ir@[C3].com, www.[C3].com/ir
        [C3] Public Relations
        [FULL NAME], [Telephone number] *(ER/C3)*

(6.12) About [C25]
        [C25] Inc. is a leading provider of comprehensive online products and services to consumers and businesses worldwide. [C25] is the No. 1 Internet brand globally [...] *(ER/C25)*

Another unique feature of the earnings releases is the presence of embedded quotes attributed to an executive of the company (example 6.13). Somewhat surprisingly, the cross-checking of these quotes in the ER corpus with the utterances of the same persons in the corresponding transcripts of the EP corpus revealed hardly any matches. In fact, of all the quotes found in the ER corpus that were cross-checked in the EP corpus, only one is exactly equivalent. Thus, the vast majority of the quotes were either produced by the speakers during some other occasion, or more likely, are instances of pseudo-quotation, typical of press releases in which the company quotes itself, attributing the words to an executive, although the quotes are actually written by other professionals, such as in-house staff or external writers (Jacobs, 1999). In one case (example 6.14), the embedded quote in the ER corpus actually refers to an utterance ostensibly made in the corresponding earnings presentation. However, cross-checking with the transcript of that call determined that it is not a verbatim quote, but instead a paraphrase that was apparently reformulated by the writer of the earnings release.

(6.13) "This quarter's performance was in line with prior year and, importantly, we continued our progress to build a unified company that will deliver superior on-going performance," said [FULL NAME], Chairman and Chief Executive Officer. *(ER/C8)*

(6.14) "If you remember, I said that 2003 would be a reset year for the company and I'm proud to say that we made progress," [C23] Chairman and Chief Executive Officer [FULL NAME] said during a conference call to discuss the results Wednesday. *(ER/C23)*

6.4 Chapter wrap-up

The macro-structure analyses described in this chapter have provided a clear generic profile of earnings presentations and earnings releases. They have shown that the two genres present some strong structural similarities, especially in terms of the most essential components or moves (e.g., key financial results and Safe Harbour statement). However, they have also highlighted the distinctive features of each genre that seem to be determined by the communicative mode (spoken vs. written) and medium (telephone vs. Internet), as well as the intended audience of the communication (carefully screened investment professionals vs. a more general public) and the role of the speaker (who actually articulates the message) vs. the writer (who reformulates the message and often inserts pseudo-quotations).

Drawing from previous research on the press release genre (McLaren & Gurău, 2005), the earnings releases analysed in this study were shown to have much in common with the generic corporate press release in terms of structural moves, even if the purpose of the latter is quite different since they do not contain reports of financial data. The fact that the earnings releases are structured along similar lines as generic corporate press releases is evidence of a certain degree of *constitutive intertextuality* (Fairclough 1992, p. 272), since the former are formulated according to the conventionalised practices of the latter. Nevertheless, the presence of unique structural features linked to the purposes and practices of the global financial community suggests that earnings releases have evolved into a distinct sub-genre of the over-arching press release genre.

With reference to the earnings presentations, some of the moves were quite similar to those found in the macrostructures of management meetings (Bargiela-Chiappini & Harris, 1995), and therefore showing some signs of *interdiscursivity* (Candlin & Maley, 1997) in relation to discourse practices of other spoken business genres. There were also instances of *manifest intertextuality* (Fairclough, 1992, p. 271). For example, in the *Introduction* move of the earnings presentations when the speakers state the Safe Harbour disclaimer, they often refer listeners to other sources in the form of printed text. In addition, during the *Financial overview* and *Financial details* moves of the earnings presentations, listeners are frequently instructed to refer to hard-copy or computerised visual supports. On the whole, the intertextual and interdiscursive nature of both earnings presentations and earnings releases seems to reflect a cohesive professional community that has shaped its own distinctive discourse instruments and practices.

The structural analysis of the two genres also reveals more about their rhetorical nature. In fact, structural moves are rhetorical units which carry out specific communicative functions (Swales, 2004). Thus, when speakers and writers impose a given sequencing of moves in their texts, they are actually steering listeners and readers towards the desired interpretation in an 'argumentative' way. Moreover, the sequencing of the key moves *Financial summary* followed by *Financial details* recalls the *claim-data-warrant* pattern associated with argumentation theory (Toulmin, 1958). In fact, the supporting statistics provided in *Financial details* function as *data*, resulting in a rhetorical strategy grounded in logic and rationality.

With this broad knowledge base of the macrostructures of the two corpora, it is now possible to embark upon a more targeted analysis of specific rhetorical features, beginning with the next chapter that will concentrate on evaluative adjectives as encoders of speakers' and writers' attitudes.

Chapter 7
Attitude: evaluative adjectives

7.1 Preliminary editing of the data

As explained in Chapter 5, to analyse evaluative adjectives both corpora (EP and ER) were tagged with the part-of-speech tagger CLAWS (Constituent Likelihood Automatic Word-tagging System) developed by UCREL (University Centre for Computer Corpus Research on Language) at Lancaster University. When dealing with an open grammatical category such as adjectives in relatively large samples of text, automatic tagging is the only viable way to carry out a reasonably complete analysis.

The tagged versions of the two corpora were queried with the text analysis software *WordSmith Tools* (Scott, 2008). Searches were performed on the general adjective tag JJ.[33] This procedure generated frequency data and concordance lines of all adjectives present in each corpora that could be sorted and then manually classified as evaluative or not according to the attitude component of Martin and White's (2005) appraisal system. The objective was to produce an exhaustive list of positively and negatively charged evaluative adjectives for each corpus that could reflect underlying rhetorical strategies of the corporate speakers and writers.

The process of distinguishing adjectives with evaluative meanings from those with non-evaluative meanings within the data was neither simple nor straightforward, and required several phases of editing. In fact, the initial queries of the two corpora based on the general adjective tag JJ returned a daunting number of items: over 7,000 in EP and over 4,000 in ER. Fortunately, the re-sorting function of the concordancer *WordSmith Tools* (Scott, 2008) allows large quantities of items to be systematically processed. This greatly facilitated the task of distinguishing adjectives that encode explicit positive or negative evaluative meanings from those that do not. In the first phase of editing, all retrieved adjectives were grouped alphabetically. This enabled me to eliminate rather easily large series of unwanted non-evaluative items from the data. For example, many adjectives were non-evaluative or neutrally descriptive, encoding meanings that are temporal (e.g., *seasonal, prior, annual, forward-looking*), geographical (e.g.,

---

[33]   This tag detects attributive adjectives that precede the head noun, as well as predicative adjectives that follow a copular verb.

American, local, international, domestic), categorical (e.g., *financial, industrial, administrative, retail, net, gross*) or general (e.g., *other, certain, various, available*). That said, we should recognise that probably any adjective can become evaluative under certain circumstances, e.g., evaluative meanings derived from specific shared knowledge or certain prosodic features. However, such meanings clearly cannot be recovered from the data used for the present study. For this reason, I concentrate only on adjectives that are more overtly evaluative.

Once the above types of non-evaluative adjectives were removed from the data, as a second phase of editing, all the remaining adjectives were examined more closely within their context of usage. The focus here was on adjectives that are not considered inherently evaluative, but could be potentially evaluative in certain situations, e.g., *competitive, accelerated, substantial, significant, growing*. To determine this possibility, it was necessary to identify the referent of each adjective, i.e., what it evaluated. This process was similarly facilitated by the resorting function which allows for a range of different sorting patterns based on words that are adjacent to the search item. Figure 7.1 illustrates a sample of concordances from *WordSmith Tools* (Scott, 2008) for the adjective *competitive* that have been resorted according to the first word on the right. As can be seen, when referring to nouns such as *advantage, compensation* and *differentiation*, *competitive* takes on a positive connotation, whereas it has a negative one with nouns such as *environment* and *developments*.

N	Concordance
1	share was up slightly despite heavy competitive activity. Pantene continued
2	member base. This strategy reflects the competitive advantage that our business
3	credit capabilities combine to create a competitive advantage which is being
4	consumer equities, equities that provide competitive advantages in each
5	gives us the power to compete in a very competitive, casual dining sector.
6	for the year. We want to pay our people competitive compensation and have
7	to retain employee talent, but maintain competitive compensation practices
8	, our results may be affected by competitive developments, the timing
9	chain projects that underscore our competitive differentiation. For example
10	solid topline results in a difficult competitive environment volume grew 4
11	ability to deal with the increasingly competitive environment for online
12	in the U.S. market has been very competitive. Even before we started our
13	fact is, today the seed industry is highly competitive. If you were a farmer, you
14	segment we continue to address our competitive issues with a strategy that's
15	indicate share gains, despite the competitive landscape, Q3 2003 office

Figure 7.1: Resorted concordances of *competitive* (Source: *WordSmith Tools*)

To further illustrate the evaluative meanings of *competitive*, in example 7.1 it is positively-charged when referring to aspects of company performance, but negatively-charged when referring to the operating environment as shown in example 7.2. Because such instances could be reasonably interpreted as evaluative, they were maintained in the data. On the other hand, in example 7.3, when referring to factors that might influence expectations, *competitive* is essentially descriptive and thus assumes a neutral meaning. Such meanings were instead removed from the data.

(7.1) Our share of details to physicians in the U.S. market has been very *competitive* [...] *(EP/C12)*

(7.2) Q3 year-over-year market share reports indicate share gains, despite the *competitive* landscape [...] *(EP/C24)*

(7.3) Actual results may differ materially from these expectations due to changes in global political, economic, business, *competitive*, market and regulatory factors. *(ER/C13)*

Some of the adjectives identified in this phase (e.g., *significant, substantial, growing, consistent*) become evaluative when their meaning shifts from quantitative (descriptive) to qualitative (evaluative), depending on what noun they modify. In example 7.4 *significant* describes quantities as large in amount, but in example 7.5 it evaluates a *development* in terms of its relevance in a positive sense. Similarly, in example 7.6, a user base is described as *growing* in terms of size, but in example 7.7 international presence is evaluated as *growing*, but more in terms of importance as a desirable attribute.

(7.4)   The project will develop upstream gas and liquids facilities [...] and *significant* quantities of associated condensate and liquefied petroleum gas. *(ER/C20)*

(7.5)   Another *significant* development in 2003 was the increase of our dividend level. *(EP/C6)*

(7.6)   Once again, our approach to investing in better products and services for consumers has [...] a *growing* user base that is good for both our advertising and premium service business. *(EP/C25)*

(7.7)   Foreign currency exchange rates continue to be a factor associated with our *growing* international presence. *(EP/C10)*

Two adjectives are particularly worthy of note: *high* and *new*. *High* typically describes sizes or amounts (e.g., *a high mountain, a high number*), but in these corpora it often took on an evaluative meaning linked to the up/down metaphor, where *up is good*, and *down is bad* (Lakoff & Johnson, 1980). *New* can similarly have a positive connotation, since what is 'new' is usually considered to be better than what is 'old'. Interestingly, the adjective *old* appears only once in the EP corpus in a descriptive non-evaluative sense, and not at all in the ER corpus, whereas *new* was among the most frequent evaluative adjectives found in both corpora. This seems to corroborate Rutherford's (2005) observation that financial discourse has an overall positive slant. The contextually-determined descriptive/non-evaluative and evaluative meanings of *high* are illustrated in examples 7.8 and 7.9, respectively. The descriptive/non-evaluative and evaluative meanings of *new* are shown in examples 7.10 and 7.11, respectively.

(7.8)   For the March quarter, organic volume is expected to be in the *high* single-digits. *(ER/C19)*

(7.9)   We have plans to open additional *high* profile stores, one in San Francisco in the spring [...] *(EP/C5)*

(7.10) Because the *new* EPS guidance is based on reported figures, goodwill amortization will now be included as an expense [...] *(EP/C20)*

(7.11) The company also announced it has identified *new* materials for future transistors designed to replace materials that have been in use for over 30 years. *(ER/C15)*

For all of the potentially evaluative adjectives discussed above, only those that appeared to have positive or negative connotations in their context of usage were maintained in the data, while those that did not were eliminated. While recognising that such a determination involves a certain degree of subjectivity, on the whole, it is a reasonably accurate way of distinguishing adjectives that carry evaluative meanings in the two corpora.

The third phase of editing entailed a series of adjustments to more finely tune the data. The evaluative adjectives remaining after the previous two editing phases were again carefully scrutinised in their surrounding co-text in order to identify polysemous items or literal vs. figurative meanings. In example 7.12, we see the polysemous adjective *outstanding* with its non-evaluative meaning of a debt that has not yet been settled in the context of accounting, while in example 7.13 *outstanding* has the evaluative meaning of distinctively excellent. Two adjectives that have quite different literal and figurative meanings are present in both corpora: *solid* in examples 7.14 (literal/non-evaluative) and 7.15 (figurative/evaluative), and *flat* in examples 7.16 (literal/non-evaluative) and 7.17 (figurative/evaluative). All instances of literal/non-evaluative meanings were removed from the data.

(7.12) Our *outstanding* long-term customer loans declined to 352 million euros from 1.1 billion euros in 2002. *(EP/C18)*

(7.13) It was an *outstanding* quarter for [C5], [...]. *(ER/C5)*

(7.14) Our laser color printers, which are based on our proprietary *solid* ink technology [...] *(EP/C24)*

(7.15) [...] we are also importantly making *solid* progress on the overall repositioning strategy [...] *(EP/C8)*

(7.16) Won 50 orders in the quarter for the new [C13] [PRODUCT], the first all-digital *flat* panel vascular imaging system [...] *(ER/C13)*

(7.17) In a down market overall, in a *flat* market for bank stocks, an
investment of $100 made in [C6] on January 1st, 2001, was
worth $238 on December 31st, 2003. *(EP/C6)*

In addition, phraseological uses of adjectives that are not of interest to this
study, i.e., *good morning/afternoon/day*, found exclusively in the EP spoken
corpus (53 occurrences), were also eliminated in this phase.

The results of the three editing phases are illustrated in Table 7.1. The
table reports both raw frequency counts (N) of the adjectives retrieved and
sorted in the various editing phases and in the normalised parameter of
number of occurrences per 10,000 words (pttw). This is important when
analysing corpora of different dimensions (i.e., word counts) in order to
achieve an accurate picture of variation. An interesting trend already emerges
from this preliminary stage of analysis. Although adjectives in general have a
higher overall frequency in the ER corpus (924 instances pttw) than the EP
corpus (764 instances pttw), the situation is reversed when we consider only
adjectives encoding evaluative meanings, with EP having 152 instances pttw
vs. ER having 91 instances pttw. Perhaps the presence of a listening audience
with the teleconference technology used in the earnings presentations
encouraged speakers to use more evaluative adjectives in comparison with
earnings release writers. This would also be supported by Biber et al.'s
(1999) finding that, generally speaking, attitudinal stance markers are
considerably more frequent in conversation than in written prose.

Phase of editing	EP (101,393) words		ER (46,715 words)	
	N	pttw	N	pttw
Pre-editing	7,750	764	4,316	924
First editing phase*	2,201	217	726	155
Second editing**	1,695	167	465	99
Third editing***	1,546	152	426	91

*   removal of non-evaluative adjectives
**   removal of potentially-evaluative adjectives used in a non-evaluative way
***   removal of non-evaluative polysemous items/literal meanings and
phraseological uses

Table 7.1: Results of preliminary editing of adjectives in EP vs. ER

The final lists of different evaluative adjectives types after the three editing
phases are shown in Appendix 3 (the EP corpus) and Appendix 4 (the ER
corpus). The first column of each table illustrates the different adjective types
found in the corpus ranked according to frequency. The second column
shows the number of occurrences of each adjective type, while the third
column indicates their positive (+) and negative (-) connotations. The

adjectives marked (+/-) can have either a positive or a negative meaning, depending on what they modified (as explained previously).

Before turning to the qualitative analysis in the next sub-section, it is interesting to note a few broad tendencies that have emerged from the data thus far. First of all, not only does the EP corpus have a higher overall frequency of evaluative adjectives (Table 7.1), but there is also a wider range of variation. There are 205 different types in EP vs. 110 different types in ER, as shown in Appendices 3 and 4. It appears that the presence of an audience encourages a more creative use of adjectives by the speakers (e.g., item 149/*fantastic*, item 167/*lingering,* item 173/*nimble*, item 190/*stellar*) in comparison with the staff writers of earnings releases who maintain a more limited range of types. In addition, in both corpora, there are relatively few evaluative adjectives carrying negative meanings, i.e., representing only 14.6 per cent in EP and 10 per cent in ER, once again supporting Rutherford's (2005) claim that financial discourse tends to place more emphasis on the positive than on the negative. Finally, if we compare the top 20 evaluative adjectives of both corpora, there is substantial overlapping, showing 11 items in common (i.e., *strong, significant, important, key, double-digit, improved/improving, positive, competitive, pleased, successful, favourable*) and both having *strong* as the most frequent evaluative adjective of all. This suggests that the language of financial disclosure can assume rather standardised ways of expressing positive and negative evaluation that transcends the spoken or written mode, even if we also find episodes of creativity, especially in the spoken corpus as discussed above. The differences in the top 20 seem to be influenced by the informality introduced by the spoken mode in EP (e.g., item 2/*good*, item 4/*great*, item 17/*terrific*) vs. more formal counterparts in ER (item 10/*premium*, item 12/*excellent*, item 14/*outstanding*). Although the latter also appear in the EP, they rank at somewhat lower positions.

7.2 Quantitative analysis

7.2.1 High-frequency adjectives

For further insights into how evaluative adjectives are used by executive corporate speakers and earnings release writers, the two most frequent items in each corpus were selected for in-depth analysis: *strong* (N=275) and *good* (N=110) in EP, and *strong* (N=89) and *double-digit* (N=23) in ER, all positive in orientation. While the adjectives *strong* and *good* can be used to evaluate something in essentially any context, *double-digit* is closely linked to the context of financial disclosure. In fact, the literal meaning of any number between 10 and 99 (i.e., a double-digit number) takes on a positive connotation when describing financial performance as an improvement of 10 points or higher, representing a highly positive result under most circumstances.

The decision to focus on these three adjectives was determined not only by their relative prominence in the corpora, but also because their frequencies were high enough to enable other types of analytical procedures to be implemented, such as collocates (i.e., words that tend to co-occur with searched items) and clusters (i.e., relatively frequent multi-word patterns containing the searched items).

Table 7.2 illustrates the nouns with which *strong, good* and *double-digit* tend to collocate. The number in parentheses is the number of times the adjectives and nouns co-occur, with minimum frequency set at five. As can be seen, *strong* collocates most frequently with growth and performance in both corpora, suggesting that these collocations have become rather standardised in financial disclosure discourse, both spoken and written. Yet *strong* also collocates with several other nouns in the EP corpus, again pointing to the idea that the spoken mode produces a richer range of vocabulary overall than the written mode. The adjective *good* in the EP corpus is instead used in a more generic way with the less domain-specific nouns *progress, start* and *year*, also reflecting the more informal tone of this interactional setting. On the other hand, *double-digit* in the ER corpus is used with more explicitly business-oriented concepts of *growth* and *earnings*.

EP corpus		ER corpus	
strong	good	strong	double-digit
growth (15)	progress (7)	growth (14)	growth (10)
performance (6)	start (6)	performance (6)	earnings (7)
results (10)	year (5)		
quarter (6)			
volume (6)			
demand (7)			
momentum (5)			

Table 7.2: Collocates of *strong, good* and *double-digit* in EP vs. ER

Table 7.3 shows the results of the cluster analysis of the same evaluative adjectives. The clusters confirm the link between *strong* and *growth* across both corpora. They also reinforce the more generic usage of *good* and the more domain-specific usage of *double-digit*.

	Three-word clusters in EP	**Three-word clusters in ER**
strong	a very strong (14) strong growth in (8) driven by strong (7) strong double-digit (6)	strong growth in (11) due to strong (5)
good	is a good (5) a very good (5) a good start (5)	-
double-digit	-	double-digit earnings growth (7)

Table 7.3: Clusters with *strong*, *good* and *double-digit* in EP vs. ER

To complement the computerised analysis of patterns with *strong*, *good* and *double-digit*, manual inspection of their concordance lines revealed some other interesting cases in the EP corpus. For example, *strong* is quite versatile, being used to evaluate numerical data (example 7.18), but also broad concepts (example 7.19). *Good* is often found in informal expressions, as shown in examples 7.20 and 7.21, reflecting the more personal side of the executive speakers.

(7.18) Sales outside the U.S. were up a very *strong* 44%, to $471 million. *(EP/C12)*

(7.19) Importantly, we believe that we have built a *strong* framework for long-term success [...] *(EP/C25)*

(7.20) And stay tuned because there will be more *good news* to come. *(EP/C24)*

(7.21) [...] and we are *in good shape* as we look at these three transactions. *(EP/C13)*

7.2.2 Positive vs. negative adjectives

As mentioned earlier, there were far more positive adjectives than negative ones in both corpora. In order to shed more light on the possible reasons for this difference, the lists of evaluative adjectives in Appendices 3 and 4 were studied carefully to identify any particular trends. Many of the positive adjectives are very strong, while the negative adjectives tend to be much less so and can, in fact, be described as relatively mild. Examples of these adjectives (listed according to frequency of occurrence) are shown in Table 7.4.

Adjective type	EP	ER
positive (strong)	great, terrific, outstanding, exceptional, huge, extraordinary, remarkable, tremendous, dramatic, amazing, record, superior, phenomenal, red-hot, theatrical, unmatched, double-barrelled, enormous, fantastic, spectacular, stellar, unparalleled, unprecedented	outstanding, exceptional, record-breaking, superior, tremendous, unmatched, great, whopping, unprecedented, unparalleled, terrific, extraordinary
negative (mild)	flat, modest, weak, disappointing, challenging, unfortunate, underperforming, anaemic, deteriorating, elusive, lingering, patchy, sluggish, troubled, uncertain	weak, flat, depressed, poor, faltering

Table 7.4: Examples of positive/negative adjectives in EP vs. ER

The table shows that the positive adjectives in both corpora are often hyperbolic in nature, i.e., they upscale reality in exaggerated ways (McCarthy & Carter, 2004). These adjectives are typically used to emphasise positive performance (examples 7.22-7.24). On the other hand, when performance was negative, attenuating adjectives are used. Not surprisingly, there are no instances of strongly negative adjectives, such as *awful*, *terrible* or *catastrophic*. Moreover, there are only three instances of *bad* in the EP corpus and none whatsoever in the ER corpus. Examples 7.25-7.27 illustrate some adjectives that are preferred in cases of negative results, i.e., *flat, patchy, uncertain* and *weak* (further mitigated with the hedge *relatively*).

> (7.22) [...] the gains in gross margin dollars were *spectacular*. *(EP/C15)*

> (7.23) Operating income surged a *whopping* 63.4 percent from the fourth quarter of 2002, [...] *(ER/C21)*

(7.24) We are pleased with the market share penetration [...] which led to *terrific* global sales of [...] *(EP/C12)*

(7.25) In Europe, the service ended the year with nearly 6.4 million members, essentially *flat* from the year-ago figure. *(ER/C23)*

(7.26) Product demand in chemicals remains *uncertain* and *patchy* across geographies [...] *(EP/C20)*

(7.27) The relatively *weak* performance of the digital media business is expected to improve [...] *(ER/C21)*

Table 7.4 also shows that a wider range of positive and negative adjectives is used by the executive speakers of the EP corpus, who are quite resourceful in their choices, perhaps because they have more at stake than the staff writers who produce the earnings releases of the ER corpus. This analysis of positive and negative evaluative adjectives has shown that corporate speakers and writers use these devices to draw attention to successes and away from failures. On this point, the professional informant noted that, as a financial analyst who has been a frequent participant in earnings conference calls, he has never heard company executives use negative hyperbolic expressions to describe performance. He added that such mild adjectives as *disappointing* often need to be interpreted by analysts more 'realistically', as corporate speakers tend to use them even when the results are actually quite negative and would warrant stronger expressions. This tendency is in line with Hager and Scheiber's (1990, p. 113) study of CEOs's letter to shareholders which highlighted similar strategies which they described as "rhetorical smoke", e.g., *a challenging year*, rather than *a bad year*.

7.2.3 Compound adjectives

Some particularly interesting uses of compound adjectives were found in both corpora. A *compound* is defined by Quirk et al. (1985, p. 1567) as "a lexical unit consisting of more than one base and functioning both grammatically and semantically as a single word" (e.g., *cost-effective* or *foreign-made* in the case of compound adjectives). Compound adjectives are often written in hyphenated form and are evidence of the high degree of productivity and creativity that often characterises the lexis of the world of business and economics (Roos, 1987). Table 7.5 provides a list of all compound adjectives, again presented according to frequency of occurrence and positive/negative connotations.

Adjective type	EP	ER
positive	double-digit, top-line, broad based, well-positioned, blue-chip, value-added, feature-rich, high-growth, red-hot, well-controlled, across-the-board, customer-centric, double-barrelled, easy-to-use, first-line, hard-working, high-margin, high-performance, high-quality, record-volume, top-performing, well-capitalized, well-defined, world-class	double-digit, broad based, top-line, high-quality, high-performance, industry-leading, record-breaking, top-end, award-winning, higher-value, revenue-producing, well-positioned, market-making, ever-growing, fast-growing innovation-driven, well-controlled, best-in-class, first-in-class, customer-centric, well-capitalized, business-building, valued-added
Negative	far-flung, low-margin, value-destroying	-

Table 7.5: Compound adjectives in EP vs. ER

As the table shows, and in line with the previous findings, positive compound adjectives are much more prominent than negative ones. Indeed, the only three negative compound adjectives *far-flung*, *low-margin* and *value-destroying* are not used to describe the company's financial performance, activities or products, but rather to characterise the negative aspects of the overall business environment. With the exception of *double-digit* and *broad-based*, compound adjectives are not among the most frequent evaluative adjectives found in the two corpora. Nevertheless, their presence illustrates the dynamic imprint they bring to financial disclosure discourse (examples 7.28-7.31).

(7.28) A shift to color and to *feature-rich* devices together with an increase [...] were the drivers of positive development. *(EP/C18)*

(7.29) [...] we intend to differentiate [C25]'s products and services by enhancing [...] and also creating *easy-to-use* products [...] *(EP/C25)*

(7.30) [C12], a leading [...]. is developing a growing portfolio of *best-in-class* pharmaceutical products by applying the latest research [...] *(ER/C12)*

(7.31) *Market-making* innovation
Building on its success, [C24] said that it's making a significant announcement later this week [...] *(ER/C24)*

It is interesting to see that some of the most creative compounds were found in the ER corpus (examples 7.30 and 7.31), perhaps due to the remoteness of the written mode that allows for greater planning and forethought that may be needed to formulate them.

7.3 Qualitative analysis

This phase of analysis focuses on the specific communicative functions of evaluative adjectives. I referred to Martin and White's (2005) appraisal framework to classify the positive/negative attitudes encoded in the adjectives according to three functions:

- *affect* (positive/negative feelings of speakers and writers)
- *judgments* (positive/negative attitudes towards behaviours in terms of esteem/sanction)
- *appreciation* (positive/negative evaluations of entities and phenomena).

While the largely descriptive analyses performed in the previous sub-sections provide insights into how evaluative adjectives are used in the two corpora under investigation, the qualitative analysis attempts to shed light on possible rhetorical strategies underlying usage. In order to render such analysis feasible, only the first 100 evaluative adjectives in each corpus (shown in Appendices 3 and 4) were selected. Although limited, this number was still broad enough to comprise both high-frequency adjectives, as well as many that occur only once or twice.

The evaluative adjectives were first cross-checked with the rather extensive lists of adjectives of *affect*, *judgment* and *appreciation* previously compiled by Martin and White (2005). *Affect* has to do with descriptions of emotions and feelings of un/happiness (e.g., *sad, glad*), in/security (e.g., *anxious, confident*) and dis/satisfaction (e.g., *bored, pleased*). Judgment refers to the esteem/sanction of behaviours associated with normality (e.g., *natural, odd*), capacity (e.g., *strong, weak*) and tenacity (e.g., *careful, inconsistent*). *Appreciation* involves the construal of reactions (e.g., *dramatic, predictable*), composition (e.g., *simple, complex*) and valuations of quality and relevance (e.g., *excellent, insignificant*). All adjectives that could not be matched to these lists were discussed with a research colleague with knowledge in the area of evaluation and specifically the appraisal model. Most could be categorised on the basis of synonymy with previously matched items. However, a few remained ambiguous as will be discussed later. The results of this classification process are shown in Table 7.6. In each category, the adjectives are again listed according to frequency of occurrence (from most to least frequent).

Adjective functions	EP	ER
affect	pleased, confident, happy, optimistic, comfortable, disappointed, excited, fortunate, proud	pleased, depressed, proud, passionate, optimistic, disappointed, confident
judgment	strong, successful, healthy, conservative, talented, robust, modest, aggressive, disciplined, fair, powerful, reasonable, relentless, respectable, careful	strong, successful, robust, weak, healthy, reasonable, aggressive, powerful, trusted, relentless, well-controlled, proven
appreciation	good, significant, great, important, key, improved, positive, solid, flat, favourable, major, terrific, difficult, top-line, new, unique, effective, critical, excellent, improving, negative, exciting, outstanding, premium, consistent, leading, nice, tough, accelerating, promising, profitable, substantial, well-positioned, exceptional, growing, huge, notable, attractive, big, comprehensive, efficient, extraordinary, meaningful, remarkable, tremendous, accelerated, dramatic, encouraging, hard, high, innovative, interesting, relevant, amazing, bad, blue-chip, considerable, dynamic, heavy, impressive, popular, record, slow, superior, valuable, value-added, adverse, appropriate, challenging, convenient, creative, deep	key, positive, significant, important, favourable, premium, excellent, negative, outstanding, leading, new, improved, improving, difficult, efficient, flat, growing, innovative, major, top-line, unique, adverse, consistent, exceptional, high-quality, solid, effective, good, high-performance, notable, industry-leading, inaccurate, impressive, record-breaking, record, superior, tremendous, top-end, unmatched, winning, award-winning, whopping, higher-value, useful, unprofitable, unprecedented, unparalleled, top, promising, terrific, profitable, poor, noteworthy, well-positioned, lean, incorrect, huge, high, ever-growing, fast-growing, great, flexible, major, faltering, extraordinary, exciting, enhanced, encouraging, eminent, dynamic, distinctive, innovation-driven, creative, compelling, clear
ambiguous	double-digit, competitive, broad-based	double-digit, competitive, market-making, broad-based, revenue-producing

Table 7.6: Functions of top 100 evaluative adjectives in EP vs. ER

As can be seen from the table, in both corpora adjectives functioning as *appreciation* are the most frequent, followed by adjectives of *judgment* and *affect*, respectively. In addition, we see that each corpus has a roughly similar number of different adjective types within each functional category with many items in common.

Adjectives of *affect* are used to describe the emotional state of the speaker in EP (or the attributed speaker in ER) who assumes the role of the company spokesperson, typically using the pronoun *we*, as shown in examples 7.32 and 7.33. However, example 7.34 shows how the adjective *depressed* is used not to describe the feelings of the speaker or writer according to the appraisal model (Martin & White, 2005), but rather the negative performance of the company. Thus, we see that in the context of financial reporting, an adjective of *affect* can take on a new meaning.

> (7.32) We are *optimistic* about our prospects in the coming year. *(EP/C15)*

> (7.33) [FULL NAME], [C1] Chairman and CEO said "We are *encouraged* by [...] and are *pleased* with our strong new bookings [...]" *(ER/C1)*

> (7.34) Polyolefins margins remained *depressed* though demand improved late in the quarter. *(ER/C20)*

Adjectives of *judgment* are quite interesting because they seem to have a distinctive function in this particular context. Rather than esteeming or sanctioning the behaviours or capacities of human beings as foreseen in the appraisal model (Martin & White, 2005), they usually evaluate inanimate financial trends either positively or negatively (examples 7.35-7.38).

> (7.35) As we exit our second consecutive year of *strong* free cash flow generation, we continue to [...] *(ER/C25)*

> (7.36) The company has one of the largest portfolios of *trusted* high-quality brands, including [...] *(ER/C19)*

> (7.37) [...] you will see of course the remarkable dip in Q3 last year which was driven [...] and by very *weak* capital markets [...] *(EP/C2)*

> (7.38) Our other performance measures grow to very *respectable* levels, including [...]. *(EP/C6)*

Adjectives of *appreciation* are used to react to phenomena (example 7.39) and evaluate quality (example 7.40), but also to provide positive commentary about quantitative results (example 7.41).

> (7.39) Since launching [PRODUCT] service, we have seen a *dramatic* acceleration in the year-over-year growth rates [...] *(EP/C25)*

> (7.40) Our marketplace provides an *unparalleled* consumer proposition. *(EP/C10)*

> (7.41) "I'm pleased to report that [C18] achieved *excellent* fourth quarter earnings results", said [FULL NAME], Chairman and CEO. *(ER/C18)*

Five items (i.e., *double-digit, competitive, broad-based, market-making, revenue-producing*) do not clearly correspond to any of the three parameters set forth the Martin and White's (2005) appraisal model, other than perhaps a vague sense of *appreciation*. For this reason, they have been classified as ambiguous. Yet these items are quite interesting as they seem to reflect the values of the financial world, i.e., companies that are dynamic, competitive and growing in quantity and/or importance (examples 7.42 and 7.43). Malavasi (2006) found a similar presence of positively-charged evaluative adjectives in banks' annual reports to convey an image of competitiveness, importance and innovativeness.

> (7.42) *Double-digit* comp growth from our stores in Malaysia and an initial franchise [...] *(EP/C7)*

> (7.43) [C22] announced three new [PRODUCT] with *industry-leading* performance of 720 MHz, breaking the company's previous industry record of 600 MHz. *(ER/C22)*

On the whole, in the context of quantitatively-oriented financial performance, it appears that executive speakers and staff earnings release writers extend the evaluative functions of Martin and White's (2005) appraisal model well beyond the sphere of human feelings and behaviours by projecting them onto non-human economic phenomena. These linguistic choices seem to produce a strengthening effect on the rhetorical dimension of the intended message.

7.4 Combined macro-micro analysis

The final phase of analysis unites the linguistic description of the evaluative adjectives (the micro dimension) with the structural analysis presented in

Chapter 6 (the macro dimension). In this way, I attempt to determine where selected evaluative adjectives tend to occur in the corpora for a better understanding of preferred patterns of usage.

Towards this aim, I used the dispersion plot function of *WordSmith Tools* (Scott, 2008) to produce a visual representation of the positions of selected evaluative adjectives throughout the transcript and text files that comprised in the two corpora. In order to provide sufficient data for the plot, I selected the two most frequent evaluative adjectives in each corpus for the combined macro-micro analysis: *strong* and *good* for EP and *strong* and *double-digit* for ER. In each case, the two adjectives were searched in tandem so that only one set of plots per corpus would be generated. The purpose was to first have a general idea of where these evaluative adjectives tend to appear, i.e., at the beginning, middle, or end of the earnings presentations or earnings releases. This was followed by manual qualitative analysis to reveal possible alignments of the evaluative adjectives within the structural moves identified in Chapter 6. The plots are reproduced in Figures 7.2 and 7.3.[34]

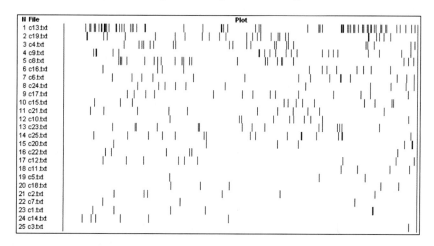

Figure 7.2: Dispersion plots of *strong/good* in EP (Source: *WordSmith Tools*)

---

[34]   The order in which the plots appear is determined by the software. The vertical lines represent single instances or clusters (thicker lines) of searched items.

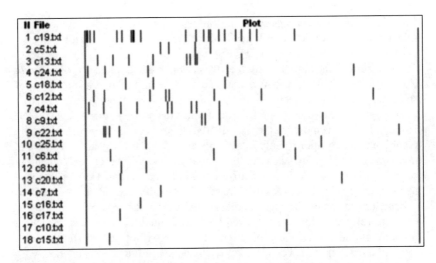

Figure 7.3: Dispersion plots of *strong/double-digit* **in ER (Source:** *WordSmith Tools*)

By comparing the two figures, we see that the two sets of evaluative adjectives show considerable variation in usage, with some individual earnings presentations and earnings releases containing many more instances than others. We should, however, keep in mind that the EP corpus is almost twice as large as the ER corpus, which clearly impacts the higher overall frequency of the searched items. Even so, variation is still evident. To look for a possible explanation, I examined the transcripts and text files of the three companies with the highest and lowest frequencies visualised in the plots to determine any possible connection between the presence or absence of the searched items and good or poor financial performance for the period reported. In other words, it seemed plausible that companies that had performed particularly well would have more instances of the three positive adjectives than those that had not. However, no correlation between the frequency of the adjectives and the level of performance was found. Thus, the differences in usage would seem to be a matter of individual styles and corporate reporting policies. Indeed, the same two companies (C13 and C19) show relatively high frequencies in their plots in both figures, suggesting that they tend to report their results with a particularly positive slant in both spoken and written form.

There are also noticeable differences in the distribution of the evaluative adjectives across the two corpora. The plots of the EP corpus (Figure 7.2) show that the items occur throughout the files from beginning to end, while the plots of the ER corpus (Figure 7.3) show that few instances occur towards the end of the files. Follow-up qualitative analysis revealed that the items are associated with certain structural moves that had been identified in Chapter 6. Figure 7.2 shows that in *strong* and *good* appear in all 25 files of the EP corpus, and are often found in the *Introduction* move. This is indicated by the concentration of vertical lines in the left-hand portion of several plots in the figure, which corresponds to this move (examples 7.44-7.46). The two evaluative adjectives are less concentrated in the *Financial overview* and the *Financial details* moves (corresponding to the central portion of the plots where there are more blank spaces), but then cluster again in the *Wrap-up* move, corresponding to the far right portion of the plots (examples 7.47-7.49). This patterning suggests that the executives responsible for delivering the initial and final segments of the earnings presentations are especially keen to leave the audience with no doubts concerning the successes achieved during the financial periods reported. Moreover, as the examples show, the moves also contain other features of positive evaluation (e.g., *significant*, *improving, strongest, double-digit, sustained*), thereby reinforcing this trend.

Introduction[35]

(7.44) Thank you and good morning, everyone, we appreciate all of you joining us for our teleconference discussing our 2003 results [...][FIRST NAME], [FIRST NAME], and [FIRST NAME] will discuss our results in greater detail in just a moment but I want to take a few minutes to highlight some of our significant accomplishments during the year [...] Net income was 10 million which is up 2.2 million or 29 percent from year earlier levels which were also very *good*. [...] *(EP/C16)*

(7.45) Good morning everyone. Just to kind of give you a recap on the fourth quarter, the economy is definitely improving. The fourth quarter sequentially was the strongest quarter of the year and we've got *strong* momentum going into '04 [...] *(EP/C13)*

(7.46) Thank you. Good morning, and welcome to the call [...]. Now, before [FIRST NAME] covers the financial results, I would like to start with a few observations about the quarter and the year. [...] Fourth quarter segment sales were 7.3 billion, up 15% with double-digit growth in every platform. We are particularly encouraged to see the *strong* volume growth, 6%, in the United States. *(EP/C9)*

---

[35]   Recall that all instances of *good* found in phraseological greetings (e.g., *good morning*) were not considered in the analysis of evaluative adjectives.

Wrap-up
(7.47) We're disappointed that we were not able, in bankruptcy court, to have a successful bid. But the core business is *good* [...] So, with that, I will take questions. Operator, [...] *(EP/C11)*

(7.48) We are positioned well to make 2004 the beginning of *strong* sustained earnings growth. This concludes our financial review for the fourth quarter and year. With that, [FIRST NAME] and I will take your questions [...] *(EP/C12)*

(7.49) And we've continued to deliver *good* profitability and very *strong* cash flow. I'd now like to move to questions and answers [...] *(EP/C20)*

With reference to the ER corpus, Figure 7.3 shows that the adjectives *strong* and *double-digit* appear in 20 out of the 25 files that make up the corpus. The plots show that they occur most frequently in far-left to centre-left portion of the plots, corresponding to the *Title*, *Subtitle* and *Summary* moves, as shown in examples 7.50-7.55. They are conspicuously less frequent in the right-hand portion of plots, which corresponds the *Conference call*, *Company info*, *Safe Harbour* and *Contact* moves, which in fact tend to report largely neutral information. The dwindling presence of these evaluative items throughout the earnings releases could be linked to the fact that these staff writers do not have an audience of listeners that they must convince in real-time via telephone, as instead occurs during earnings presentations where executives seem particularly keen to maintain rhetorical 'pressure'.

Title
(7.50) [C24] Fourth-Quarter Earnings Exceed Expectations Through *Strong* Sales of New Technology *(ER/C24)*

(7.51) [C2] Group: *Double-digit* Growth during the First Nine Months of 2003. *(ER/C2)*

Subtitle
(7.52) Growth in Cardmember Spending and Borrowing, Excellent Credit Quality and Higher Client Assets Reflect *Strong* Momentum in Key Businesses *(ER/C4)*

(7.53) *Double-digit* sales growth *(ER/C24)*

Summary
(7.54) Fairfield, Conn., January 16, 2004 - [C13] achieved record earnings [...] the company announced today. "[C13] had a solid

2003, with eight of 13 businesses delivering *double-digit* earnings growth for the year," said [C13] Chairman and CEO [FULL NAME]. *(ER/C13)*

(7.55) STAMFORD, Conn., Jan. 27, 2004 -- [C24/Electronic Equipment] Corporation (NYSE: [C24]) [C24] Corporation announced today better-than-expected fourth-quarter earnings that reflect *strong* sales of the company's industry-leading color systems [...] *(ER/C24)*

Close examination of the five text files of the ER corpus where *strong* and *double-digit* did not appear revealed the presence of alternative adjectives (e.g., *record, record-breaking, significant*) in the same three moves, thus confirming the tendency to concentrate positive evaluation at the beginning of these texts.

7.5 Chapter wrap-up

The results of the various types of analysis undertaken in this chapter have provided numerous insights into the rhetorical dimension of evaluative adjectives by corporate speakers and writers. On a descriptive level, evaluative adjectives are more frequent and show higher variation in the EP corpus in comparison with the ER corpus, probably due the more interactional teleconference environment. This idea is supported by Biber's (2006) study that found higher frequencies of attitudinal stance markers in spoken registers of academic discourse as compared to written ones.

Positively-charged adjectives are particularly prominent in the two corpora, thus in line with the findings of studies that investigated other forms of written financial communication (Garzone, 2005b; Hyland, 2005; Rutherford, 2005; Piotti, 2006). The two corpora also contain many instances of creative compounds and hyperbolic positive adjectives, in line with findings by Roos (1987). With particular reference to the latter, the professional informant provided some useful insights, commenting that highly positive evaluation is fairly standard in earnings presentations. However, he also added that the use of such expressions is not necessarily completely unwarranted. For example, an *amazing quarter* usually means that the company did in fact perform very well. He further explained that most of the analysts in the teleconference audience are able to gauge the reality of the situation on the basis of empirical data already in their possession at the time of the conference call, as well as their previous experience with the company executives in question. Indeed, he noted that some simply have a more upbeat speaking style and wider range of vocabulary than others.

The qualitative analysis of evaluative adjectives based on Martin and White's (2005) appraisal framework suggests that the quantitative orientation of financial disclosure leads to patterns of usage that are rather different from those found in everyday conversation. In particular, values such as *affect* and *judgment* often refer to economic data rather than the feelings of speakers and writers and the behaviours of human beings. In this way, the corporate speakers and writers succeed in maintaining a strong rhetorical effect across the entire message.

The combined macro-micro analysis showed that three key evaluative adjectives (i.e., *strong, good* and *double-digit*) are associated with certain structural moves. In the EP corpus, they characterise the initial (*Introduction*) and final (*Wrap-up*) moves. Interestingly, the tendency of evaluative adjectives to cluster towards the final segment of discourse has also been observed in another rhetorically-oriented genre, i.e., newspaper editorials where they are used to launch a strong final appeal to readers (Morley, 2004).

In the ER corpus, evaluative adjectives are instead concentrated in the initial moves (*Title, Subtitle* and *Summary*) and are rather scarce in the final moves containing informative text that does not focus on performance (e.g., *Company info, Contacts*). The difference in the distributional patterns of evaluative adjectives between the two corpora seems to be impacted by the presence of an audience in the EP corpus and the generic structure of the ER corpus that typically places less persuasive content at the end of the texts.

The next chapter is dedicated to the analysis of concessive connectives, representing the *engagement* component of Martin and White's (2005) appraisal framework. Although concessive connectives are perhaps less overtly rhetorical than the adjectives that have been analysed in this chapter, they are nonetheless important linguistic devices used by speakers and writers to steer perceptions of how propositions are intended to be construed.

Chapter 8
Engagement: concessive connectives

8.1 Preliminary editing of the data

As anticipated in Chapter 5, 15 concessive connectives were selected for the investigation of the linguistic expression of *engagement* in the two corpora. These items were processed with *WordSmith Tools* (Scott, 2008) in order to generate concordance lines that could be further analysed both quantitatively and qualitatively. However, the concordance output of three of the items (i.e., *while*, *still* and *yet*) required extensive editing in order to remove unwanted non-concessive temporal meanings. Therefore, before reporting the overall results of the analysis of concessive connectives, I first explain how I carried out this editing process and how some of the more challenging aspects were dealt with.

In most cases, the distinction between temporal and concessive meanings could be rather easily determined from the immediate context of usage, but also from certain grammatical cues. With reference to *while*, temporal meanings were distinguished when it was possible to logically paraphrase the connective with *at the same time* (example 8.1), a phrase which actually co-occurred in several cases (example 8.2).[36] Moreover, as the examples illustrate, temporal meanings of *while* were often signalled by the presence of a verb in the present continuous tense. All such instances of temporal meaning were eliminated from the analysis.

(8.1) I would characterize 2001 [...] and 2003 as the year in which we began to harvest the initial results of our efforts *while* continuing to reinvest in the future. *(EP/C25)*

(8.2) We continue to roll out the [C10] playbook to our growing international market, *while at the same time* identifying new opportunities overseas. *(EP/C10)*

Of interest to this study are instead *concessive* meanings, where the process of conceding can be placed within the broader context of argumentation. More specifically, when speakers or writers recognise some vulnerability in a

---

36   Lyons (1995) considers paraphrasing to be a valid technique for determining and distinguishing meanings of lexical items.

claim that will also be evident to their interlocutors, the very concession serves to strengthen their own position by demonstrating a sense of fairness or objectivity, thereby achieving a heightened "rhetorical effect" (Couper Kuhlen & Thompson, p. 383). For example, in a situation in which a particular goal is not achieved, the statement *While we made a very strong effort, we did not achieve our goal* seems to have more persuasive force than *We made a very strong effort to achieve our goal* with no concessive element that recognises failure, weakness or vulnerability.

Concessive uses of *while* were identified by paraphrasing with *even if* or *even so*. This is seen in example 8.3, where the writer uses *while* to first convey the stronger proposition before conceding the weaker one. However, there were some instances in which the temporal/concessive distinction was not so clear-cut. In example 8.4, the speaker seems to indicate two contemporaneous events (temporal meaning), but also to reinforce the first proposition that concedes an incomplete state of affairs with a second one that points out some degree of compliance. I opted to include such items since there appears to be at least some degree of 'concessive intention' on the part of speakers and writers.

(8.3)   […] we identified that *while* our core business was strong, based on the performance of our most recent classes, our selection process needs to be significantly altered. *(ER/C7)*

(8.4)   *While* our efforts are ongoing, we have shared information with the regulators throughout that process […] *(EP/C4)*

It was also interesting to note the variation in the positioning of the subordinate clauses introduced by *while*. In examples 8.1 and 8.2 where *while* has a temporal meaning, the subordinate clause comes after the main clause. On the other hand, in examples 8.3 and 8.4 where *while* has a concessive meaning, it precedes the main clause which may foreground either the stronger proposition as in example 8.3 or the weaker (or conceded) one as in example 8.4.

Similar criteria were used to distinguish *still* and *yet* used as adverbs of time (to be eliminated from the data) from their concessive uses (to be included in the data). These different functions of *still* and *yet* have been discussed by Ranger (2007, p.178), who categorises them as *aspectual* and *argumentative*, respectively.[37] In example 8.5, *still* clearly has a temporal

---

[37]   According to Lyons (1995), *aspect* is a non-deictic grammatical category that refers to temporal notions, such as duration, punctuality, completion and frequency.

meaning, whereas in example 8.6 it is used in a context of concession to put forward a stronger proposition that offsets the previously conceded weakness, and could be paraphrased with *even so* or *nevertheless*. Again, some instances presented a certain amount of fuzziness. In example 8.7, the speaker is referring to something that needs to be accomplished in the future (further signalled by the adverb *yet*), but also makes a concession concerning the performance of the company. While recognising the potential subjectivity of this interpretation, I opted to include such borderline cases in the analysis when at least some concessive meaning seemed to emerge.

(8.5)   The main data from that study are *still* immature and require more clinical events in patients before a full analysis can be completed. *(EP/C14)*

(8.6)   In Western Europe, currency appreciation will likely restrain growth, but we *still* expect to see higher GDP and manufacturing growth rates than last year. *(EP/C9)*

(8.7)   Our team is pleased with our efficiency improvements over the last few years, but we *still* haven't achieved the industry average for that measure yet. *(EP/C6)*

In the case of *yet*, distinguishing between temporal and concessive uses proved to be somewhat less problematic, also due to more distinctly different structural properties or grammatical features, as illustrated by example 8.8 (adverb of time with present perfect tense) and example 8.9 (concessive connective as the coordinating element of a compound sentence).

(8.8)   No funding decision has been made *yet*. *(EP/C9)*

(8.9)   The results of these efforts are encouraging, *yet* we're striving for even greater progress. *(EP/C1)*

8.2 Quantitative analysis

Table 8.1 illustrates the distribution of the 15 concessive connectives selected for investigation across the two corpora based on the concordance output. The data are again presented in both raw frequency counts and in the normalised parameter of number of occurrences per 10,000 words (pttw).

Concessive connective	EP (101,393 words)		ER (46,715 words)	
	N	pttw	N	pttw
However	63	6.2	11	2.4
While	62	6.1	9	1.9
But (sentence-initial)	37	3.6	-	-
Although	36	3.5	1	0.2
Despite	31	3.1	8	1.7
Still	26	2.5	2	0.4
Yet	6	0.6	-	-
Whereas	5	0.5	-	-
Though	3	0.3	1	0.2
Even though	1	0.1	-	-
Even so	1	0.1	-	-
Even if	-	-	1	0.2
In spite of	1	0.1	1	0.2
Nevertheless	2	0.2	-	-
Notwithstanding	1	0.1	-	-
Total	276	27.1	34	7.2

Table 8.1: Concessive connectives in EP vs. ER

By comparing the two totals, it can be seen that concessive connectives were noticeably more frequent in the EP corpus (27.1 occurrences pttw) than in the ER corpus (7.2 occurrences pttw). Even if we remove the item sentence-initial *but* (which not surprisingly appeared only in the spoken EP corpus as will be discussed later), the concessive connectives were still more than three times as frequent in the EP corpus (23.5 instances pttw) vs. the ER corpus (7.2 instances pttw). This strong overall difference was in fact suggested by the initial elaboration of the corpora with the semantic tagger *WMatrix* (Rayson, 2008) which returned the *Grammatical_bin* domain that contains concessive connectives as key in the EP corpus, but not in the ER corpus (see Chapter 5).

This result contrasts sharply with previous studies in which relatively formal concessive connectives were found to be highly characteristic of written prose. In Biber et al.'s (1999, p. 887) comparison of connectives such as *however*, *nevertheless,* and *yet* (which they call *linking adverbials*) in conversation vs. academic prose, these items were found to be considerably more frequent in the latter. Similarly, both Taboada (2006) and Partington (2007) found that formal concessive connectives such as *although*, *despite*, and *whereas* were quite common in corpora of newspaper texts. Thus, given this trend, it is rather surprising to find such a high overall frequency of these items in the spoken earnings presentations as compared to the written earnings releases. This is especially true when we consider that in other respects the language in the earnings presentations presents numerous informal conversation-like elements. In fact, it contains many first names, contracted forms, colloquial expressions and makes extensive use of first and second person pronouns in order to engage directly with the audience of investment analysts listening in via telephone. In Chapter 7, we also saw evidence of more informality in the choice of evaluative adjectives in EP vs. ER. Thus, the corporate speakers' use of these relatively formal concessive connectives stands in stark contrast to the overall informal tone of the speech event. This suggests that concessive connectives have an important function in this communicative context that merits further consideration.

It is also interesting to note that the earnings presentations contain a much wider range of concessive connectives than the earnings releases. Out of the total of 15 items searched, in the ER corpus only 8 different items appear, while in the EP corpus, the speakers use 14 different items, some of which are rare in most spoken language (e.g., *notwithstanding*, *nevertheless*). It could be that the executives are also keen to demonstrate their personal 'verbal prowess' to listeners, and thereby make a more favourable impression on them.

After analysing the concessive connectives with the concordancer tool, they were processed with other features of *WordSmith Tools* (Scott, 2008) to identify possible common collocates, clusters, and patterns. However, this analysis did not produce any results of interest, likely due the relatively low frequencies involved.

In terms of individual items, from Table 8.1 it is evident that *however* and *while* are particularly popular choices, ranking at the top of the frequencies found across both corpora. As the most prominent concessive connectives, in the next section these items will be examined extensively in order to shed more light on their rhetorical functions, the underlying motivations for their usage, as well as differences observed between the corpora. In addition, some particularly interesting uses of other concessive connectives will be discussed.

8.3 Qualitative analysis

8.3.1 *However* and *while*

The in-depth study of all the instances of these concessive connectives across both corpora within their contexts of usage revealed a rich articulation of specific rhetorical functions within the local context of usage, beyond their conventional concessive meanings. Across the two corpora, I identified eight different rhetorical functions:

1. highlighting a positive result;
2. offsetting a negative result;

3. expressing confidence in the future;
4. conceding future uncertainty;
5. mitigating a positive result;
6. conceding a negative result;
7. explaining a procedure or result;
8. pointing out a direct contrast.

These rhetorical functions largely mirror the two communicative purposes of financial disclosure genres: to inform (by providing and explaining information) and to persuade (by underlining past success and predicting future ones, and by mitigating failures). In particular, the persuasive purpose is reflected in how corporate speakers and writers use these devices in a dialogically-oriented way to express their own stances based on the stances they anticipate from their interlocutors, i.e. *engagement* in Martin and White's (2005) terms.

In order to control for the reliability of the above-listed functional categories, I asked two colleagues to classify samples of items from the corpora according to these functions. Their categorisations largely corresponded to mine; the few discrepancies of opinion that arose were discussed until agreement was reached.

The rhetorical analysis of *however* and *while* in the EP corpus vs. the ER corpus is illustrated in Table 8.2. Under the EP and ER columns, the number of occurrences corresponding to each function is listed (N), with the relative percentage of the total occurrences of the item in the corpus (from Table 8.1) indicated in parentheses (%).

Rhetorical functions	EP		ER	
	N	(%)	N	(%)
However				
- explaining a procedure or result	16	(25.4)	2	(18.2)
- conceding future uncertainty	14	(22.2)	4	(36.3)
- highlighting a positive result	11	(17.5)	1	(9.1)
- offsetting a negative result	10	(15.9)	2	(18.2)
- expressing confidence in the future	7	(11.1	1	(9.1)
- conceding a negative result	3	(4.7)	-	-
- mitigating a positive result	2	(3.2)	1	(9.1)
- pointing out a direct contrast	-	-	-	-
Total	63	(100.0)	11	(100.0)
While				
- pointing out a direct contrast	28	(45.1)	6	(66.7)
- explaining a procedure or result	13	(20.9)	-	-
- expressing confidence in the future	7	(11.4)	-	-
- conceding future uncertainty	5	(8.1)	-	-
- offsetting a negative result	5	(8.1)	2	(22.2)
- highlighting a positive result	3	(4.8)	1	(11.1)
- conceding a negative result	-	-	-	-
- mitigating a positive result	-	-	-	-
- ambiguous	1	(1.6)	-	-
Total	62	(100.0)	9	(100.0)

Table 8.2: Rhetorical analysis of *however* and *while* in EP vs. ER

As can be seen from the table, the concessive connective *however* was highly multi-functional, performing seven (in EP) and six (in ER) of the eight rhetorical functions identified. The only function that *however* did not serve in either corpus was *pointing out a direct contrast*. In the EP corpus in particular, 25.4 per cent of the occurrences had the function of *explaining a procedure or result* (example 8.10). In these cases, the corporate speakers are careful to rationalise their explanations very explicitly, perhaps as a way to anticipate and discourage possible challenges from the audience. In the ER corpus, a similar usage was found in two of the eleven occurrences of *however* (example 8.11). Therefore, *however* seems to be the concessive connective of choice when speakers and writers are keen to explain their assessment of the situation in order to persuade their interlocutors more effectively.

    (8.10) I'm sorry, these debt and debt-per-sub figures do include the effects of partial redemption or our 9 1/8% senior notes and our issuance of a 3 percent convertible note to SEC […]. *However,*

these figures do not include the effects of the issuance and sale of
$2.5 billion in senior notes [...] (*EP/C11*)

(8.11) The Company continues to expect total integration expense of
$75 million in fiscal 2003 through fiscal 2005. *However*, due to
its ability to achieve integration objectives more quickly than
originally anticipated, it is increasing its projected integration
expense in fiscal 2004 from the $26 million previously estimated
to $45 million [...] (*ER/C8*)

In both corpora, another key function of *however* was *conceding future
uncertainty*, representing 22.2 per cent and 36.3 per cent of the total
occurrences in EP and ER, respectively. This function is illustrated in
examples 8.12 and 8.13. It is interesting to note that in the ER corpus, this
function was always found in the *Safe Harbour disclaimer* move, as example
8.13 shows.

(8.12) [...] what we believe today to be appropriately conservative
assumptions. *However*, there's a high level of uncertainty
surrounding fluctuations in the Euro, pound, yen, and Canadian
dollar foreign exchange rates [...]. (*EP/C3*).

(8.13) These statements are based on current expectations and currently
available information. *However*, since these statements are based
on factors that involve risks and uncertainties, the company's
actual performance and results may differ materially from those
described or implied by such forward-looking statements.
(*ER/C17*)

The next three most frequent functions were all reflections of how corporate
speakers and writers can manipulate *however* to evoke or reinforce a positive
evaluation: *expressing confidence in the future* (example 8.14), *highlighting a
positive result* (example 8.15), *offsetting a negative result* (example 8.16).
With particular reference to the third function, a similar usage of *however*
was found by Bondi (2004) in a corpus of academic research articles to
highlight the writer's stance in argumentative episodes of a concession of
some weakness followed by a strengthening counter claim. Therefore,
however seems to be a particularly effective device for persuading
interlocutors, regardless of the communicative settings.

(8.14) The major risks and uncertainties associated with this outlook are
sustained increases in oil and natural gas prices or a faltering
U.S. economic expansion. *However*, with the strength of the

recovery and its current momentum, [C9] is confident that the economic conditions in 2004 are positive for its businesses. *(ER/C9)*

(8.15) On the top line, stacking brings largely additive value. *However,* the big reward isn't on the top line; it is clearly evident in our margins. *(EP/C17)*

(8.16) [...] [PRODUCT] prices have been slow since November. *However* we see very strong sync [PRODUCT] prices and thus we have raised the proportion of sync [PRODUCT] out of the total of [PRODUCT] a little bit. *(EP/C21)*

There were very few instances of *however* being used to *concede a negative result* (example 8.17) and *mitigate a positive result*, perhaps to present a 'realistic' picture (example 8.18). This contrasts with Rogers' (2000) study in which CEOs were careful to do this during live meetings with investment analysts. It could be that the physical distance introduced by the telephone medium in these earnings presentations attenuated the perceived need for such 'transparency'.

(8.17) The mobile infrastructure industry sentiment has improved over the recent month. *However,* due to the much shortened operator investment cycles over the last year, visibility remains low. *(EP/C18)*

(8.18) In Q4 the [indiscernible] has shown an extraordinary sequential growth of 17%, which marks two consecutive quarters of elevated corporate growth. *However,* a sub-sequential megabyte per system growth of 2%, reaching 394 megabytes, has triggered weaker [PRODUCT] prices towards the end of the quarter. *(EP/C21)*

With reference to *while*, as Table 8.2 shows, this item served a more limited range of functions, particularly in the ER corpus. In contrast to *however* which never functioned to *point out a direct contrast*, this was instead the most common function of *while* in both corpora, accounting for 45.1 per cent and 66.7 per cent of the occurrences in EP and ER, respectively. This function is illustrated in examples 8.19-8.21, where *while* is used to contrast two entities according to some specific and well-defined difference, i.e., different percentages of increase in shipments vs. revenue in example 8.19, a decrease in U.S. sales vs. an increase in out-side U.S. sales in example 8.20, and different people who will speak in example 8.21. In all three, *while* does not carry any particular rhetorical force linked to concession. Caenepeel (1997) refers to this function of *while*, also found in newspaper texts, as *contrastive parallelism* for the neutral comparison of two entities. Example 8.21 illustrates a particularly interesting non-rhetorical context, where it would seem entirely appropriate to use the simple conjunction *and* to explain to listeners who will be presenting what. The fact that the speaker has chosen the more formal and explicit *while* to emphasise a simple contrast seems to give the utterance a more 'sophisticated' tone, perhaps designed to reflect positively on the speaker himself.

(8.19) Total education channel unit shipments increased 8% from the year ago quarter, *while* revenue was up 20% driven by strong growth in higher education. *(EP/C5)*

(8.20) U.S. sales of [PRODUCT] decreased 6 percent, to $171.1 million, *while* sales outside the United States increased 28 percent, to $73.5 million. *(ER/C12)*

(8.21) *While* [FIRST NAME] will provide a thorough financial overview, I would like to review two primary areas in the context of our 2003 results. *(EP/C25)*

Most of the other functions of *while* were found in the EP corpus, with *explaining a procedure or result* accounting for 20.9 per cent of the occurrences (example 8.22). In this case, the speaker is explaining aspects of the procedure that will be used during the question and answer session that follows the earnings presentations.

(8.22) *While* we will attempt to respond to as many of your questions as possible before we end the call, we do have a limited amount of time. *(EP/C4)*

Although less frequent, other functions of *while* were *expressing confidence in the future* (example 8.23), *conceding future uncertainty* (example 8.24), *offsetting a negative result* (example 8.25), and *highlighting a positive result* (example 8.26). One or two instances of the last two functions were also found in the ER corpus. These functions that convey greater rhetorical force are considered by Caenepeel (1997) to be instances of *contrastive framing*, which unlike *contrastive parallelism* described above, always have an evaluative slant.

(8.23) *While* we remain committed to our five-by-five goal, we are well positioned to fulfill our EPS growth trajectory of annual double-digit growth for 2006 to 2010. *(EP/C14)*

(8.24) *While* we are cautiously optimistic, it is not possible to accurately predict demand and therefore our results could differ […] *(EP/C3)*

(8.25) *While* we were posting a shortfall by the end of last year of around 1.7 billion, we now have a surplus of approximately 10 billion […] *(EP/C2)*

(8.26) And [PRODUCT] in China, *while* in the very early stages of growth, added over 1 million new users during the quarter […] *(EP/C10)*

One instance of *while* was classified as functionally ambiguous. In example 8.27, there seem to be three functions being served at the same time: *explaining a procedure, expressing confidence for the future* and *offsetting a negative situation*. Of particular interest is the combination of *while* with *however*, which seems to reinforce the speaker's intention to pre-empt any potential challenges from the audience about an issue that he appears to be reluctant to discuss.

(8.27) Following our fourth quarter performance review, we will take your questions. However, *while* we are as confident as we can be in our position concerning the current [PRODUCT] patent litigation, we are not going to get into the specifics of how the trial currently underway is going. *(EP/C12)*

To conclude this qualitative analysis of *however* and *while*, it is important to mention that other lexical items found within the episodes of usage may also be seen as contributing to the various rhetorical functions that were identified. For instance, in the above example, the positively-charged item *confident*, the phrase *we are not going to get into the specifics*, and the negatively-charged items *litigation* and *trial* also come into play when *expressing confidence for the future, explaining a procedure*, and *offsetting a negative situation*. Yet the fact that virtually all the utterances/sentences with *however* and *while* could be re-phrased using the simple coordinating conjunction *but* suggests that these concessive connectives do indeed serve a distinct rhetorical function that heightens the persuasive force of the discourse.

8.3.2 Other concessive connectives

The other concessive connectives found in the two corpora were much less frequent than *however* and *while*, but their usage still presented some interesting rhetorical trends. The item *although* was used in the EP corpus (N=36) essentially for the same function as *while*, e.g., *explaining a procedure or result* (example 8.28), *conceding future uncertainty* (example 8.29), *offsetting a negative result* (example 8.30). However, unlike *while*, *although* was never used to point out a simple contrast and thus seems to have greater rhetorical force in this context.

> (8.28) *Although* ROE went down, again it's really because ROE is on a net income basis [...]. In reality it should really be going up, really in context. *(EP/C21)*

> (8.29) *Although* we anticipate special items related to both restructuring, and [NAME] separation during the year these cannot be reasonably estimated at this time. *(EP/C9)*

> (8.30) *Although* our mobile results in the fourth quarter were excellent overall, we were disappointed that we did not begin shipping in Dothan as planned. *(EP/C15)*

As previously mentioned, sentence-initial *but* was found exclusively in the spoken earnings presentations (N=37). This is probably because it is generally considered stylistically inappropriate to use simple conjunctions (e.g., *but, and, or, so*) at the beginning of sentences in relatively formal written genres. However, the fact that *but* was transcribed in this position seemed to signal its concessive rather than coordinating function. In example 8.31, we see how *but* in sentence-initial position is used to offset a negative result by countering it with a positive comment.

> (8.31) Today, only about 20 percent of our business is in developing markets, compared to 25 to 45 percent for our major competitors. *But* we're catching up, making good progress against this large growth opportunity. *(EP/C19)*

The item *despite* was found in both corpora, even if not in particularly large numbers (31 instances in EP and 8 instances in ER). However, *despite* was always used to highlight situations in which results had been positive even when the company was faced with serious challenges (examples 8.32 and 8.33), drawing even more attention to its successes.

(8.32) *Despite* a tough economy, we were able to reduce charge offs from a very low 2002 level of .09 percent of average loans to .04 percent for the year 2003. *(EP/C16)*

(8.33) The strong results of the first half of the year, *despite* widespread competitive activity, confirm our belief that we have the right strategies to deliver sustainable growth […] *(ER/C19)*

In the EP corpus, the item *still* (N=26) was typically used as an alternative concessive connective to *however* in order to offset negative results, often in combination with *but* (example 8.34). The few instances of *yet* as a concessive connective in the EP corpus (N=6) reflected largely the same function (example 8.35).

(8.34) Nonperforming loans have a slight increase due to one past due loan that is currently in workout mode *but* we're *still* at the top of our peer group […] *(EP/C16)*

(8.35) I am not trying to lightly dismiss the task that we have ahead of us to manage [PRODUCT] effectively, *yet* the reality is that much of our organization is focused on the growth from our seeds and traits businesses. *(EP/C17)*

The few occurrences of *whereas* (N=5) found in the EP corpus were used exclusively to signal a simple contrast, without any particularly persuasive intentions, as shown in example 8.36. This is worthy of note because *whereas* is traditionally considered to be interchangeable with *while*. However, evidence from the previous analysis of *while* shows that in this interactional context, this concessive connective is often used in an overtly rhetorical way and serves a range of different functions beyond mere contrast.

(8.36) Spain, for example, is almost entirely driven by new business *whereas* in France our risks are shrinking […] *(EP/C2)*

The other items that were found (mostly in EP) were quite rare, with only one or two occurrences. However, it is interesting to look at how two particularly formal items were used by corporate speakers, seeming to want to call special attention to a personal and complimentary assessment (example 8.37), or to appear particularly eloquent (example 8.38).

(8.37) This additional profitability has been moderated somewhat by a small reduction in the planted acres of corn. *Nevertheless*, I feel that our Brazilian team has delivered a very nice upswing in our seed business. *(EP/C17)*

(8.38) Looking at [PRODUCT] operating expenses, *notwithstanding* holiday seasonality, the credit card funding mix remained constant with Q3 at 55%. *(EP/C10)*

8.4 Combined macro-micro analysis

In order to understand how concessive connectives might be linked to certain structural moves, dispersion plots were generated for *however* as the most frequent concessive connective across both corpora. The series of plots for EP and ER are reproduced in Figures 8.1 and 8.2, respectively. From the figures, we see not only that *however* occurs in only 9 out of 25 text files in ER vs. 16 out 25 transcript files in EP. In addition, in the ER corpus, *however* is relatively infrequent in the initial portions of the plots, whereas it appears throughout the plots of the EP in a more uniform manner.

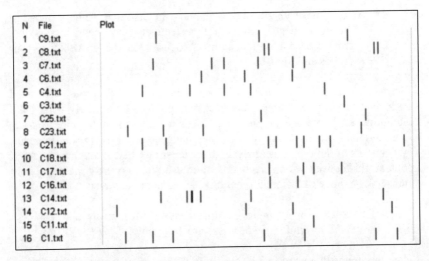

Figure 8.1: Dispersion plots of *however* in EP (Source: *WordSmith Tools*)

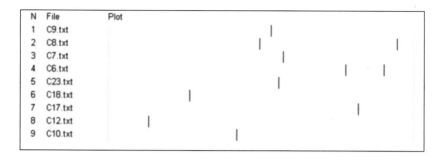

Figure 8.2: Dispersion plots of *however* in ER (Source: *WordSmith Tools*)

Follow-up qualitative analysis showed that in the ER corpus, the relatively few occurrences of *however* are mostly in structural moves associated with future activities (*Outlook*) and cautionary language about forward-looking statements (*Safe Harbour disclaimers*) that concede future uncertainty, as shown in examples 8.39 and 8.40, respectively. On the other hand, in the EP corpus, in addition to these moves, *however* was also present in the initial moves of presentations, including the *Introduction, Financial Overview* and *Financial details* where they are used by speakers for more complex reasons. In example 8.41, *however* seems to be used to demonstrate the speakers' verbal 'flair', since it actually seems rather superfluous in this context. In examples 8.42-8.43, it is used more rhetorically to explain and justify the speakers' own positions and therefore persuade the audience more effectively.

Business Outlook
(8.39) Based on current conditions, the Company does not expect to record a provision for loan and lease losses in 2004. *However*, the actual amount of the provision for loan and lease losses depends on determinations of credit risk that are made near the end of each quarter *(ER/C6)*

Safe Harbour
(8.40) These statements are based on current expectations and currently available information. However, since these statements are based on factors that involve risks and uncertainties, the company's actual performance and results may differ materially from those described [...] *(ER/C17)*

Introduction
(8.41) Welcome, everyone, and thanks for joining with us today. As usual, the majority of my opening remarks will focus on the

results for the fourth quarter, as you are already familiar with our results for the three prior quarters of the year. *However*, during the Q&A period, [FIRST NAME] and I will be happy to respond to any questions. *(EP/C4)*

Financial overview
(8.42) Thank you, [FIRST NAME]. [...] I am going to begin with some commentary on our first-quarter results and [FIRST NAME] will cover the financial details [...] Diluted earnings per share for the quarter with 33 cents compared to 27 cents in the first-quarter last year. *However*, as described in our news release our results included a benefit of six cents per share from a reduction in reorganization liability [...] *(EP/C1)*

Financial details
(8.43) Thank you, [FIRST NAME]. I will review the major components of the 5 cent year-over-year decline in earnings [...] Had that been the entire story, fourth quarter earnings per share would have been 56 cents, well above the prior year. *However*, our fourth quarter results did also reflect the same head winds we had faced all year. [...] *(EP/C9)*

Thus, it appears that, unlike the remote written production process of the earnings releases, the real-time interactional environment of the earnings presentations afforded the executive speakers with greater opportunities to exploit *however* to engage their interlocutors in a 'dialogue' to forcefully communicate their message, while anticipating and pre-empting potential challenges at the same time.

8.5 Chapter wrap-up

The analysis of concessive connectives in this chapter has shown how corporate speakers and writers use concessive connectives as resources of *engagement*, or devices through which speakers and writers construe meanings against the "heteroglossic backdrop of prior utterances, alternative viewpoints and anticipated responses" (Martin &White, 2005, p. 97).

The fact that concessive connectives were on the whole much more prominent in the EP corpus in comparison with the ER corpus could be determined by who actually produces the discourse. Earnings releases are typically written by lower-level professionals (e.g., company press officers) who are perhaps less directly impacted by financial disclosure issues, and thus less 'rhetorically-motivated' than the top executives who deliver the earnings presentations. According to Den Hartog and Verburg (1997) executives are intensely involved in shaping the corporate identity and are often seen as company spokespeople or figureheads. Thus, they have a great deal at stake on both the professional and personal levels. The idea that executives are prone to engage in overtly persuasive discourse is also supported by Hyland (2005) and Garzone (2005a), who both found high frequencies of concessive connectives in CEOs' letters to shareholders.

The qualitative analysis of the key concessive connectives *however* and *while* revealed their markedly rhetorical and argumentative dimension. In line with the findings of Hyland (1998) for CEOs' letters and Lassen (2006) for press releases, concessive connectives are used here by corporate speakers and writers to carefully explain their assessment of situations and events. In this way, they construct their arguments so rationally that it is difficult to challenge them. In addition, like evaluative adjectives (Chapter 7), concessive connectives are also used in a manipulative way to draw attention away from the negative and towards the positive. As Garzone (2005a, p. 136) states with reference to CEOs' letters, "concessive constructions enable the writer to present negative propositions in concomitance with positive facts, thus neutralising the potentially detrimental effect of wholly negative disclosures". Similarly, Hager and Scheiber (1990, p. 119) suggest that statements that begin with expressions such as *Despite the...* in CEOs' letters to shareholders are "red flags" that signal the need for readers to be aware of attempts on the part of corporate writers to gloss over poor performance.

Such rhetorical usage of concessive connectives in financial disclosure genres clearly reflects Fairclough's (2001, p. 164) notion of *strategic discourse* which is motivated by instrumental goals. Interestingly, it is in contrast with Vergaro's (2008) study which found that concessive constructions were used in business letters primarily for reasons of politeness. This difference suggests that the 'high-stake' nature of financial disclosure encourages corporate speakers especially to exploit concessive connectives to impose their own evaluations, while pre-empting and thus discouraging possible alternative viewpoints. In this way, they are able to position themselves and the companies they represent in the best possible light. Indeed, since a similar strategy-oriented usage has been found in written financial genres (Hyland, 1998; Garzone, 2005a; Maat, 2007), concessive connectives may well represent a characterising feature that is extremely important for corporate speakers and writers to master. This has clear implications for novices aspiring to become professionals who engage in activities of financial disclosure, particularly for non-native speakers of English who may need special training in order to become more aware of how concessive connectives can be used strategically.

With particular reference to the earnings presentations, a comment made by the professional informant concerning the information that is presented by the executives seems to support this notion. He mentioned that many of the "most sophisticated participants", (i.e., some investment analysts) "have already digested the material and rippled the key information through their own financial models". The executive presenters are therefore likely to be aware of pre-conceived stances among their audience and, in response, make especially strong efforts to put forth their viewpoints.

The combined macro-micro analysis also supports the idea that the executive speakers of the EP corpus are particularly skilled at using concessive connectives to steer audiences towards their interpretation of reality. Indeed, we find highly rhetorical uses of *however* that occur already in the initial structural moves of the discourse, which instead does not happen in the ER corpus.

Thus far, we have seen how rhetoric in earnings presentations and earnings releases is encoded through evaluative adjectives (to convey attitudes) and concessive connectives (to engage interlocutors by anticipating and re-directing their viewpoints). The next chapter will be dedicated to linguistic expressions that serve to adjust or graduate the rhetorical force of discourse, i.e., intensifiers and mitigators, representing the resource of *graduation* described in Martin and White's (2005) appraisal framework.

Chapter 9
Graduation: intensifiers and mitigators

9.1 Preliminary editing of the data

The third type of evaluative language accounted for in the appraisal model is *graduation*, meaning linguistic resources that adjust the evaluative force of discourse (Martin & White, 2005). More specifically, I focus on devices used to upscale (intensifiers) or downscale (mitigators) evaluative meanings. It is important to point out that evaluative force refers not only to *intensification*, but also *quantification* (ibid., p. 140), even if the authors recognise a certain degree of overlapping between the two. However, on the whole, devices of intensification assess the degree of intensity of a quality or process (e.g., *extremely*, *slightly*), while devices of quantification assess the amount of an entity in terms of size, number, weight and proximity, (e.g., *small, many, distant*). This study will be limited to the analysis of the degree intensification, which may be either upscaled (with *intensifiers*) or downscaled (with *mitigators*) and will therefore not deal specifically with evaluative resources of quantification. In selecting which types of resources within Martin and White's (2005) framework to focus on this study, I decided to give priority to resources of intensification as they seem to have more potential for expressing rhetorical meanings than resources of quantification.

As anticipated in Chapter 5, a set of 15 lexical items functioning as intensifiers and mitigators was established on the basis of indications from Martin and White (2005), as well as direct hands-on work with the two corpora, i.e., both preliminary overviews of the printed versions and automatic searches with *Wordsmith Tools* (Scott, 2008). To recapitulate, these intensifiers (N=6) and mitigators (N=9) are as follows:

intensifiers: *quite, very, really, extremely, simply, tremendously*
mitigators: *slightly, somewhat, pretty, a bit, rather, reasonably, fairly, relatively, just*

The above-listed items were searched across both corpora using the concordancer tool. From the resulting output, it was evident that some preliminary editing was needed, as there were instances of various items that did not function to intensify or mitigate what followed. *Rather* was found not only as a mitigating adverb (example 9.1), but also in the conjunction phrase *rather than* to distinguish two sentential elements (example 9.2) and as a contrastive connective (example 9.3). *Really* was sometimes an intensifier of enthusiasm (example 9.4), but other times carried the literal meaning, paraphrasable with *in reality* (example 9.5). All instances of these two items that did not clearly encode mitigation or intensification, respectively, were removed from the data.

(9.1)   […] the market expenses went up a little bit and therefore the profit is *rather* flat. *(EP/C21)*

(9.2)   Examples disclosed at CES include our development work on a device we call the [PRODUCT] that is focused on the consumption of digital content *rather than* the creation of it. *(EP/C15)*

(9.3)   We are not leaving or closing our operations in any metropolitan area but, *rather*, consolidating within existing locations. *(EP/C1)*

(9.4)   Likewise, it is *really* nice to have Latin America now at the beginning of our fiscal year and to have the improved performance in Brazil at our back. *(EP/C17)*

(9.5)   Although ROE went down, again it's *really* because ROE is on a net income basis […] *(EP/C21)*

The item *just* was particularly complex. Several instances conveyed meanings that did not seem to be evaluative. Some could be paraphrased as *a short time ago* (example 9.6), or *only* in a quantitative sense (example 9.7), or *only* in the sense of posing limits to proposed actions (example 9.8). These meanings that did not reflect the intensification or mitigation of qualities were removed. Moreover, when *just* did serve to adjust the force of evaluation, it was sometimes an intensifier to emphasise or upscale the evaluation (example 9.9) and other times a mitigator (example 9.10) to downscale an assessment and could be paraphrased by *a bit* or *slightly*. Thus, it was necessary to classify *just* as both an intensifier and a mitigator.

(9.6)   Our expectation is that with experience physicians will extend this patient base […] consistent with adoption pattern that I *just* described. *(EP/C14)*

(9.7)   Advertising revenues grew *just* 2% in 2003, similar to what our industry peers experienced. *(EP/C23)*

(9.8)   We have listed the activities with which I think you are all familiar so I do not need to repeat them. If you *just* look at the graphs that is the combined ratio for 2002 [...] *(EP/C2)*

(9.9)   [Product] had another great quarter and a great year. Revenue up 7 and op profit up 14. *Just* a terrific fall season [...] *(EP/C13)*

(9.10) "Continued strong asset management enabled us to increase cash by $225 million to *just* under $4.8 billion." *(ER/C5)*

Similarly, *pretty* could be an intensifier (when paraphrasable by *very*) or a mitigator (when paraphrasable by *fairly*).[38] These different uses are illustrated in examples 9.11 and 9.12, respectively.

(9.11) Operating profit, it is a *pretty amazing* story here. *(EP/C21)*

(9.12) So overall earnings were down 15% which is a *pretty good* progress offsetting the lack of terminations. *(EP/C13)*

9.2 Quantitative analysis

After the above-illustrated adjustments were made to the data, frequency counts were taken of the remaining occurrences of intensifiers and mitigators and are presented in Table 9.1 in both raw frequency counts and the normalised parameter of instances per ten thousand words (pttw).

---

[38]   To make this distinction, prosodic signals would have been quite useful. However, since audio files of the transcripts were not available (see Chapter 5), this was not possible. I therefore relied on the surrounding co-text for clues and also solicited feedback from a research colleague.

Graduation marker	EP (101,393 words)		ER (46,715 words)	
	N	pttw	N	pttw
Intensifiers				
very	187	18.4	5	1.0
really	24	2.4	-	-
quite	16	1.6	1	0.2
just	15	1.5	-	-
simply	9	0.9	-	-
extremely	7	0.7	2	0.4
pretty	6	0.6	-	-
tremendously	2	0.2	1	0.2
Subtotal	266	26.3	9	1.8
Mitigators				
slightly	40	3.9	8	1.7
pretty	20	1.9	-	-
somewhat	17	1.7	3	0.6
just	13	1.3	3	0.6
relatively	10	1.0	2	0.4
a bit	9	0.9	-	-
fairly	6	0.6	-	-
rather	2	0.2	-	-
reasonably	1	0.1	2	0.4
Subtotal	118	11.6	18	3.7
Grand total	384	37.9	27	5.5

Table 9.1: Intensifiers and mitigators in EP vs. ER

A clear trend that emerges from the data is the overall much higher frequency of both intensifiers and mitigators in EP (37.9 instances pttw) vs. ER (5.5 instances pttw), as seen by comparing the grand totals. In the case of intensifiers, the difference is extremely marked: 26.3 pttw in EP vs. 1.8 pttw in ER. Most of this difference can be traced to the item *very* (18.4 pttw in EP vs. 1.0 pttw in ER), which skews the results considerably. In Biber et al.'s (1999) work that contrasted more generic types of spoken vs. written discourse (represented by conversation and academic prose, respectively), *very* was found to be equally common in both (ibid., p. 565). Therefore, the scarcity of *very* in ER is somewhat surprising. Like academic prose, earnings releases can be described as a relatively formal written genre and it would thus seem reasonable to also find a fair number of instances of *very*.

Follow-up contextual analysis of *very* in the ER corpus revealed that three of the five instances are actually found in embedded quotes (example 9.13). This suggests that, unlike other types of formal written discourse, earnings release writers tend to avoid using even this most common intensifier and associate it mainly with instances of speech.

> (9.13) "We are *very* pleased with the strength of our fourth quarter and year-end results [...]" said [FULL NAME], chief financial officer , [C25] *(ER/C25)*

Also evident from Table 9.1 is the wider range of intensifiers used in EP vs. ER, with eight vs. four different types, respectively. This trend is instead generally in line with Biber et al. (1999, p. 564), who also found greater variation in intensifiers (which they call *amplifiers*) in conversation vs. academic prose. Perhaps the limited variety of intensifiers in ER is a reflection of a more standardised and conventional approach on the part of staff earnings release writers as compared to a more creative approach of executive speakers of the earnings presentations.

As Table 9.1 shows, mitigators are also considerably more frequent in EP (9.6 pttw) vs. ER (3.7 pttw), as well as more varied. Again using Biber et al. (1999) as a benchmark, such items (which they call *downtoners* or *non-amplifiers*) were instead found to be generally more common in academic prose than in conversation (ibid., p.567).[39] Therefore, their higher frequency in EP is somewhat surprising. Closer examination of the concordance lines showed that the most frequent mitigator in both corpora, *slightly*, is used exclusively to refer to numerical data, as shown in examples 9.14 and 9.15. In the appraisal framework (Martin & White, 2005), *slightly* is listed as evaluative resource of *intensification.* However, the fact that it is found in both corpora only to mitigate the assessment of quantity suggests that in financial disclosure it has a very specific function that is closely linked to the reporting of numerical data, which is quite different from its more vague meaning when referring to qualities or processes (e.g., *I feel slightly sad, We were slightly delayed*).

> (9.14) [Product] is expected to represent approximately 65% of [C18] net sales with gross margins similar but operating margins *slightly higher* than the former [C18] [PRODUCT]. *(EP/C18)*

> (9.15) Reported operating margin as a percentage of net sales *increased slightly. (ER/C19)*

---

[39] The exceptions are *pretty* and *nearly* that were more frequent in conversation than in academic prose (Biber et al., 1999, p. 568).

If we look at the usage of intensifiers vs. mitigators within each corpus, an interesting trend emerges. While intensifiers are more than twice as frequent as mitigators in EP (26.3 pttw vs. 11.6 pttw), the opposite is true in ER, where mitigators outnumber intensifiers (3.7 pttw vs. 1.9 pttw). From a closer look at the concordance output, we see that the executive speakers of the EP corpus often upscale positive remarks (examples 9.16-9.17), but less frequently comment on negative performance which, at any rate, they tend to mitigate (example 9.18-9.19).

> (9.16) And because of these efforts, [C10]'s performance in Q4 was *simply phenomenal. (EP/C10)*

> (9.17) So we feel like we're in a *tremendously strong* position here. *(EP/C13)*

> (9.18) […] we had 1.84% for net profit for the third quarter. It's *pretty flat* but because of very good reasons. *(EP/C21)*

> (9.19) On page 29 you can see the development of impairments and corresponding write-ups, we have still *a fairly high level* of impairment in Q3 […] *(EP/C2)*

On the other hand, there are more mitigators in the ER corpus, mainly referring to numerical quantities (e.g., *slightly* in example 9.15), but also to performance more generally as shown in example 9.20. Only nine intensifiers were found in this corpus, six of which occur in embedded quotes (example 9.21). Apparently, the staff writers of earnings releases are much less inclined to pepper their texts with intensifiers than the executive speakers of earnings presentations. With the exception of embedded quotes attributed to executive speakers, the remaining text of the earnings releases tends to have a much more restrained style, with very little upscaling. Again, the remoteness of the written mode and less important professional status of the staff writers could be a plausible explanation.

> (9.20) The *relatively weak* performance of the Digital Media business is expected to improve as demand for flat-panel, high-definition and digital TVs starts to gain momentum. *(ER/C21)*

> (9.21) […] said [FULL NAME], [C12] president, chairman and chief executive officer. "Our new product launches - [PRODUCT], [PRODUCT] and [PRODUCT] - performed *extremely well* in their first year on the market with combined sales in excess of $500 million" *(ER/C12)*

I conclude this sub-section with a particularly interesting case found in the EP corpus that somewhat paradoxically combines the mitigator *a bit* with the highly positive evaluative adjective *terrific* (example 9.22). This serves to highlight just how creative and 'upbeat' the executive presenters can be when it comes to trying to persuade listeners.

> (9.22) The core volume across the whole portfolio of Commercial was up 12% ex aviation, so *a terrific bit* of momentum there. *(EP/C13)*

9.3 Qualitative analysis

For a better understanding of how intensifiers and mitigators are used in earnings presentations and earnings releases, it seemed useful to determine which type of entity or phenomenon they referred to. Towards this aim, I made use of Martin and White's (2005, pp. 141-142) three semantic categories of intensification which, in turn, correspond to specific lexico-grammatical features:

- Upscaling/downscaling of *qualities*: pre-modification of an adjective or adverb (e.g., *very good, rather nicely*);
- Upscaling/downscaling of *verbal processes*: adverbial modification of a verb group (e.g., *we are really encouraged, it can be reasonably estimated*);
- Upscaling/downscaling of *modalities*: pre-modification of an adjective or an adverb (e.g., *relatively often, quite possible*).

The tagged versions of the two corpora were searched for the same 15 intensifiers and mitigators with the concordancer of *Wordsmith Tools* (Scott, 2008). The concordance lines were then resorted according to the referents of intensifiers and mitigators, which were also tagged according to grammatical form (e.g., adjective, adverb, verb). In this way, it was possible to identify the *quality*, *verbal process* or *modality* that was being intensified or mitigated. To illustrate this process, Figure 9.1 shows a screenshot of a small sample of tagged concordances for the intensifier *very* in the EP corpus, tagged RG for general adjective. The concordances have been resorted according to the first word to the right, i.e., the referent of *very*, thus identifying the adjectives *comfortable, competitive, complex, confident, conservative* (tagged JJ) as the qualities that have been intensified.

N	Concordance
9	For_IF now_RT ._. we_PPIS2 are_VBR very_RG comfortable_JJ that_CST
10	the_AT third_MD quarter_NN1 and_CC very_RG comfortable_JJ that_CST
11	success_NN1 in_II this_DD1 very_RG competitive_JJ market_NN1
12	to_TO compete_VVI in_II a_AT1 very_RG competitive_JJ ._, casual_JJ
13	_NP1 market_NN1 has_VHZ been_VBN very_RG competitive_JJ ._. Even_RR
14	were_VBDR in_II some_DD cases_NN2 very_RG complex_JJ ._. And_CC
15	see_VV0 we_PPIS2 are_VBR very_RG confident_JJ of_RR21
16	._. Again_RT this_DD1 is_VBZ very_RG conservative_JJ ._.
17	we_PPIS2 have_VH0 a_AT1 very_RG conservative_JJ

Figure 9.1: Resorted concordances of *very* (Source: *WordSmith Tools*)

The results of the analysis of the 15 intensifiers and mitigators are illustrated in Table 9.2. In the columns under EP and ER, the number of occurrences found in the semantic category is listed (N), along with the relative percentage of the total occurrences of the item found in the corpus (from Table 9.1) indicated in parentheses (%). As can be seen, the table reports only two semantic categories (*qualities* and *verbal processes*) because there were no instances of intensifiers or mitigators that modified *modalities* (e.g., *quite possible, very likely, fairly certain, rather often*) in either corpus. The complete absence of this type of intensification or mitigation deserves further comment. Apparently, the executive speakers and earnings release writers prefer to restrain from upscaling or downscaling when entertaining the possibility or the frequency of phenomena, perhaps to avoid committing themselves to positions that may prove wrong in the future. Yet given the importance of cautioning against potentially different outcomes in financial disclosure (e.g., mandatory *Safe Harbour* disclaimers described in Chapter 7), this attitude is not surprising.

	EP				ER			
	Qualities		Verb. Proc.		Qualities		Verb. Proc.	
	N	(%)	N	(%)	N	(%)	N	(%)
Intensifiers								
very	179	(95.7)	8	(4.3)	5	(100.0)	-	-
really	2	(8.3)	22	(91.7)	-	-	-	-
quite	16	(100.0)	-	-	1	(100.0)	-	-
just	7	(46.7)	8	(53.3)	-	-	-	-
simply	2	(22.2)	7	(77.8)	-	-	-	-
extremely	5	(71.4)	2	(28.6)	2	(100.0)	-	-
pretty	6	(100.0)	-	-	-	-	-	-
tremendously	1	(50.0)	1	(50.0)	1	(100.0)	-	-
Subtotal	218	(82.0)	48	(18.0)	9	(100.0)	-	-
Mitigators								
slightly	25	(62.5)	15	(37.5)	-	-	8	(100.0)
pretty	18	(90.0)	2	(10.0)	-	-	-	-
somewhat	7	(41.2)	10	(58.8)	-	-	3	(100.0)
just	11	(84.6)	2	(15.4)	1	(33.3)	2	(66.7)
relatively	10	(100.0)	-	-	2	(100.0)	-	-
a bit	4	(44.4)	5	(55.6)	-	-	-	-
fairly	6	(100.0)	-	-	-	-	-	-
rather	2	(100.0)	-	-	-	-	-	-
reasonably	-	-	1	(100.0)	-	-	2	(100.0)
Subtotal	83	(70.3)	35	(29.7)	3	(16.7)	15	(83.3)

Table 9.2: Categories of intensifiers/mitigators in EP vs. ER

9.3.1 Intensifiers

By comparing the percentages and subtotals of intensifiers used with qualities and verbal processes, we see that in EP most are used to upscale qualities, and therefore modify adjectives (examples 9.23-9.24). As could be expected, the item *very* is used almost exclusively to upscale qualities or verbal processes in positive contexts. Out of 187 total occurrences, only five are negatively-oriented (e.g., *a very difficult environment*).

(9.23) "For the year, […] we started with a *very healthy* balance sheet […]" (*ER/C22*)

(9.24) Here we have listed for you the example of the eastern European companies, *fairly strong double-digit* growth. (*EP/C2*)

This trend was also confirmed by the cluster analysis of *very* in the EP corpus, the only item among the intensifiers and mitigators present in sufficient frequencies to generate clusters. Table 9.3 lists the five clusters that were detected, four of which are seen to have an overtly positive tone.

Three-word clusters	N
a very strong	14
a very good	6
very strong quarter	5
very pleased with	5
we are very	8

Table 9.3 Clusters with the item *very* in EP

Three intensifiers in EP – *really, just* and *simply* - are exceptions to this general trend as they were used more often to upscale verbal processes, accounting for 91.7 percent, 77.8 percent and 53.3 percent of all occurrences, respectively (examples 9.25-9.27). This usage tends to render the utterances quite dynamic and therefore more intensely rhetorical. Indeed, in example 9.27, we even find a sports metaphor (i.e., *just hitting it out of the park*) that serves to further reinforce the upscaling function of *just*, in this case used as an intensifier.

> (9.25) More importantly, we're well-aware that our challenge is *not simply to deliver* growth for one or two years, but to make the appropriate investment and capital allocation in the long term. *(EP/C25)*

> (9.26) [Product] sales and profits *are really surging. (EP/C21)*

> (9.27) [Product] ratings are up significantly and [PRODUCT] *is just hitting* it out of the park and exceeding plan. *(EP/C13)*

9.3.2 Mitigators

By comparing the percentages and subtotals of the mitigato*r*s, we see that in EP they are used more frequently to attenuate qualities, while in ER they refer more to verbal processes. However, the most frequent mitigator in both corpora, *slightly*, is actually used to downscale quantities rather than qualities before adjectives and adverbs, and verbal processes when present in a verb group, as explained earlier and illustrated in examples 9.14 and 9.15, respectively. In the EP corpus, *just* as a mitigator was also used much in the same way (example 9.28) and is perhaps a more colloquial alternative to *slightly. Somewhat* downscales both qualities and verbal processes in EP (examples 9.29 and 9.30, respectively), but only verbal processes in ER (example 9.31). It is interesting to see that, in the EP corpus, the executive speakers use the relatively formal *somewhat* in a quite sophisticated way that recalls an academic style. This item has been noted in editorials of academic journals (Giannoni, 2007), where it is used mainly to mitigate criticism. Yet the corporate speakers and writers seem to have a different purpose in mind, i.e., to downplay negative performance in a verbally refined way which seems to give more credibility to the speakers (examples 9.29 and 9.30). The mitigator *a bit* is used with both semantic categories, but is found only in EP (example 9.32), perhaps due to its more colloquial nature.

> (9.28) Our current view is that mobile infrastructure market in euro terms *contracted by just over 15%. (EP/C18)*

> (9.29) You may recall that last year's coating season was *somewhat disappointing. (EP/C9)*

> (9.30) Institutional sales levels which *have suffered somewhat* as a result of our historical investment performance improved during the quarter. *(EP/C4)*

> (9.31) In the third quarter of 2003, [PRODUCT] prices *moderated somewhat* to average $4.89 per million Btu. *(ER/C20)*

> (9.32) Chipset units *were up a bit*, and set a revenue coming off a very strong Q3. *(EP/C15)*

9.4 Combined macro-micro analysis

The combined macro-micro analysis in this section concentrates on the two most frequent items in the EP corpus: the intensifier *very* (N=187) and the mitigator *slightly* (N=40). In the ER corpus, none of the intensifiers and mitigators appeared in sufficient frequencies to produce any detectable patterns in dispersion plots, which could then be integrated with further analysis within structural moves (Chapter 6).

As can be seen from Figure 9.2, *very* occurs in 23 out of the 25 files that comprise the EP corpus and is rather well distributed throughout the presentations. However, in several cases, it occurs more frequently in the initial and/or final parts.

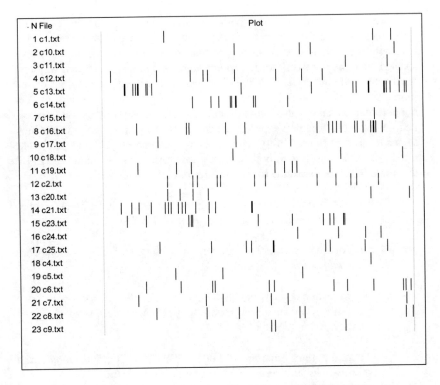

Figure 9.2 Dispersion plots of *very* in EP (Source: *WordSmith Tools*)

The structural patterning of *very* in the earnings presentations was quite similar to the structural patterning of evaluative adjectives described in Chapter 7. *Very* appears most frequently in the *Introduction* and *Wrap-up* moves, corresponding to the portions of the plots on the far left and far right ends, respectively. This usage is illustrated in examples 9.33-9.36. As with evaluative adjectives, this patterning reaffirms the idea that the executives responsible for delivering the initial and final segments of the earnings presentations often adopt a strong rhetorical tone to impress their audiences. Interestingly, the five instances of *very* that occurred in the ER corpus were only found in the *Summary* move, and usually in embedded quotes (example 9.13), with none whatsoever in the final moves of the earnings releases. This again points to the skilful exploitation of this intensifier by the executives delivering the earnings presentations to maintain a high level of persuasion throughout the discourse.

Introduction

(9.33) [...] Without further ado let's kick off the conference call. I would like to start off by saying that the management is *very happy* to announce that the results for Q4 in terms of revenues and operating profits have reached a historical high. [...] *(EP/C21)*

(9.34) Thank you and good morning, everyone, we appreciate all of you joining us for our teleconference discussing our 2003 results. We *very much appreciate* your interest in our Company. [...] Net income was 10 million which is up 2.2 million or 29 percent from year earlier levels which were also *very good*. [...] *(EP/C16)*

Wrap-up

(9.35) [...] And most important, we have *very good hard-working employees*, dedicated to building value at [C6]. That concludes my comments for this afternoon, and [FIRST NAME] and I would now like to take questions. *(EP/C6)*

(9.36) [...] We believe that we're making steady progress towards building a company that can compete *very well* in the U.S. retail food industry and that can deliver growth and higher performance We'd like to take your questions. *(EP/C8)*

Figure 9.3 reproduces the dispersion plot of *slightly* in EP, which appears in 15 out of the 25 files that comprise the corpus. Unlike *very* (Figure 9.2), this item does not often occur at the beginning and at the very end of the presentations (corresponding to the *Introduction* and *Wrap-up* moves), but occurs more in the centre to the right-hand portions of the plot, corresponding to the *Financial details* move which directly precedes the *Wrap-up* move.

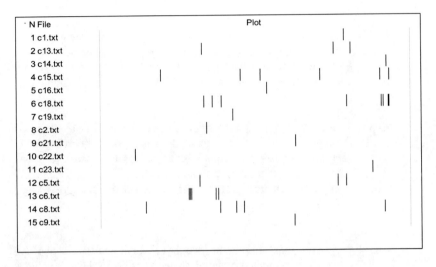

Figure 9.3: Dispersion plots of *slightly* in EP (Source: *WordSmith Tools*)

Qualitative analysis of the concordance lines showed that *slightly* is most often used by the executive speaker responsible for explaining numerical data (typically the CFO), as shown in examples 9.37-9.38. This pattern is very much in line with the previous result showing that *slightly* is used to mitigate exclusively assessments of quantity (see sub-section 9.1). Thus, we see a very consistent numerical orientation of *slightly* from both the quantitative analysis of the frequency counts and the qualitative analysis of the structural moves.

<u>Financial details</u>
(9.37) [...] Our income tax rate in '04 will be approximately 36.7%, *slightly* higher than the 36% fiscal 2003 rate. Now I'd like to turn it back to [FIRST NAME]. *(EP/C8)*

(9.38) Flash units were approximately flat, but ASPs were *slightly* higher as average densities continued to improve [...] With that, let me turn the meeting back over to [FIRST NAME]. *(EP/C15)*

9.5 Chapter wrap-up

The quantitative, qualitative and combined macro-micro analyses undertaken in this chapter have revealed some interesting trends in how intensifiers and mitigators are used in the discourse of financial disclosure. On a quantitative level, both devices are much more frequent in the EP corpus in comparison with the ER corpus. Unlike the written medium of the earnings releases, the more interactional spoken teleconference medium seems to encourage executive speakers to 'turn up the rhetorical volume' in keeping with their high professional status. While this is not surprising in the case of intensifiers to emphasise positive performance, mitigators are also more frequent in EP vs. ER, although they are more characteristic of written prose (Biber et al. 1999).

In both corpora, the most frequently occurring mitigator is *slightly*, which is used exclusively to downscale the evaluation of quantities. This result is to some extent at odds with the appraisal model (Martin & White, 2005), where *slightly* is broadly classified as mitigator of *intensification* referring to qualities, processes and modalities, and not *quantification* referring to entities.[40] While these authors recognise some blurring between the two concepts, the fact that *slightly* was found only with reference to quantity may indicate that in financial disclosure it functions to assess quantity rather than intensity.

Another way in which intensifiers and mitigators are used in the two corpora that is not in alignment with the appraisal model (Martin & White, 2005) is seen in the complete lack of these features being used to modify modalities (e.g., *quite possible, very likely, fairly certain*), which is instead quite common in other communicative contexts, e.g., academic writing (Hinkel, 2002; Hyland, 2005). This may be due to the financial nature of the two genres examined in this study, where it is of paramount importance to avoid problematic issues of credibility and legality that may arise when actual outcomes differ from forecasted expectations.

The combined macro-micro analysis showed that the intensifier *very* in the EP corpus tends to occur in the same structural moves (i.e., *Introduction* and *Wrap-up*) where we find evaluative adjectives (Chapter 7). This tends to confirm the highly specialised use of such rhetorical devices by the expert executive speakers. In contrast, the mitigator *slightly* is more prevalent in the *Financial details* move, where speakers provide in-depth explanations of financial data.

With this chapter, the analysis of rhetorical features in the EP and ER corpora has now come full-circle, beginning with evaluative adjectives as resources of *attitude* (Chapter 7), concessive connectives as resources of *engagement* (Chapter 8) and intensifiers and mitigators as resources of *graduation* in this chapter. Along the way, I have used both quantitative and qualitative methods to describe these features according to form, function and

---

[40]   The authors actually make a very fine distinction: *a slight disappointment* encodes a quantified entity, but *slightly disappointing* encodes an intensified quality.

referents in order to gain more insights into evaluation as a ubiquitous rhetorical element of spoken and written interpersonal communication. As Linde (1997, p.167) aptly remarks "In order to understand the practice of evaluation, an analysis must specify what is evaluated, and how."

In the final chapter, I conclude the study by drawing general conclusions, summarising the most significant results, re-positioning the research within the broader panorama of business discourse and suggesting possible topics for further research. I also discuss applications of the findings in English for business and finance teaching contexts, as well as implications for professionals involved in the process of financial disclosure in corporate settings.

Chapter 10
Final considerations

10.1 Contributions of the study

The objective of this study was to contrastively analyse two corpora that represent relatively new genres of financial discourse: spoken earnings presentations (delivered via teleconferencing) vs. written earnings releases (published on the Internet). Particular attention was paid to the rhetorical strategies used by corporate speakers and writers to influence the interpretations of their audiences of listeners and readers and how these are, in turn, impacted by the technology-mediated settings. Given the broad scope of this objective, in order to carry out a sufficiently exhaustive analysis, it was necessary to develop a three-pronged analytical approach that includes not only 'top-down' and 'bottom-up' textual analysis (Brown & Yule, 1983), but also ethnographically-inspired contacts with a professional informant from the corporate world. This multi-faceted analysis proved to be particularly useful for investigating such socially-situated types of discourse.

The top-down approach was based on techniques of discourse analysis (van Dijk, 1977) and genre analysis (Swales, 1990; Bhatia, 1993). These two research frameworks provided the analytical tools needed to identify the global macro-structures of texts and the various rhetorical moves that carry out specific communicative functions. Because of the newness of earnings calls and earnings releases as two text types that have thus far received little attention from linguists, it was important to first establish and compare their macro-structures and rhetorical patterning in order to understand how they constitute genres in their own right.

To complement the top-down approach, the application of techniques from corpus linguistics enabled me to investigate rhetorical features also at the micro-level across the two corpora, in other words, from the 'bottom-up'. At a very basic level, this is seen in the way the earnings presentations and earnings releases were collected and compiled into two comparable corpora and prepared for automated analytical procedures with text analysis software (cf. Pearson, 1998; Sinclair, 2001; Partington, 2004). More specifically, it is seen in the range of different analytical methods that were applied, including concordancing, dispersion plots and word clusters that facilitated in-depth and exhaustive analyses of key linguistic elements (cf. Scott, 2008; Leech, 2005). Without these tools, it would not have been feasible to analyse rhetorical features in the comprehensive way that was accomplished in this study. On the interpretive level, the influence of corpus linguistics can be seen largely in the use of other large corpora of spoken and written language (cf. Biber et al., 1999) as benchmarks to provide insights into the quantitative results that emerged from the computer-assisted methods.

On a methodological level, this study has underscored the importance of combining various types of quantitative and qualitative analytical procedures when studying the rhetorical dimension of spoken and written texts. In addition, it has shown how a corpus approach can be exploited to the maximum to investigate the linguistic features of specialised texts used in professional contexts, beginning with the identification of two key but thus far neglected financial genres, and followed by their collection and compilation into two specially designed corpora. Another novel aspect of the analysis was the use of both part-of-speech and semantic tagging as a research tool. Previous work involving these procedures has relied mainly on million-word corpora developed and tagged within the framework of very large-scale projects, such as the British National Corpus (BNC), the International Corpus of English (ICE) and Longman Corpus of Spoken and Written English (Biber et al., 1999). However, I hope to have shown that the tagging procedure is feasible and can be very valuable even when working with small self-collected corpora.

The study has also highlighted the usefulness of consulting with informants when analysing discourse that is produced and consumed in particular professional communicative contexts. With reference to corporate settings, discourse analysts typically do not have knowledge of the procedures and other contingent factors involved in corporate communication that serve to shed light on the linguistic phenomena that emerge from a study. The financial analyst who served as my professional informant for this study provided important information about financial disclosure events. His insights regarding the communicative process and the participant relationships enabled me to draw some conclusions that would not have been possible otherwise. As a frequent participant of earnings calls, the informant confirmed the overall regularity of their generic structure, as well as the strong impact of ICT. Indeed, he observed that such technologically-mediated forms of communication are destined to rise as they can provide progressively more cost-effective and flexible solutions for companies. Moreover, the informant's 'insider' knowledge of the dynamics of this communicative context was valuable for interpreting the use of rhetorical language.

It is important to recognise that the three-pronged approach reviewed above builds on several important and interrelated theoretical orientations for the study of language in use, namely systemic functional linguistics (Halliday, 1985), interactional sociolinguistics (Goffman, 1981), the ethnography of communication (Hymes, 1972) and critical discourse analysis (Fairclough, 2001). All of these orientations that foreground the social contexts in which authentic language is produced and received are therefore highly relevant to language research that focuses on variation in speech and writing in professional settings. Indeed, each has to some degree informed this study, proving useful to interpret the findings of the various analyses that were undertaken, as will be briefly discussed below.

As mentioned in Chapter 4, Hallidayan systemic functional linguistics is at the base of Martin and White's (2005) appraisal model which I applied to investigate rhetorical strategies across the two corpora. This theoretical framework allowed me to identify not only the forms of rhetorical features, but also their functions, seen in the decidedly functional slant of the qualitative analyses carried out in Chapters 7, 8 and 9.

From interactional sociolinguistics, I drew on the notion of "participation framework" (Goffman, 1981. p. 137), i.e., an articulation of different roles that may be assumed by discourse participants beyond the traditional ones of *speaker* or *writer*. For example, during the earnings presentations the speakers also took on the role of the authoritative company figurehead/spokesperson, in contrast to the staff writers of earnings releases whose role could be described as 're-elaborators' of financial information provided by other internal sources. The interactional sociolinguistic perspective was therefore helpful to shed light on the complexity of roles that emerged from the earnings presentations and earnings releases, as well as the motivations underlying their rhetorical features.

The analysis also incorporated principles of the ethnography of communication (Hymes, 1972) which emphasises the need to consider contextual factors outside the text itself (e.g., setting, participants, purpose, mode, channel, tone) in order to interpret linguistic forms and functions, and to collect information from other sources (e.g., discourse participants) in order to interpret the findings more accurately. The latter characteristic is in fact reflected in the reliance on the professional informant from the world of finance whose input contributed considerably to this study.

Finally, the principles of critical discourse analysis (Fairclough, 2001; van Dijk, 1996), i.e., how language reflects power and dominance in society and how it contributes to shaping and reproducing ideologies, were useful for interpreting the findings of the analysis from a rhetorical perspective. According to van Dijk (1996), corporate discourse is also involved in propagating ideology, albeit in a more indirect way since it is usually less public. Nevertheless, he affirms that corporate discourse "is ultimately vastly influential through its consequences for the socio-economic implications of the ethnic status quo" (ibid., p. 95). Critical discourse analysis is useful for a better understanding of how discourse participants attempt to influence readers or listeners in professional contexts where persuasion is the underlying force that drives the interaction. This was the case with the participants of earnings presentations and earnings releases who appeared to use value-laden expressions (i.e., evaluative adjectives, intensifier and mitigators) and 'manipulative' concessive connectives strategically for this purpose.

With reference to the communicative settings represented by earnings presentations and earnings releases corpora, the study contributes to enhancing our understanding of increasingly important forms of professional communication distributed by ICT-mediated channels (i.e., teleconferencing and the Internet) for the purpose of financial disclosure. Their ICT-driven nature reflects the theoretical concepts of multimodality, i.e., the integration of different semiotic resources to produce texts, and multimediality, i.e., the integration of different technologies to transmit texts (Shortis, 2001; Thibault, 2000; Kress & van Leeuwen, 2001). In the case of earnings presentations, we find not only the mode of speech, but also writing and visual images in the form of pre-distributed printed or digital texts, through which the speakers communicate the message, which is then transmitted by the audio and visual media through which the listeners receive the message. The earnings releases are instead distributed via the Internet, thereby replacing the conventional print forms supplied to journalists. They thus constitute a new press release genre with technology-influenced features, such as hypertext links to other financial documents and non-linear structures that are tailored to Internet navigation (cf. Askehave & Ellerup Nielsen, 2005; Crystal, 2006; Garzone et al., 2007). The concepts of multimodality and multimediality also come into play when interpreting the findings of the structural analyses. The macro-structures of both the earnings presentations and the earnings releases were impacted by their ICT environments in that the presence of certain rhetorical moves was actually determined by both mode and medium. Thus, the study shows how the multimodal and multimedial properties of ICT can contribute to reshaping the traditional discursive practices of the corporate community.

The earnings presentations and earnings releases investigated in this study were produced by companies for the purpose of financial disclosure, i.e., the public release of financial information (Gibbins et al., 1990). This has become a vital aspect of corporate communication in order for companies to remain viable in an increasingly competitive and globalised business environment (cf. Rogers, 2000; Brown et al., 2004; Saatchi, 2007). The fact that I had the opportunity to collect two corpora of language designed specifically for this aim is further testimony to the importance that companies place on financial disclosure to keep stakeholders informed and to promote a favourable corporate image. Indeed, as pointed out in Chapter 2, companies dedicate a great deal of effort and resources to the production of documentation for financial disclosure, both in written and spoken form.

The priority given to the financial disclosure component of corporate communication is also seen in the use of English in all the earnings presentations and earnings releases, regardless of the nationality of the companies and the discourse participants involved, lending further support to the idea that using English as *lingua franca* is essential if companies want to be successful global competitors (Louhiala-Salminen, 1996; Nickerson, 2005; Graddol, 2006).

The analytical focus of this study centred on the rhetorical dimension of earnings presentations and earnings releases, with particular reference to the construct of evaluation, i.e., how speakers and writers intervene in propositions to express personal feelings, attitudes and stance. In recent years, we have witnessed a growing interest in the concept of evaluation as a crucial dimension of interactive and interpersonal discourse (cf. Biber et al., 1999; Hyland, 1999; Thompson & Hunston, 2000; Martin & White, 2005). This study has shown that in the high-stakes interactional context of financial disclosure where companies are keen to both inform and persuade audiences, evaluative language plays a prominent role and may well be a distinguishing characteristic of earnings presentations and earnings releases that complements their basic informative purpose, in line with the idea that persuasion and information often co-exist in the corporate world (Bhatia, 2005). This strategic role of evaluation in the two corpora was determined by analysing them on the basis of Martin and White's (2005) appraisal model that is able to detect rhetorical features of language from various angles, covering a wide variety of linguistic features. These include not only inherently evaluative lexical items (e.g., positive/negative adjectives), but also elements that enable speakers and writers to position their own ideas and opinions in relation to those of others (e.g., concessive connectives), as well as elements that upscale or downscale qualities and processes (e.g., intensifiers and mitigators). Following in the footsteps of previous researchers who have enhanced our understanding of rhetorical language in corporate settings (Garzone, 2005a; Rutherford, 2005; Piotti, 2009), by applying Martin and White's (2005) framework to produce a broad-spectrum study, I hope to have made a further contribution.

Within the wider panorama of corporate discourse research, this study has advanced our knowledge of key rhetorical features of two innovative genres that are destined to play an increasingly important role as ICT becomes the driving force behind corporate communication of the future. This is also suggested by some recent work on other new technology-mediated business genres (cf. Poncini, 2007; Ruiz-Garrido & Ruiz-Madrid, 2011). With particular reference to the earnings presentations that focus on executive speech, the findings of this study help to redress the imbalance of existing business discourse research that has thus far privileged mainly written genres, such as letters (e.g., Vergaro, 2008), emails (e.g., van Mulken & van der Meer, 2005; Gimenez. 2006) and reports, (e.g., Ruiz-Garrido, 2001; Yeung, 2007), or dialogic spoken genres such as meetings (e.g.,

Bargiela Chiappini & Harris, 1995; Poncini, 2004) and negotiations (e.g., Charles, 1996). At the same time, the present study has clearly benefited from this important earlier work, which was particularly useful for identifying structural patterns and suggesting possible elements and approaches for the linguistic analysis of rhetorical strategies in the two corpora.

This research must also be situated in work that has been carried out in the narrower area of financial discourse. Given the crucial role of financial disclosure in modern business activities, studies of this nature have become increasingly relevant. However, the majority of this type of research has dealt with written financial documentation, such as annual reports (e.g., Ruiz-Garrido et al., 2005; Rutherford, 2005), CEOs' letters and Chairmen's statements (e.g., Skulstad, 1996; Thomas, 1997; Nickerson & De Groot, 2005; Piotti, 2006). Work on spoken financial genres is instead quite limited. Thus, the in-depth description and interpretation of the rhetorical features of earnings presentations offered by this study represents a step forward in this under-researched area.

With reference to the written earnings releases, other work on the press release genre (e.g., Jacobs, 1999; McLaren & Gurău, 2005; Lassen, 2006) has been very useful to inform the analysis and interpret the findings. Indeed, thanks to their work, this study has succeeded in identifying Internet-published earnings releases as a distinct genre. Although they may share some features with other types of press releases, ICT-mediated earnings releases have emerged as an important new tool for financial communication in today's modern enterprises.

10.2 The research questions revisited

To summarise the most salient findings of the various analyses undertaken in the present study, I now return to the original research questions set forth in Chapter 1. The first research question sought to determine distinguishing organisational features of earnings releases vs. earnings presentations in terms of their macro-structures, using techniques of traditional discourse analysis. As comparable genres with the same communicative purpose (i.e., to inform stakeholders of the current financial status and future outlook of the company, and to persuade them of the company's worth), they present some structural similarities and share several moves which communicate key information (e.g., descriptions of financial results and the Safe Harbour statement). However, each genre also contains some distinctive structural features. For example, only the earnings presentations include a preliminary move in which the teleconference operator opens the call to the participants and a final move in which the last speaker opens up the floor for questions from the investment analysts who are listening on the telephone line. On the other hand, moves that give general information about the company, upcoming conference calls and media contacts are found only in the earnings releases which are addressed to a wider audience of Internet users. In addition, the presence of embedded quotes attributed to company executives in the releases (which typically do not match utterances in the corresponding calls) signals their different authorship, e.g., by a staff press officer rather than by the executives themselves. We can thus conclude that, although similar in purpose and in content, earnings presentations and earnings releases have unique structural features that are determined by their diverse communicative contexts.

The macro-structure analysis of the two corpora reflects elements of interdiscursivity (Candlin & Maley, 1997), as they share some of the same structural features of other types of discourse, i.e., the business meeting (Bargiela-Chiappini & Harris, 1995) and press releases found in discourse domains other than business (Jacobs, 1999; Lassen, 2006). Features of intertextuality (Fairclough, 1992) are also present. For example, earnings presentations are formulated following some of the conventionalised practices of generic corporate press releases. In addition, both earnings presentations and the earnings releases contain explicit references to other texts.

The second research question focused on the rhetorical strategies expressed in the two corpora, or more specifically on the distinguishing rhetorical features of earnings releases vs. earnings presentations. This aspect was explored using Martin and White's (2005) appraisal model for the analysis of evaluative language, where evaluation is articulated into the constructs of *attitude, engagement* and *graduation*. Attitude was investigated through the use of evaluative adjectives by the corporate speakers and writers. There are strong differences between the EP corpus and the ER corpus, with the former having both a higher frequency and wider variety of evaluative adjectives. Follow-up qualitative analysis suggested that this difference can be attributed to the more interactional teleconference setting of earnings presentations as compared to the remote written medium of the earnings releases. However, the two corpora are similar in their much greater use of positive adjectives with respect to negative ones, as well as several instances of creative compounds and hyperbolic adjectives. This usage was linked to the dynamic nature of business discourse in general and the rhetorical skills of the corporate writers and speakers, with the latter being particularly well-versed in this type of rhetorical language. In addition, the level of informality introduced by the interactional audio channel seems to also impact especially the creative and 'upbeat' choices of the executive speakers, who seem to carve out a distinct role that showcases their authority and leadership.

The functional analysis of the evaluative adjectives in the two corpora was also based on Martin and White's (2005) appraisal model. However, some patterns of usage do not fully correspond to the model as originally conceptualised by the authors, likely due to the quantitative focus of financial reporting in both earnings presentations and earnings releases. In particular, aspects of attitude such as *affect* and *judgment* often refer to assessments of financial performance, and not to emotions of the speakers and writers and the behaviours of human beings, as foreseen in the appraisal model (ibid.) Thus, how corporate speakers and writers convey attitudes in the discourse of financial disclosure appears to follow some unique trends that are determined by the specific nature of the content and the communicative purpose.

Concessive connectives were then analysed as markers of *engagement*. These items have higher frequencies in the EP corpus with respect to the ER corpus, despite the fact that they have been reported to be typically more common in written discourse (Biber et al., 1999). During their presentations, the corporate executives intensively and extensively exploit concessive connectives. The follow-up qualitative analysis indicated that this may be a finely-tuned rhetorical strategy used by executives to engage prospective investors while imposing their own views and explanations of the company's financial situation. The fact that concessive connectives are on the whole much more prominent in the EP corpus in comparison with the ER corpus could also be linked to the producer of the discourse. Earnings releases are typically written by lower-level professionals (e.g., staff press officers) who are perhaps less directly impacted by financial disclosure issues, and thus less 'rhetorically-motivated' than the top executives who deliver the earnings presentations. Moreover, in the EP corpus, the wider variety of concessive connectives, including some typically prose-like choices (e.g., *notwithstanding*) seems to reflect the desire of executives to portray themselves as sophisticated and highly-proficient public speakers.

The final component of Martin & White's (2005) appraisal model, *graduation*, was investigated though the use of intensifiers and mitigators in the earnings presentations and earnings releases. From the quantitative perspective, these features are much more frequent in the EP corpus in comparison with the ER corpus, and similar to the findings for evaluative adjectives reported in Chapter 7. Again, the more interactional spoken teleconference medium as compared to the written earnings releases seems to stimulate greater use of these rhetorical devices.

The analysis of intensifiers and mitigators also revealed some interesting discrepancies with the appraisal model (Martin & White, 2005). In both corpora, the most frequently occurring mitigator *slightly* is used exclusively to downscale assessments of quantities. Thus, in financial reporting *slightly* would perhaps be better classified as an adjuster of quantity and not of intensity. In addition, there are no instances of intensifiers and mitigators that refer to modalities (e.g., *quite possible, very likely*), which is instead frequent in other communicative settings (Hinkel, 2002; Hyland, 2005). This seems to be impacted by the high degree of uncertainty surrounding financial performance and the desire of speakers and writers to avoid taking categorical stances, since they could possibly be proved wrong in a later moment.

The third research question aimed to shed light on how the structural and rhetorical features of earnings releases and earnings presentations combine into distinct communicative patterns. More specifically, this was an effort to unite the analysis of the macro-structures of the two corpora illustrated in Chapter 6 with the micro-level analysis of evaluative resources undertaken in Chapters 7, 8, and 9. In each of these chapters, there is a section dedicated specifically to findings of the combined macro-micro analysis. With reference to evaluative adjectives (Chapter 7, sub-section 7.4), some interesting differences were found in the distributional patterns of the two corpora for three prominent evaluative adjectives, i.e., *strong, good* and *double-digit*. In the EP corpus, *strong* and *good* are particularly frequent not only in the initial move (*Introduction*), but also in the final move (*Wrap-up*). This seems to reflect the executive speakers' efforts to maintain high levels of 'persuasive pressure' on the audience of investment analysts throughout the presentations. In the ER corpus, *strong* and *double-digit* are also frequent in the initial moves (*Title, Subtitle* and *Summary*), but quite sparse in the final moves (e.g., *Company info, Contacts*), which contain less rhetorical and mainly informative texts produced by staff press release writers.

The combined analysis of the most frequent concessive connective *however* (Chapter 8, sub-section 8.4) showed that in the earnings presentations this item occurs from the very beginning and continues throughout the discourse. This tends to reinforce its rhetorical function in this interactional context, whereby the speakers use *however* to pre-empt possible challenges by first imposing their own stances. In contrast, in the earnings releases the relatively few instances of *however* carry out a largely textual function, without a particular rhetorical force.

With reference to resources of *graduation* (Chapter 9, sub-section 9.4, in the EP corpus the intensifier *very* tends to occur in the same structural moves as evaluative adjectives (i.e., *Introduction* and *Wrap-up*), thereby reinforcing their strategic use by executive speakers. On the other hand, *slightly* appears most often in the *Financial details*, in line with its exclusive function of explaining numerical data.

The final research question dealt with the impact of the ICT environments of the earnings presentations and the earnings releases on their rhetorical features. This issue has already emerged to some degree throughout the various analyses that have been carried out. As we have seen, the structural analyses revealed that several moves across both genres are motivated by their technology-mediated communicative contexts, or more specifically, the teleconference medium of the earnings presentations and the Internet medium of the earnings releases. The higher frequency of evaluative adjectives, concessive connectives and intensifiers/mitigators in the earnings presentations seem to reflect the presenters' attempts to take advantage of the technology that allowed them to engage more directly with the listeners for persuasive purposes. On the other hand, in the earnings releases, the presence of hypertext links to other sources of information allows these companies to manage the disclosure of financial information in an efficient and flexible way that fits their particular needs. However, the absence of an audience with whom to engage on a more direct level seems to be linked to a more textual and less rhetorical use of concessive connectives. Thus, ICT has been shown to have an important role in the crafting of the rhetorical dimension of these genres of financial disclosure.

10.3 Limitations of the study

Because this study was based on two small specialised corpora, the findings cannot be broadly generalised. Yet they can serve as a reference source or guidelines for similar types of discourse studies in specific domains of language. It is also important to recognise that the rhetorical features dealt with (i.e., evaluative adjectives, concessive connectives and intensifiers/mitigators) could each be investigated in a considerably more in-depth way by focusing on only one of them. For example, one could examine other forms of evaluative lexis beyond adjectives (e.g., adverbs, nouns, verbs), other cohesive relations beyond concession (e.g., additive, causal, temporal) and other forms of intensification (e.g., the use of repetition and metaphors). Each of these areas could easily become a full-length study in its own right. Nevertheless, by opting to analyse the rhetorical dimension of earnings presentations and earnings through selected features representing each of the three components of Martin and White's (2005) appraisal model, I have tried to offer a reasonably broad picture of the rhetorical dimension of these two technology-mediated financial genres which are relative newcomers to the constellation of corporate genres.

With reference to the ethnographically-inspired component of the analysis, for this study I had access to only one professional informant. It would have undoubtedly been useful to interview other investment analysts for a broader perspective. However, according to my professional informant (with whom I have a familiar relationship), it is highly unlikely that investment analysts would be willing to discuss anything related to their work with an unknown 'outsider', given the high-risk nature of their jobs and the possible legal implications for the organisations involved. Moreover, the circumstances surrounding the special authorisation to download the earnings presentations transcripts prevented me from establishing direct contacts with the actual participants, even if their names were indicated in the original versions of the transcripts. Clearly, in this case I was not permitted to contact these company executives, nor was it even feasible given the fact that they represent large multinational corporations whose communications tend to be strictly controlled. Concerning the earnings releases downloaded freely from the Internet, the identities of the writers of these documents were not decipherable. Although names and contact information at times appeared in the *Contact* move of some earnings releases (see Chapter 6), we cannot be sure that these corresponded to their actual authors.

The situation described above illustrates that access to authentic discourse in the corporate world continues to be a challenge for linguists working in this area, particularly when the discourse deals with performance-related issues. Gaining access to the top executives or press officers of high-profile multinational corporations and then asking them to discuss their rhetorical strategies relating to sensitive financial matters may prove to be quite difficult. However, if this could be accomplished - perhaps through informal contacts or personal relations - it would no doubt yield important information about the processes and attitudes involved in producing these texts, along the lines of Sleurs and Jacobs' (2005) ethnographic case study of the lengthy process that led to the production of a press release by a Belgian bank, or Garcés-Conejos Blitvich and Fortanet-Gómez's (2009) contrastive analysis of Spanish and US résumés that was effectively informed by members of upper management who actually review these texts to make hiring decisions. This would not only enhance our knowledge of how and why corporate speakers and writers use certain rhetorical features in spoken and written texts used for financial disclosure, but also shed light on the resources and processes involved in their production.

On a more positive note, the increasing implementation of ICT by companies may lead to more opportunities to carry out this type of research. Indeed, since the time that the two corpora used for this study were collected, more and more companies have begun to post financial information on their websites where it is freely available. This typically includes mandatory financial reports and earnings press releases. However, it is now possible to sporadically find some materials from earnings presentations, such as summaries or partial transcripts in pdf format and accompanying Powerpoint slides for a limited time on the websites of some companies, mainly those that operate in the technology sector, In addition, recently we have begun to see Internet services that post some financial documentation of companies. For example, *Seeking Alpha* is a website that provides information and documentation about the US stock market including some earnings call transcripts, although not consistently in complete form. Fortunately, the general trend seems to be moving in the direction of greater availability of various types of financial information, and not only limited to professional operators, but also accessible to a wider audience.

10.4 Prospects for further research

The findings of this study suggest some other topics that would warrant further investigation. While this analysis has focused on rhetorical features in two technology-mediated genres of financial disclosure that differ according to communicative mode, it would be very interesting to look at the differences in rhetorical language between the 'technological' and 'traditional' versions of the same genre. Although some work has been done in this area, focusing mainly on differences in the structural features of print vs. web-mediated genres (Catenaccio, 2007), there has not been a study that targets rhetorical aspects. For example, one could investigate how writer stance emerges in print earning releases distributed to the media vs. earnings releases published on the Internet, or speaker stance in live vs. teleconference financial events. Such studies would also provide interesting diachronic perspectives on how rhetorical language in these genres may evolve over time as a result of changing communicative media.

Studies that take a narrower focus would also be worthwhile. For instance, an in-depth discourse analysis of a more limited number of earnings presentations vs. earnings releases would undoubtedly reveal additional knowledge about their structural composition, beyond the more general profiles that emerged from this study. For example, it might be possible to identify not only recurring structural *moves*, but also the subordinate level of *steps* within the *moves*, allowing for higher level of articulation of the rhetorical functions performed by even smaller units of discourse (Swales, 1990). An extended qualitative analysis of this type would provide more insights into the generic structures of earnings presentations and earnings releases. In the case of spoken earnings calls, it would also be interesting to shift the focus from the monologic executive presentations to the dialogic question and answer sessions that follow them which were not dealt with in this study. An investigation of this interactional component could shed light on how corporate speakers may exploit different rhetorical strategies when speaking directly with the financial analysts via telephone, particularly when faced with questions that they do not wish to answer (cf. Hollander et al., 2009).

Another type of analysis that would be best undertaken on a smaller scale concerns how corporate speakers and writers communicate positive and negative results in relation to actual business outcomes. A detailed study of the rhetorical language found in 'good news' vs. 'bad news' earnings presentations and earnings releases, along the lines of Clatworthy & Jones' (2003) study of accounting narrative texts, would no doubt yield extremely interesting results. Indeed, the need for corporations to engage in careful impression management is likely to be even more crucial in ICT-mediated financial communication which often reaches audiences in real time. My professional informant confirmed that analysts typically publish their forecasts based on information obtained during earnings calls presentations immediately, and the same information usually becomes available to the general public within 24 hours. Thus, companies need to set a rhetorical tone that avoids triggering unfavourable rumours and market speculation that could have serious economic consequences for the company and its stakeholders, especially when results are less than positive.

In addition to the three rhetorical features focused on in this study, there were others present in earnings presentations and earnings releases that would merit more attention. In fact, during the many phases of qualitative hands-on analysis, I noticed other characteristics that could reflect rhetorical strategies on the part of speakers and writers, such as vocatives in the form of first names in the EP corpus, the presence of embedded quotes attributed to company executives in the ER corpus and various participant roles encoded by first and second person pronouns, which have been shown to be important manifestations of speaker and writer identity in corporate settings (Thomas, 1997; Poncini, 2004; Ruiz-Garrido et al., 2006). To expand insights into how textual connectives are used rhetorically, other linking devices could be investigated. In particular, there was a strong presence of *resultative connectives* (Hyland, 1998, p. 235) that appeal to the interlocutor's sense of rationality (e.g., *as a result, therefore*) in an argumentative or persuasive context.

Finally, the use of English as a *lingua franca* that involves both native and non-native speakers and/or writers of financial communications is another aspect that could be further explored. In this analysis, among the executive speakers of the earnings presentation, there were a few non-native speakers of English, but they were not systematically represented throughout the EP corpus (see Chapter 5). For the earnings releases, it was not possible to determine the language background of their anonymous writers. For these reasons, the language background variable was deemed to be beyond the scope of this study and was therefore not taken into consideration when interpreting the findings. Nevertheless, given the increasingly global nature of financial discourse, it would be useful to understand more about differences in the rhetorical strategies of native vs. non-native speakers of English in corporate settings. This type of analysis could help to identify particularly effective rhetorical strategies, but also alert us to those that may be less effective, or even result in miscommunication. Clearly, to carry out such research it is necessary to be able to systematically collect data that represents financial communications produced by native and non-native speakers whose language backgrounds can be verified, which often presents considerable challenges for language researchers (cf. Cho & Yoon, 2013). Yet it is clearly worth an effort to move towards such interculturally-oriented research, even if on a case study basis where information about individual participants may be easier to obtain. This would be especially important in light of its implications for instructional contexts involving non-native speakers of English who aspire to work in the area of global finance, as will be discussed in the next section.

10.5 Pedagogical implications

Beyond an in-depth description of the rhetorical strategies of corporate speakers and writers, this study offers insights for higher education instructional settings that target students of business and finance. More specifically, the results can be used to inform business, organisational or management communication courses that are typically part of the core curriculum of both undergraduate and graduate business degree programmes. Strong communication skills remain a top priority for both students and the professional community (Gray, 2010; Zhao & Alexander, 2004). In particular, communication ranked among the academic subjects perceived as most important for undergraduate students of finance by Fortune 1000 CFOs (Collier & Wilson, 1994), and should comprise specific speaking and listening skills for participation in teleconferencing events (Grosse, 2004). While the more recent corporate communication textbooks at least mention audio/video teleconferencing (cf. Adler & Marquardt Elmhorst 2008; Munter 2009), they do not provide sufficient information about their rhetorical features or include activities to help students learn them in order to become effective communicators in contexts of ICT-mediated financial reporting. The findings of this study can be exploited in corporate communication courses that aim to achieve this goal.

Another instructional setting that could greatly benefit from this research is English for Business Studies (hereinafter EBS) that targets learners who are native speakers of other languages. In higher education, many international business and finance students aspire to work in professional environments where a good knowledge of spoken and written forms of financial disclosure in English is imperative. They therefore need to be taught the language of the authentic communicative instruments and processes used for this purpose, particularly in light of the predominant role of English as the *lingua franca* of international business (Louhiala-Salminen, 1996; Nickerson, 1999; Scollon & Scollon, 2001; Palmer-Silveira et al., 2006). The insights that have emerged from this study about the rhetorical features of financial disclosure genres can be used to help these learners acquire this competence. In the following paragraphs, I suggest some practical ways to achieve this objective.

At the level of course planning and preparation, it is important for EBS instructors in higher education to be aware of the two genres analysed in this study and their key role in the financial world. Because traditional EBS textbooks do not incorporate learning activities based either on earnings presentations or earnings releases, instructors could create their own by using Internet sources to access samples and then adapt them for use in the classroom. For example, students could be introduced to the conference call as a communicative event. They could then be provided with materials and activities prepared from webcasts of authentic earnings presentations replayed on the Internet to help them understand their structure and content. A similar activity could be prepared for written earnings releases. In this case, students could be asked to procure an earnings release from a company website for themselves and then analyse its various components. As a more advanced activity, students could contrastively analyse the two genres, describing their key structural and linguistic differences.

The findings of this study can also find applications in EBS courses concentrating on the development of specific communicative skills for corporate settings. When learning how to give oral presentations, it is important to use rhetorical language appropriately. Paying particular attention to the features investigated in this study, students could prepare a spoken earnings presentation using a written earnings release as a source of input. When focusing on aural comprehension, students could be introduced to the rhetorical dimension of evaluative adjectives, textual connectives and intensifiers/mitigators by having them listen to extracts of executive presentations in earnings presentations replayed on the Internet, while pointing out how these features are used by speakers in transcripts produced from the audio files. In addition, the lists of evaluative adjectives that were generated from the various phases of analysis could be used as a source of learning activities to help non-native speakers expand their vocabulary with innovative and alternative linguistic forms that are typically used by native speakers in the context of financial disclosure.

Table 10.1 suggests some additional specific learning activities that might be included in a teaching unit dedicated to financial disclosure in an EBS instructional setting. As the proposed activities have been developed for non-native speakers of English who are studying to work in global finance where they will use English as a *lingua franca*, the activities are designed to encompass and reinforce the four basic communicative skills in English language teaching, i.e., reading, writing, listening and speaking. In addition, they aim to build ICT expertise and rhetorical abilities that are important for professionals in the corporate world.

Targeted competence	Examples of learning activities
Awareness of the communicative instruments used for purposes of financial	- Brainstorming followed by mini-lecture to introduce the concept of financial disclosure: purpose, types, forms, trends - Discussion of assigned readings on the topic of financial disclosure - Group task: surf the Internet to discover various types of spoken and written forms of mandatory/voluntary financial disclosure of a selected company
Familiarity with earnings releases as a key written form of financial disclosure	- Mini-lecture/class discussion to introduce the use of press releases in corporate communication - Reading an earnings release with follow-up comprehension questions - Group task: analyse key linguistic and structural features of the earnings release of a selected company - Vocabulary exercises based on the earnings release to learn key lexical items for written financial disclosure - Group project: produce an earnings release based on the numerical performance data of a selected company
Familiarity with earnings presentations as a key oral form of financial disclosure	- Mini-lecture/class discussion to introduce the use of conference calls for corporate communication - Listening to a webcast earnings presentation while following the corresponding transcript - Group task: analyse key linguistic and structural features of the transcripts and accompanying Powerpoint slides of a selected company - Vocabulary exercises based on the transcripts to learn key lexical items for oral financial disclosure - Group project: perform a mock earnings presentation accompanied by prepared Powerpoint slides
Development of rhetorical awareness and abilities for financial communications	- Analysis of earnings calls transcripts and earnings releases to raise awareness of language used by corporate leaders and spokespeople to persuade and steer interpretations - Comparison of persuasive strategies found in written earnings releases and spoken earnings presentation - Analysis of the rhetorical styles of various company leaders representing different business sectors - Group project: produce persuasive oral and written financial texts that effectively incorporate rhetorical strategies based on evaluative adjectives, concessive connectives and intensifiers/mitigators

Table 10.1: Learning activities for financial disclosure in EBS

The activities described in the table represent new and advanced-level skills for learners of business English that likely go beyond what is found in most EBS courses. A key challenge is to find ways to incorporate such additional topics and activities into the curricula of EBS courses in universities in non-English-speaking countries which, in my experience, are often reduced to the minimum in terms of credits allocated within business degree programmes, with a corresponding limited number of hours actually available for teaching. A possible solution could be offered by CLIL (Content and Language Integrated Learning), where a foreign language, i.e., not the native language of learners, is used as the medium to teach non-language content, typically by instructors who are also not native speakers of the language in question. CLIL has been identified as a viable and cost-effective solution to provide learners with additional language exposure beyond what is possible in traditional language courses (Marsh, 2003). In this case, EBS instructors could enlist the support of non-native speakers of English who teach content courses in the areas of finance and corporate communication. They could be encouraged to collaborate by teaching in English the parts of their courses that focus specifically on financial disclosure. In this way, today's international business students would have more opportunities to come into contact with important forms of financial disclosure before they encounter them in an English-speaking workplace.

To wrap up this section, I would like to highlight a quote from my professional informant which underscores the importance of learning how to communicate effectively in the financial world. With reference to his own experience, he stated:

> *"There's a whole mode of corporate communication that you need to know to be credible. If you sound overly scientific, academic or verbose, you lose credibility. You need to have different ways of saying things, using both plain-speak and wit. One thing that impressed me when walking into meetings fresh out of business school was how experts were able to say things is a way that resonates. Communication is one of the most important skills in business."*

10.6 Professional applications

To conclude this final chapter, I would like to discuss some ways in which the analysis of the rhetorical dimension of oral and written forms of financial disclosure may be useful for professionals in the corporate world. An indication that companies are paying increasing attention to the effectiveness of the language they use in their financial communications can be seen in some recent scholarly literature in the fields of finance and accounting which has called for more research on the role of language in financial disclosure

(Beyer et al. 2010, Berger 2011). However, the limited amount of research that has to some extent addressed the language of ICT-mediated voluntary financial disclosure has produced rather sporadic results, without providing a systematic analysis of rhetorical strategies that could be fruitfully exploited by the professionals involved in producing these key financial texts (e.g., Matsumoto et al., 2006; Larcker & Zakolyukina, 2010). In contrast, the findings of this study offer a panorama of various rhetorical strategies used in the financial communications of major multinationals. These could be exploited in different ways. First of all, the findings could serve as guidelines for other organisations, particularly smaller ones that are in the process of developing their own forms of voluntary financial disclosure. In addition, companies that operate in sectors that correspond to those included in this study may be interested in discovering how their competitors use rhetorical strategies in financial communications, which could then lead to adjustments to improve the effectiveness of their own. The results of the various phases of analysis could also be utilised in the context of professional training in the area of corporate communication, specifically for staff that need to learn how to produce effective financial disclosure documentation.

Beyond the specific results that have been presented in this volume, the study also suggests how companies could carry out systematic analyses of their own communications to monitor their rhetorical effectiveness. Indeed, professionals who are involved in activities of financial disclosure could themselves use computer-assisted textual analysis as a way to improve their communications that target investors and other important stakeholders. The type of text analysis software that was utilised for this study is increasingly accessible and user-friendly. It can therefore be exploited by users who are not necessarily language specialists, but nonetheless have a need for tools that can help them acquire in-depth insights into how language is used in their particular sphere of communication. Such interdisciplinary applications could serve to enhance the effectiveness of corporate communication in general, and more specifically, financial reporting. For example, the staff members that prepare financial documentation could collect and maintain databases of their written and spoken texts to be submitted to corpus software for elaboration. It would be relatively easy and straightforward to generate profiles of rhetorical key features contained in the documentation. Using a program such as *WMatrix* (Rayson, 2008), it is possible to opt for a simple interface mode that quickly identifies key words and key semantic domains within a given text with a one-click procedure. Engaging in this type of analysis regularly over time would allow companies to detect patterns in how rhetorical language is used, and whether or not it may have any impact on financial performance. Such analysis could also be extended to accessible financial documentation of competitors, thus enabling a company to become aware of new trends in rhetorical uses of language that may lead to better financial results. Finally, at the level of managerial communication, the existence of a database that enables the tracking of rhetorical features found in a company's financial documentation could be useful in situations of management turnover, helping incoming executives to gain an understanding of the rhetorical tone set by previous management during earnings presentations with which they may want to gauge their own.

In conclusion, this study has provided numerous insights into the rhetorical dimension of two important ICT-mediated genres that are clearly on the rise in the financial world. In addition, it has shown how the findings can be used in instructional settings as input for 1) teachers to assist in the design of courses and the preparation of materials, and 2) learners to help them master the skills they need for future success in the world of international finance. Finally, the study has offered some resources and tools that can be used by professionals working in the area of financial communication to improve the quality of the oral and written documents that they produce.

References

Ädel, A. (2006). *Metadiscourse in L1 and L2 English*. Amsterdam/Philadelphia: John Benjamins.

Adler, R. B., & Marquardt Elmhorst, J. (2008). *Communicating at work. Principles and practices for business and the professions*. New York, NY: McGraw-Hill.

Agar, M. H. (1996). *The professional stranger: An informal introduction to ethnography*. San Diego, CA: Academic Press.

Aijmer, K. (2005). Evaluation and pragmatic markers. In E. Tognini-Bonelli & G. Del Lungo Camiciotti (Eds.), *Strategies in academic discourse* (pp. 83-96). Amsterdam/Philadelphia: John Benjamins.

Aijmer, K., & Altenberg, B. (1996). Introduction. In K. Aijmer, B. Altenberg, & M. Johansson (Eds.), *Language in contrast: Papers from a symposium on text-based cross-linguistic studies* (pp. 11-16). Lund: Lund University Press.

Amernic, J., & Craig, R. (2006). *CEO-speak: The language of corporate leadership*. Montreal & Kingston: McGill-Queen's Press.

Anderson, L., & Bamford, J. (Eds.) (2004). *Evaluation in oral and written academic discourse*. Rome: Officina Edizioni.

Andrus, J. (2013). Rhetorical discourse analysis. In C. Chapelle (Ed.), *The encyclopedia of applied linguistics* (pp. 4975–4981). Malden, MA: Wiley-Blackwell.

Argenti, P. (2009). *Corporate communication* (5th ed.). New York, NY: McGraw-Hill.

Argenti, P., & Forman, J. (2002). *The power of corporate communication: Crafting the voice and image of your business*. New York, NY: McGraw Hill.

Argenti, P., Howell, R. A., & Beck, K. A. (2005). The strategic communication imperative. *MIT Sloan Management Review, 46*(3), 83-89.

Argondizzo, C., & Plastina, A. F. (2004). E-mail TextTalk in institutional discourse. *Textus, XVII*(1), 89-109.

Askehave, I., & Ellerup Nielsen, A. (2004). Web-mediated genres. A challenge to traditional genre theory (Working Paper No. 6). Retrieved from Aarhus University Research Publications website: http://pure.au.dk/portal/en/organisations/8000/publications.html.

Askehave, I., & Ellerup Nielsen, A. (2005). What are the characteristics of digital genres? Genre theory from a multi-modal perspective. *Proceedings of the 38th Annual Hawaii Conference on System Sciences, Honolulu, HI*. Retrieved from http://www.computer.org/csdl/proceedings/hicss/2005/index.html.

Bakhtin, M. M. (1986). The problem of speech genres. In C. Emerson & M. Holquist (Eds.), *Speech genres and other late essays* (pp. 60-102). Austin, TX: The University of Texas Press.

Baldry, A. (2000). English in a visual society: comparative and historical dimensions in multimodality and multimediality. In A. Baldry (Ed.), *Multimodality and multimediality in the distance learning age* (pp. 41-89). Campobasso: Palladino Editore.

Bargiela-Chiappini, F. (Ed.) (2009). *The handbook of business discourse.* Edinburgh: Edinburgh University Press.

Bargiela-Chiappini, F., & Harris, S. J. (1995). Towards the generic structure of meetings in British and Italian Managements. *Text, 15*(4), 531-560.

Bargiela-Chiappini, F., & Harris, S. J. (1997). *Managing language: The discourse of corporate meetings.* Amsterdam/Philadelphia: John Benjamins.

Bargiela-Chiappini, F., & Nickerson, C. (1999). Business writing as social action. In F. Bargiela-Chiappini & C. Nickerson (Eds.), *Writing business: Genres, media and discourses* (pp. 1-32). Essex: Pearson Education Limited.

Barlow, M. (2004). *MonoConc 2.0.* Houston, TX: Athelstan.

Barrett, D. J. (2012). *Leadership communication.* New York, NY: McGraw-Hill.

Baron, N. S. (1998). Letters by phone or speech by other means. The linguistics of email. *Language and Communication 18*(2), 133-170.

Bazerman, C. (1994). Systems of genres and enactments of social intentions. In A. Freedman & P. Medway (Eds.), *Genre and new rhetoric* (pp. 79-101). London: Taylor & Francis.

Beattie, V., Dhanani, A., & Jones, M. J. (2008). Investigating presentational change in U.K. annual reports: A longitudinal perspective. *Journal of Business Communication, 45*(2), 181-222.

Bednarek, M. (2006). *Evaluation in media discourse.* London and New York: Continuum.

Bell, A. (1991). *The language of news media.* Oxford: Blackwell.

Bell, D. M. (2007). Sentence initial "and" and "but" in academic writing. *Pragmatics, 17*(2), 183-202.

Berger, P. (2011). Challenges and opportunities in disclosure research – A discussion of 'The financial reporting environment: review of the literature'. *Journal of Accounting and Economics, 51*(1-2), 204-218.

Beyer, A., Cohen, D. A., Lys, T. Z., & Walther, B. R. (2010). The financial reporting environment: review of the recent literature. *Journal of Accounting and Economics, 50*(2-3), 296-343.

Bhatia, V. K. (1993). *Analysing genre. Language use in professional settings.* Essex: Longman.

Bhatia, V. K. (2002). A generic view of academic discourse. In J. Flowerdew (Ed.), *Academic discourse* (pp. 21-39). London: Pearson Education Limited.

Bhatia, V. K. (2004). *Worlds of written discourse. A genre-based view.* London and New York: Continuum.

Bhatia, V. K. (2005). Genres in business contexts. In A. Trosborg & P. E. Flyvholm Jørgensen (Eds.), *Business discourse: texts and contexts* (pp. 17-39). Bern: Peter Lang.

Bhatia, V. K. (2008). Genre analysis, ESP and professional practice. *English for Specific Purposes, 27*(2), 161-174.

Bhatia, V. K. (2010). Interdiscursivity in professional communication. *Discourse & Communication, 21*(1), 32-50.

Biber, D. (2006). Stance in spoken and written university registers. *Journal of English for Academic Purposes, 5*(2), 97-116.

Biber, D. (2008, June 4-5). *Merging corpus linguistic and discourse analytic research goals.* Paper presented at the 3rd International LABLITA Workshop on Corpus Linguistics, Florence, Italy.

Biber, D., & Finegan, E. (1988). Adverbial stance types in English. *Discourse Processes, 11*(1), 1–34.

Biber, D., Conrad, S., Reppen, R., Byrd, P., & Helt, M. (2002). Speaking and writing in the university: A multidimensional comparison. *TESOL Quarterly, 36*(1), 9-48.

Biber, D., Johansson, S., Leech, G., Conrad, S., & Finegan, E. (1999). *Longman grammar of spoken and written English.* Essex: Longman.

Bilbow, G. T. (1997). Spoken discourse in the multicultural workplace in Hong Kong: Applying a model of discourse as 'impression management'. In F. Bargiela-Chiappini & S. Harris (Eds.), *The languages of business: An international perspective* (pp. 21-48). Edinburgh: Edinburgh University Press.

Bitzer, L. (1968) The rhetorical situation. *Philosophy and Rhetoric, 1*(1), 1-14.

Bondi, M. (1999). *English across genres: Language variation in the discourse of economics.* Modena: Il Fiorino.

Bondi, M. (2004). The discourse function of contrastive connectors in academic abstracts. In K. Aijmer & A-B. Stenström (Eds.), *Discourse patterns in spoken and written corpora* (pp. 139-156). Amsterdam/Philadelphia: John Benjamins.

Bonet, E., Czarniawaska, B., McCloskey, D., & Siggaard Jensen, H. (2011). Preface. In E. Bonet, B. Czarniawaska, D. McCloskey, & H. Siggaard Jensen (Eds.), *Second conference on narratives and management research: Management and persuasion* (pp. 7-13). Barcelona: Esade.

Boubaker, S., Lakhal, F., & Nekhili, M. (2012). The determinants of web-based corporate reporting in France, *Managerial Auditing Journal*, *27*(2), 126 – 155.

Bragg, S. M. (2011). *The new CEO corporate leadership manual: Strategic and analytical tools for growth*. Hoboken, NJ: Wiley.

Brown, G., & Yule, G. (1983). *Discourse analysis*. Cambridge: Cambridge University Press.

Brown. S., Hillegeist, S. A., & Lo, K. (2004). Conference calls and information asymmetry. *Journal of Accounting and Economics, 37*(3), 343-366.

Bushee, B. J., Matsumoto, D., & Miller, G. S. (2003). Open versus closed conference calls: the determinants and effects of broadening access to disclosure. *Journal of Accounting and Economics, 34*(1-3), 149-180.

Caenepeel, M. (1997). *Putting while in context* (Research Paper). Retrieved from University of Edinburgh Human Communication Research Centre website: http://groups.inf.ed.ac.uk/hcrc_publications/.

Canagarajah, S. (1999). *Resisting linguistic imperialism in English teaching*. Oxford: Oxford University Press.

Candlin, C. N., & Maley, Y. (1997). Intertextuality and interdiscursivity in the discourse of alternative dispute resolution. In B-L. Gunnarsson, P. Linell, & B. Nordberg (Eds.), *The construction of professional discourse* (pp. 201-222). Essex: Addison Wesley Longman.

Catenaccio, P. (2006). Looking beyond today's headlines: The Enron crisis from press release to media coverage. In M. Bondi & J. Bamford (Eds.), *Managing interaction in professional discourse: Intercultural and interdiscoursal perspectives* (pp. 159-172). Rome: Officina Edizioni.

Catenaccio, P. (2007). New(s) genres and discursive identity: the changing face of press releases in the age of the Internet. In G. Garzone, G. Poncini, & P. Catenaccio, (Eds.), *Multimodality in corporate communication* (pp. 55-72). Milan: FrancoAngeli.

Chafe, W. L. (1985). Linguistic differences produced by speaking and writing. In D.R. Olson, N. Torrance, & A. Hilyard (Eds.), *Literacy, language and learning* (pp. 105-123). Cambridge: Cambridge University Press.

Chafe, W. L. (1986). Evidentiality in English conversation and writing. In W. Chafe & J. Nichols (Eds.), *Evidentiality: The linguistic encoding of epistemology* (pp. 261-272). Norwood, NJ: Ablex.

Chakorn, O. (2008). Rhetorical appeals in Thai annual reports: An investigation of the authority's language in the executive letter during Asia's economic crisis. *The Association for Business Communication Special Topics Conference. Business Discourse. Los Angeles, CA*. Retrieved from http://businesscommunication.org/conventions/abc-convention-proceedings/.

Chanal, V., & Tannery, F. (2011). The leader's strategy communication: A rhetorical approach. In E. Bonet, B. Czarniawaska, D. McCloskey, & H. Siggaard Jensen (Eds.), *Management and Persuasion. Second Conference on Narratives and Management Research*, 103-124, Barcelona: Esade.

Channell, J. (1994). *Vague language.* Oxford: Oxford University Press.

Charles, M. (1996). Business negotiations: Interdependence between discourse and the business relationship. *English for Specific Purposes, 15*(1), 19-36.

Cheng, W., Greaves, C., & Warren, M. (2006). From N-gram to skipgram to concgram. *International Journal of Corpus Linguistics, 11*(4), 411-433.

Cho, H., & Yoon, H. (2013). A corpus-assisted comparative genre analysis of corporate earnings calls between Korean and native-English speakers. *English for Specific Purposes, 32*(3), 170-185.

Clatworthy, M., & Jones, M. J. (2003). Financial reporting of good news and bad news: Evidence from accounting narratives. *Accounting and Business Research, 33*(3), 171-185.

Clifton, J. (2012). A discursive approach to leadership: Doing assessments and managing organizational meanings, *Journal of Business Communication, 49*(2) 148-168.

Collier, B., & Wilson, M. (1994), What does a graduate need? Evidence from the careers and opinions of CFOs, *Financial Practice and Education, 4*(2), 59-65.

Connor, U. M., & Moreno, A. I. (2005). Tertium comparationis: A vital component in contrastive rhetoric research. In P. Bruthiaux, D. Atkinson, W. G. Eggington, W. Grabe, & V. Ramanathan (Eds.), *Directions in applied linguistics essays in honor of Robert B. Kaplan* (pp. 155-164). Clevedon: Multilingual Matters.

Couper Kuhlen, E., & Thompson, S. A. (2000). Concessive patterns in conversation. In E. Couper Kuhlen & B. D. Kortmann (Eds.), *Cause, condition, concession, contrast: Cognitive and discourse perspectives* (pp. 381-410). Berlin: Walter De Gruyter.

Crawford Camiciottoli, B. (2009) 'Just wondering if you could comment on that': indirect requests for information in corporate earnings calls. *Text & Talk, 29*(6), 661–681.

Crawford Camiciottoli, B. (2010) Earnings calls: exploring an emerging financial reporting genre. *Discourse & Communication, 4*(4), 343-359.

Crawford Camiciottoli, B. (2011). Ethics and ethos in financial reporting: Analyzing persuasive language in earnings calls. *Business Communication Quarterly, 74*(3), 298-312.

Crystal, D. (1997). *English as a global language.* Cambridge: Cambridge University Press.

Crystal, D. (2003). *A dictionary of linguistics and phonetics* (5th ed.). Oxford: Blackwell.

Crystal, D. (2006). *Language and the Internet* (2nd ed.). Cambridge: Cambridge University Press.

David, C. (1999). Words of women: A study of executives' rhetorical strategies. In F. Bargiela-Chiappini & C. Nickerson (Eds.), *Writing business: Genres, media and discourses* (pp. 153-177). Essex: Pearson Education Limited.

de Bruin, R. (1999). *Communication financière: image et marketing de l'entreprise*. Paris: Editions Liaison.

Del Lungo Camiciotti, G., & Tognini-Bonelli, E. (2004). *Academic discourse. New insights into evaluation*. Bern: Peter Lang.

Deller, D., Stubenrath, M., & Weber, C., (1999). A survey on the use of the Internet for investor relations in the USA, the UK and Germany. *The European Accounting Review, 8*(2), 351-364.

Den Hartog, D. N., & Verburg, R. M. (1997). Charisma and rhetoric: Communicative techniques of international business leaders. *The Leadership Quarterly, 8*(4), 355-397.

Drew, P. (2004). Integrating qualitative analysis of evaluative discourse with the quantitative approach of corpus linguistics. In Del Lungo Camiciotti, G. & Tognini-Bonelli, E. (2004). *Academic discourse. New insights into evaluation* (pp. 217-229). Bern: Peter Lang.

Drolet, A., & Morris, M. W. (2000). Rapport in conflict resolution: accounting for how face-to-face contact fosters mutual cooperation in mixed-motive conflicts. *Journal of Experimental Social Psychology, 36*(1), 26-50.

Du-Babcock, B. (2004, May 20-22). *An analysis of a video-conferencing project: Intercultural communication, administration and student reactions*. Paper presented at the 6th Association for Business Communication European Convention, Milan, Italy.

Eggins, S. (1994). *An introduction to systemic functional linguistics*. London: Pinter.

Englebretson, R. (Ed.) (2007). *Stance-taking in discourse*. Amsterdam/Philadelphia: John Benjamins.

Enos, T. (Ed.) (1996). *Encyclopedia of rhetoric and composition: communication from ancient times to the information age*. New York, NY: Taylor & Francis.

Ettredge, M., Richardson, V. J., & Scholz, S. (2002). Dissemination of information for investors at corporate web sites. *Journal of Accounting and Public Policy, 21*(4-5), 357-369.

Fairclough, N. (1992). Intertextuality in critical discourse analysis. *Linguistics and Education, 4*(3-4), 269-293.

Fairclough, N. (2001). *Language and power* (2nd ed.). Harlow: Longman.

Fairclough, N. (2003). *Analysing discourse. Textual analysis for social research.* London and New York: Routledge.

Feely, A. J., & Harzing, A. W. (2003). Language management in multinational companies. *Cross Cultural Management, 10*(2), 37.

Firth, A. (1996). The discursive accomplishment of normality. On 'lingua franca' English and conversation analysis. *Journal of Pragmatics, 26*(2), 237-259.

Flowerdew, J. (2002). Ethnographically-inspired approaches to the study of academic discourse. In J. Flowerdew (Ed.), *Academic discourse* (pp. 235-252). London: Pearson Education Limited.

Fortanet-Gómez I. (2008). Evaluative language in peer review referee reports. *Journal of English for Academic Purposes, 7*(1), 27-37.

Fox, R. (1999). The social identity of management ergolect. *English for Specific Purposes, 18*(3), 261-278.

Frankel, R., Johnson, M., & Skinner, D. J. (1999). An empirical examination of conference calls as a voluntary disclosure medium. *Journal of Accounting Research, 37*(1), 133-150.

Fraser, B. (1996). Pragmatic markers. *Pragmatics, 6*(2), 167-191.

Freedman, A., & Medway, P. (Eds.) (1994). *Genre and the new rhetoric.* London: Taylor & Francis.

Garcés-Conejos Blitvich, P. (2007). Conference calls, the business meetings of the 21st century: A multi-layered approach to an emerging genre. In P. Bou Franch, A. E. Sopeña Balordi, & A. Briz Gómez (Eds.), *Pragmática, Discurso y Sociedad. Quaderns de Filologia Estudis Lingüístics XII* (pp. 57-75). València: Universitat de València.

Garcés-Conejos Blitvich, P. & Fortanet-Gómez, I. (2009). The presentation of self in résumés: An intercultural approach. *English for Specific Purposes across Cultures, 5*, 69-90.

Garcia, T. (2007, August 1). Internet's role in financial disclosure debated. *PR Week.* Retrieved from http://www.prweek.us/.

Garzone, G. (2005a). Pragmatic and discoursal features of annual executive letters: observations on the rhetorical and evaluative function of concessive constructions. In M. Bondi & N. Maxwell (Eds.), *Cross-cultural encounters: Linguistic perspectives* (pp. 130-141). Rome: Officina Edizioni.

Garzone, G. (2005b). Letters to shareholders and Chairman's statements: Textual variability and generic integrity. In P. Gillaerts & M. Gotti (Eds.), *Genre variation in business letters* (pp. 147-178). Bern: Peter Lang.

Garzone, G., Poncini, G., & Catenaccio, P. (2007). Introduction. In G. Garzone, G. Poncini, & P. Catenaccio (Eds.), *Multimodality in corporate communication* (pp. 7-12). Milan: FrancoAngeli.

Geertz, C. (1973). *The interpretation of cultures.* New York, NY: Basic Books.

Geisler, C. (2001). Textual objects: Accounting for the role of texts in the everyday life of complex organizations. *Written Communication, 18*(3), 296-325.

Giannoni, D. S. (2007). Metatextual evaluation in journal editorials. *Textus, XX*(1), 57-81.

Gibbins. M., Richardson, A., & Waterhouse, J. (1990). The management of corporate financial discourse: opportunism, ritualism, policies and processes. *Journal of Accounting Research, 28*(1), 121-143.

Gimenez, J. C. (2006). Dynamic evolution: An exploration of textual change in business e-mails. In G. Del Lungo Camiciotti, M. Dossena, & B. Crawford Camiciottoli (Eds.), *Variation in business and economics discourse: Diachronic and generic perspectives* (pp. 69-83). Rome: Officina Edizioni.

Goffman, E. (1981). *Forms of talk.* Oxford: Basil Blackwell.

Gotti, M. (2005). English across communities and domains: Globalising trends and intercultural contacts. In M. Bondi & N. Maxwell (Eds.), *Cross-cultural encounters: Linguistic perspectives* (pp. 11-32). Rome: Officina Edizioni.

Graddol, D. (2006). *English next. Why global English may mean the end of 'English as a Foreign Language'.* London: The British Council. Retrieved from http://www.britishcouncil.org/learning-research-englishnext.htm.

Gray, F. E. (2010). Specific oral communication skills desired in new accountancy graduates. *Business Communication Quarterly, 73*(1), 40-67.

Grosse, C. U. (2004). English business communication needs of Mexican executives in a distance-learning class. *Business Communication Quarterly, 67*(1), 7-23.

Gunnarsson, B-L. (1998). Round table: where to in the description of academic discourse. In P. Evangelisti Allori (Ed.), *Academic discourse in Europe: Thought processes and linguistic realisations* (pp. 156-159). Rome: Bulzoni Editori.

Gunnarsson, B-L. (2005). The organization of enterprise discourse. In A. Trosborg & P. E. Flyvholm Jørgensen (Eds.), *Business discourse: Texts and contexts* (pp. 83-109). Bern: Peter Lang.

Hager, P. J., & Scheiber, H. J. (1990). Rhetorical smoke and mirrors. The rhetoric of corporate annual reports. *Journal of Technical Writing and Communication, 20*(2), 113-130.

Halliday, M. A. K. (1978). *Language as a social semiotic.* London: Edward Arnold.

Halliday, M. A. K. (1985). *An introduction to functional grammar*. London: Edward Arnold.

Halliday, M. A. K. (1989). *Spoken and written language*. Oxford: Oxford University Press.

Halliday, M. A. K. & Hasan, R. (1976). *Cohesion in text*. London/New York: Longman.

Henry, A., & Roseberry, R. L. (2001). Using a small corpus to obtain data for teaching a genre. In M. Ghadessy & A. Henry (Eds.), *Small corpus studies and ELT: Theory and practice* (pp. 93-133). Amsterdam/Philadelphia: John Benjamins.

Heuboeck, A. (2009). Some aspects of coherence, genre and rhetorical structure and their integration in a generic model of text. *University of Reading Language Studies Working Papers*, *1*, 35-45. Retrieved from http://www.reading.ac.uk/english-language-and-applied-linguistics/Research/elal-research-language-publications.aspx.

Hinkel, E. (2002). *Second language writers' text*. Mahway, NJ: Lawrence Erlbaum.

Hollander, S., Pronk, M., & Roelofsen, E. (2009). Does silence speak? An empirical analysis of disclosure choices during conference calls. *Journal of Accounting Research*, *48*(3), 531-563.

Hood, S. (2010), *Appraising research: Evaluation in academic writing*. Basingstoke: Palgrave MacMillan.

House, J. (2003). English as a lingua franca: A threat to multilingualism? *Journal of Sociolinguistics*, *7*(4), 556-578.

Huhtinen, T. P. (2008). *Oral rhetoric and rhetorical invention in investor relations. The anatomy of a quarterly conference call* (Master's Thesis, University of Tampere, Finland). Retrieved from http://tutkielmat.uta.fi/.

Hunston, S. (2004). Counting the uncountable: Problems of identifying evaluation in a text and in a corpus. In A. Partington, J. Morley, & L. Haarman (Eds.), *Corpora and discourse* (pp. 157-188). Bern: Peter Lang.

Hunston, S. (2011) *Corpus approaches to evaluation. Phraseology and evaluative language*. New York and London: Routledge.

Hunston, S., & Thompson, G. (Eds.) (2000). *Evaluation in text: Authorial stance and the construction of discourse*. Oxford: Oxford University Press.

Hyland, K. (1998). Exploring corporate rhetoric: Metadiscourse in the CEO's letter. *The Journal of Business Communication, 35*(2), 224-245.

Hyland, K. (1999). Disciplinary discourses: Writer stance in research articles. In C. N. Candlin & K. Hyland (Eds.), *Writing: Texts, processes and practices* (pp. 99-121). London: Sage.

Hyland, K. (2000). *Disciplinary discourses: Social interactions in writing.* Harlow: Longman.

Hyland, K. (2004). Engagement and disciplinarity: The other side of evaluation. In Del Lungo Camiciotti, G. & Tognini-Bonelli, E., *Academic discourse. New insights into evaluation* (pp. 13-30). Bern: Peter Lang.

Hyland, K. (2005). *Metadiscourse: Exploring interaction in writing.* London: Continuum.

Hyland, K. (2013). Genre and discourse analysis in language for specific purposes, In C. Chapelle (Ed.), *The encyclopedia of applied linguistics* (pp. 2281–2288). Malden, MA: Wiley-Blackwell.

Hyland, K., & Sancho Guinda, C., (2012). *Stance and voice in written academic genres.* Basingstoke: Palgrave MacMillan.

Hymes, D. (1972). Models of the interaction of language and social life. In J. Gumperz & D. Hymes (Eds.), *Directions in sociolinguistics: The ethnography of communication* (pp. 35-17). New York, NY: Holt, Rhinehart and Winston.

IBM España. (2005). *Best practices in public relations. An analysis of online pressrooms in leading companies around the world.* Madrid: Departamento de Comunicación IBM España. Retrieved from http://www.globalpr.org/knowledge/features/bestpractices.pdf.

Isaksson, M. (2005). Ethos and pathos representations in mission statements: Identifying virtues and emotions in an emerging business genre. In A. Trosborg & P. E. Flyvholm Jørgensen (Eds.), *Business discourse: Texts and contexts* (pp. 111-138). Bern: Peter Lang.

Izutsu, M. N. (2008). Contrast, concessive, and corrective: Toward a comprehensive study of opposition relations. *Journal of Pragmatics*, *40*(4), 646–675.

Jacobs, G. (1999). *Preformulating the news.* Amsterdam/Philadelphia: John Benjamins.

Jeanjean, T., Lesage, C., & Stolowy, H. (2010). Why do you speak English (in your financial statements). *International Journal of Accounting*, *45*(2), 200-223.

Johnson, G., & Scholes, K. (1999). *Exploring corporate strategy. Text and cases* (5th ed.). Harlow: Prentice Hall.

Jorgensen R. D., & Wingender, J. R. (2004). A survey on the dissemination of earnings information by large firms. *Journal of Applied Finance*, *14*(1), 351-364.

Kennedy, G. (1998). *An introduction to corpus linguistics.* London: Longman.

Kilgarriff, A., Rychly, P., Smrz, P., & Tugwell, D. (2004). *The Sketch Engine.* Proc EURALEX 2004, Lorient, France. pp. 105-116. http://www.sketchengine.co.uk.

Kress, G., & van Leeuwen, T. (2001). *Multimodal discourse. The modes and media of contemporary communication.* London: Arnold.

Labov, W. (1972). *Sociolinguistic patterns.* Philadelphia, PA: University of Pennsylvania Press.

Lakoff, R. (1973). Hedges: A study in meaning criteria and the logic of fuzzy concepts. *Journal of Philosophical Logic, 2*(4), 458-508.

Lakoff, G., & Johnson, M. (1980). *Metaphors we live by.* Chicago and London: The University of Chicago Press.

Larcker, D. F., & Zakolyukina, A. A. (2010). Detecting deceptive discussions in conference calls (Working Paper No. 83). Stanford Graduate School of Business and the Rock Center for Corporate Governance. Retrieved from http://papers.ssrn.com/sol3/papers.cfm?abstract_id=1572705.

Laskin, A. V. (2009). A descriptive account of the investor relations profession. A national study. *The Journal of Business Communication, 46*(2), 208-233.

Lassen, I. (2006). Is the press release a genre? A study of form and content. *Discourse Studies, 8*(4), 503-530.

Lassota Bauman, M. (1999). The evolution of Internet genres. *Computers and Composition, 16*(2), 269-282.

Leech, G. (2005). Adding linguistic annotation. In M. Wynne (Ed.), *Developing linguistic corpora: A guide to good practice* (pp. 17-29). Oxford: Oxbow Books.

Linde, C. (1997). Evaluation as linguistic structure and social practice. In B-L. Gunnarsson, P. Linell, & B. Nordberg (Eds.), *The construction of professional discourse* (pp. 151-172). London: Longman.

Linell, P. (1998). *Approaching dialogue: Talk, interaction and contexts in dialogical perspectives.* Amsterdam/Philadelphia: John Benjamins.

Louhiala-Salminen, L. (1996). The business communication classroom vs. reality. What should we teach today? *English for Specific Purposes, 15*(1), 37-51.

Louhiala-Salminen, L. (2002). The fly's perspective: Discourse in the daily routine of a business manager. *English for Specific Purposes, 21*(2), 211-231.

Louhiala-Salminen, L., & Charles, M. (2006). English as the lingua franca of international business communication: Whose English? What English? In I. Fortanet-Gómez, J. C. Palmer-Silveira, & M. F. Ruiz-Garrido (Eds.), *English for intercultural and international business communication. Theory, research and teaching* (pp. 27-54). Bern: Peter Lang.

Louhiala-Salminen, L., Charles, M., & Kankaanranta, A. (2005). English as a lingua franca in Nordic corporate mergers: Two case companies. *English for Specific Purposes, 24*(4), 401-421.

Luzón, M. J., Campoy, M. C., Del Mar Sánchez, M., & Salazar, P. (2007). Spoken corpora: New perspectives in oral language use and teaching. In M. C. Campoy & M. J. Luzón (Eds.), *Spoken corpora in applied linguistics* (pp. 1-28). Bern: Peter Lang.

Lyons, J. (1977). *Semantics. vol. 1.* Cambridge: Cambridge University Press.

Lyons, J. (1995). *Linguistic semantics. An introduction.* Cambridge: Cambridge University Press.

Maat, H. P. (2007). How promotional language in press releases is dealt with by journalists. Genre mixing or genre conflict? *The Journal of Business Communication, 44*(1), 59-95.

Malavasi, D. (2006). Annual reports: An analysis of lexical evaluation across sections. In M. Bondi & J. Bamford (Eds.), *Managing interaction in professional discourse: Intercultural and interdiscoursal perspectives*, (pp. 147-158). Rome: Officina Edizioni.

Marais, M. (2012). CEO rhetorical strategies for corporate social responsibility (CSR). *Society and Business Review, 7*(3), 223-243.

Marschan-Piekkari, R., Welch, D., & Welch, L. (1999). In the shadow: the impact of language on structure, power and communication in the multinational. *International Business Review, 8*(4), 421–440.

Marsh, D. (2003). The relevance and potential of content and language integrated learning (CLIL) for achieving MT + 2 in Europe. *ELC Information Bulletin 9.* Retrieved from http://www.celelc.org/archive/Information_Bulletins/index.html.

Marston, C. L. (1996). The organization of the investor relations function by large UK quoted companies. *Omega, 24*(4), 477-488.

Marston, C. (2004). *A survey of European investor relations.* Edinburgh: The Institute of Chartered Accountants of Scotland. Retrieved from http://icas.org.uk/.

Martin, J. R. (2000). Beyond exchange: Appraisal systems in English. In S. Hunston & G. Thompson (Eds.), *Evaluation in text: Authorial stance and the construction of discourse* (pp. 142-175). Oxford: Oxford University Press.

Martin. J. R., & White, P. R. R. (2005). *The language of evaluation. Appraisal in English.* Houndsmills, Basingstoke: Palgrave MacMillan.

Matsumoto, D.A., Roelofsen, E., & Pronk, M. (2006). *Managerial disclosure vs. analyst inquiry: an empirical investigation of the presentation and discussion portions of earnings-related conference calls* (Working paper). Retrieved from SSRN website: http://ssrn.com/abstract=943928.

Mauranen, A. (2001). Reflexive academic talk: Observations from MICASE. In R. C. Simpson & J. M. Swales (Eds.), *Corpus linguistics in North America. Selections from the 1999 symposium* (pp. 165-178). Ann Arbor, MI: The University of Michigan Press.

Mauranen, A. (2002). A good question: Expressing evaluation in academic speech. In G. Cortese & P. Riley (Eds.), *Domain-specific English: Textual practices across communities and classrooms* (pp. 115-140). Bern: Peter Lang.

McArthur, T. (Ed.) (1992). *The Oxford companion to the English language.* New York, NY: Oxford University Press.

McCarthy, M. J. (1998). *Spoken language and applied linguistics.* Cambridge: Cambridge University Press.

McCarthy, M. J. (2004). *Touchstone. From corpus to coursebook.* Cambridge: Cambridge University Press.

McCarthy, M. J., & Carter, R. A. (2004). 'There's millions of them': Hyperbole in everyday conversation. *Journal of Pragmatics, 36*(2), 149-184.

McCloskey, D. (1992). The rhetoric of finance. In M. Murray, P. Newman, & J. Eatwell (Eds.), *The new Palgrave dictionary of money and finance* (pp. 350–352). London: Macmillan Press.

McEnery, A., & Wilson, A. (1996). *Corpus linguistics.* Edinburgh: Edinburgh University Press.

McLaren Y., & Gurău, C. (2005). Characterising the genre of the corporate press release. *LSP and Professional Communication, 5*(1), 10-29.

McLaren-Hankin, Y. (2007). Conflicting representations in business media texts: The case of PowderJect Pharmaceuticals plc. *Journal of Pragmatics, 39*(6), 1088-1104.

Miller, C. R. (1984). Genre as social action. *Quarterly Journal of Speech, 70*(2), 151-167.

Miller, D. R. (2004). 'Truth, justice and the American way': The appraisal system of judgement in the U.S. House debate on the impeachment of the President, 1998. In P. Bayley, (Ed.), *Cross-cultural perspectives on parliamentary discourse* (pp. 271-300). Amsterdam & Philadelphia: John Benjamins.

Mitra, A., & Cohen, E. (1999). *Analyzing the web: Directions and challenges.* In S. Jones (Ed.), *Doing Internet research. Critical issues and methods for examining the net* (pp. 179-202). London: Sage.

Morley, J. (2004). The sting in the tail: Persuasion in English editorial discourse. In A. Partington, J. Morley, & L. Haarman (Eds.), *Corpora and discourse* (pp. 239-255). Bern: Peter Lang.

Munter, M. (2009). *Guide to managerial communication. Effective business writing and speaking* (8th ed.). Upper Saddle River, NJ: Prentice Hall.

Murphy, A. (2004). A hidden or unobserved presence? Impersonal evaluative structures in English and Italian and their wake. In A. Partington, J. Morley, & L. Haarman (Eds.), *Corpora and discourse* (pp. 205-220). Bern: Peter Lang.

Nickerson, C. (1999). The use of English in electronic mail in a multinational corporation. In F. Bargiela-Chiappini & C. Nickerson (Eds.), *Writing business: Genre, media and discourses* (pp. 35-56). Essex: Pearson Educational Limited.

Nickerson, C. (2005). English as a lingua franca in international business contexts. *English for Specific Purposes, 24*(4), 367-380.

Nickerson, C., & De Groot, E. (2005). Dear Shareholder, Dear Stockholder, Dear Stakeholder: The business letter genre in the Annual General Report. In P. Gillaerts & M. Gotti (Eds.), *Genre variation in business letters* (pp. 325-346). Bern: Peter Lang.

Ochs, E. (1979). Planned and unplanned discourse. In T. Givón (Ed.), *Syntax and semantics. Volume 12. Discourse and syntax* (pp. 51-80). New York, NY: Academic Press.

Palmer, F. (1979). *Modality and the English modals.* London/New York: Longman.

Palmer-Silveira, J. C., Ruiz-Garrido, M. F., & Fortanet-Gómez I. (2006). Introduction: Facing the future of intercultural and international business communication (IIBC), In I. Fortanet-Gómez, J.C. Palmer-Silveira, & M.F. Ruiz-Garrido (Eds.), *English for intercultural and international business communication. Theory, research and teaching* (pp. 9-24). Bern: Peter Lang.

Palmieri, R. (2008). Argumentative dialogues in mergers & acquisitions (M&As): Evidence from investors and analysts conference calls. *L'analisi Linguistica e Letteraria XVI*(2), 859-872.

Partington, A. (1998). *Patterns and meanings: Using corpora for language research and teaching.* Amsterdam/Philadelphia: John Benjamins.

Partington, A. (2003). *The linguistics of political argument. The spin-doctor and the wolf-pack at the White House.* London: Routledge.

Partington, A. (2004). Corpora and discourse, a most congruous beast. In A. Partington, J. Morley, & L. Haarman (Eds.), *Corpora and discourse* (pp. 11-20). Bern: Peter Lang.

Partington, A. (2007). Irony and reversal of evaluation. *Journal of Pragmatics, 39*(9), 1547-1569.

Pearson, J. (1998). *Terms in context.* Amsterdam/Philadelphia: John Benjamins.

Piotti, S. (2006). Relevance and reliability in economic and financial reporting: An analysis of CEOs' letters and Chairmen's Statements. In G. Del Lungo Camiciotti, M. Dossena, & B. Crawford Camiciottoli (Eds.), *Variation in business and economics discourse: Diachronic and generic perspectives* (pp. 115-125). Roma: Officina Edizioni.

Piotti, S. (2009). The rhetoric of financial and accounting reporting. A corpus-driven analysis of hedging in company annual reports. In D. Torretta, M. Dossena, & A. Sportelli (Eds.), *Proceedings of the 23rd*

AIA Conference Bari, 20-22 September 2007. Forms of migration, migrations of forms (pp. 290-302). Bari: Progedit.

Poncini, G. (2002). Investigating discourse at business meetings with multicultural participation. *IRAL, 40*(4), 345-373.

Poncini, G. (2004). *Discursive strategies in multicultural business meetings.* Bern: Peter Lang.

Poncini, G. (2007). Corporate podcasts and blogs: exploring the voices of emerging genres. In G. Garzone, G. Poncini, & P. Catenaccio (Eds.), *Multimodality in corporate communication* (pp. 147-166). Milan: FrancoAngeli.

Poncini, G., & Hiris, L. (2012). *CEO letters of securities brokerage firms in times of financial market distress* (Departmental Working Paper No. 2012-4). Retrieved from Department of Economics, Management and Quantitative Methods, University of Milan website: http://www.demm.unimi.it/ecm/home/ricerca.

Ponton, D. M. (2011). *For arguments' sake: Speaker evaluation in modern political discourse.* Newcastle: Cambridge Scholars Publishing.

Quirk, R., Greenbaum, S., Leech, G., & Svartvik, J. (1985*). A comprehensive grammar of the English language.* London/New York: Longman.

Radner, G. (2003, August 1). Web-based meetings as a strategic communications tool. *PR Week.* Retrieved from http://www.prweek.com/uk/.

Räisänen, C. (1999). *The conference forum as a system of genres.* Gothenberg: Acta Universitatis Gothoburgensis.

Ranger, G. (2007). Continuity and discontinuity in discourse. Notes on yet and still. In A. Celle & R. Huart (Eds.), *Connectives as discourse landmarks* (pp. 177-194). Amsterdam/Philadelphia: John Benjamins.

Rayson, P. (2008). From key words to key semantic domains. *International Journal of Corpus Linguistics, 13*(4), 519-549.

Reinsch, N. L., & Turner, J. W. (2006). Ari, U R There? Reorienting business communication for a technological era. *Journal of Business and Technical Communication, 20*(3), 339-356.

Roelofsen, E. (2010). *The role of analyst conference calls in capital markets* (Doctoral Dissertation, Erasmus University, The Netherlands). Retrieved from http://repub.eur.nl/dissertations.

Rogan, R. G., & Simmons, G. A. (1984). Teleconferencing. *Journal of Extension, 22*(5). Retrieved from http://www.joe.org/journal-archive.php

Rogers, P. (2000). CEO presentations in conjunction with earnings announcements: Extending the construct of organizational genre through competing values profiling and user-needs analysis. *Management Communication Quarterly, 13*(3), 426-485.

Rogerson-Revell, P. (2007). Using English for international business: A European case study. *English for Specific Purposes 26*(2), 103-120.

Roos, E. (1987, August 16-21). *The vocabulary of the language of business and economics.* Paper presented at the 8th Annual Meeting of the International Association of Applied Linguistics, Sydney, Australia. (Eric Document Reproduction Service No. ED302081)

Ruiz-Garrido, M. F. (2001). Formats of a business report: A practical case in the classroom. In J.C. Palmer, S. Posteguillo, & I. Fortanet-Gómez (Eds.), *Discourse analysis and terminology in language for specific purposes* (pp. 185-194). Castelló: Publicacions de la Universitat Jaume I.

Ruiz-Garrido, M. F., Fortanet-Gómez, I., & Palmer-Silveira, J. C. (2006, August 29 –September 2). *Introducing British and Spanish companies to investors: Building the corporate image through the chairman's statement.* Paper presented at the ESSE-8 Conference, London, UK.

Ruiz-Garrido, M. F., Palmer-Silveira, J. C., & Fortanet-Gómez, I., (2005). Discursive strategies in annual reports: The role of visuals. In A-M. Bülow-Møller (Ed.), *Proceedings of the Association for Business Communication 7th European Conference, Copenhagen, Denmark.* Retrieved from http://www.businesscommunication.org/conventions/.

Ruiz-Garrido, M. F., & Ruiz-Madrid, M. N. (2011) Corporate identity in the blogosphere: The case of executive weblogs. In V.K. Bhatia & P. Evangelisti Allori, (Eds.), *Discourse and identity in the professions. Legal, corporate and institutional citizenship* (pp. 103-126). Bern: Peter Lang.

Rutherford, B. A. (2005). Genre analysis of corporate annual report narratives. A Corpus-linguistics based approach. *Journal of Business Communication, 42*(4), 349-378.

Ryan T. M., & Jacobs C. A. (2005). *Using investor relations to maximize equity valuation.* Hoboken, NJ: Wiley.

Saatchi, E. (2007). The discourse of voluntary disclosures in quarterly conference calls: Implications for investor relations. In M. Bait & M.C. Paganoni (Eds.), *Discourse and identity in specialized communication. Conference proceedings* (pp. 100-103). Milano: Lubrina Editore.

Scollon, R. (2000). Generic variability in news stories in Chinese and English: A contrastive discourse study of five days' newspapers. *Journal of Pragmatics, 32*(6), 761-791.

Scollon, R., & Scollon, S. W. (2001). *Intercultural communication* (2nd ed.). Oxford: Blackwell.

Scott, M. (2008). *WordSmith tools version 5.0.* Liverpool: Lexical Analysis Software.

Seidlhofer, B. (2000). Mind the gap: English as mother tongue vs. English as a lingua franca. *Vienna English Working Papers 9*(1), 51-69. Retrieved from http://anglistik.univie.ac.at/research/views/.

Sheehan, B. (2005). Europe switches to US-style disclosure rules. *Global Finance, 19*(3), 18-19.

Shortis, T. (2001). *The Language of ICT*. London: Routledge.

Sinclair, J. Mc. (1991). *Corpus, concordance and collocation*. Oxford: Oxford University Press.

Sinclair, J. Mc. (2001). Preface. In M. Ghadessy & A. Henry (Eds.), *Small corpus studies and ELT: Theory and practice* (pp. vii-xv). Amsterdam/Philadelphia: John Benjamins.

Skinner, D. J. (2003). Should firms disclose everything to everybody? A discussion of 'Open versus closed conference calls: the determinants and effects of broadening access to disclosure'. *Journal of Accounting and Economics, 34*(1-3), 181-187.

Skulstad, A. S. (1996). Rhetorical organization of chairmen's statements. *International Journal of Applied Linguistics, 6*(1), 43-62.

Sleurs, K. & Jacobs, G. (2005). Beyond preformulation: An ethnographic perspective on press releases. *Journal of Pragmatics, 37*(8), 1251-1273.

Sokół, M. (2011, October 6-8). *Attitudinal positioning on a business e-forum: Towards the new standards of (im)politeness?*. Paper presented at Int-Eval: International workshop on the evaluative function of language: Evaluation across text types and cultures, Madrid, Spain.

Steen, G. (1999). Genres of discourse and the definition of literature. *Discourse Processes, 28*(2), 109-120.

Strobbe, I., & Jacobs, G. (2005). E-releases: A view from linguistic pragmatics. *Public Relations Review, 31*(2), 289-291.

Stubbs, M. (1983). *Discourse analysis*. Oxford: Blackwell.

Stubbs, M. (2007). An example of frequent English phraseology: Distributions, structures and functions. In R. Facchinetti (Ed.), *Corpus linguistics, 25 years on* (pp. 89-106). Amsterdam/New York: Rodopi.

Svennevig, J. (2011). Leadership style in managers' feedback in meetings. In J. Angouri & M. Marra (Eds.), *Constructing identities at work* (pp. 17-39). London: Palgrave.

Swales, J. M. (1990). *Genre analysis. English in academic and research settings*. Cambridge: Cambridge University Press.

Swales, J. M. (1998). *Other floors, other voices. A textography of a small university building*. Mahwah, NJ: Lawrence Erlbaum.

Swales, J. M. (2004). *Research genres. Explorations and applications*. Cambridge: Cambridge University Press.

Taboada, M. (2006). Discourse markers as signals (or not) of rhetorical relations. *Journal of Pragmatics, 38*(4), 567-592.

Tannen, D. (1993). Introduction, In *Framing in discourse*, D. Tannen (Ed.), 3-13. Oxford: Oxford University Press.

Tarca, A., (2004). International Convergence of Accounting Practices: Choosing between IAS and US GAAP, *Journal of International Financial Management and Accounting, 15*(1), 60-91.

Tasker, S. C. (1998a). Technology company conference calls: A small sample study. *Journal of Financial Statement Analysis, 4*(1), 6-14.

Tasker, S. C. (1998b). Bridging the information gap: Quarterly conference calls as a medium for voluntary disclosure. *Review of Accounting Studies, 3*(1-2), 137–167.

Tench, R. (2003). Public relations writing - a genre-based model. *Corporate Communications: An International Journal, 8*(2), 139-146.

Thibault, P. J. (2000). The multimodal transcription of a television advertisement: Theory and practice. In A. Baldry (Ed.), *Multimodality and multimediality in the distance learning age* (pp. 311-385). Campobasso: Palladino Editore.

Thomas, J. (1997). Discourse in the marketplace: The making of meaning in annual reports. *The Journal of Business Communication, 34*(1), 47-66.

Thompson, G. & Hunston, S. (2000). Evaluation: An introduction. In S. Hunston & G. Thompson (Eds.), *Evaluation in text: Authorial stance and the construction of discourse* (pp. 1-27). Oxford: Oxford University Press.

Thompson, T., & Alba-Juez, L. (Eds.) (forthcoming) *Evaluation in context*. Amsterdam/Philadelphia: John Benjamins.

Tognini-Bonelli, E. (2001). *Corpus linguistics at work*. Amsterdam/Philadelphia: John Benjamins.

Toulmin, S. (1958). *The uses of argument*. Cambridge: Cambridge University Press.

Trosborg, A. (2000). The inaugural address. In A. Trosborg (Ed.), *Analysing professional genres* (pp. 121-144). Amsterdam/Philadelphia: John Benjamins.

Trosborg, A., & Flyvholm Jørgensen, P. E. (Eds.). (2005). *Business discourse. Texts and contexts*. Bern: Peter Lang.

van Dijk, T. (1977). Pragmatic macro-structures in discourse and cognition. In M. de Mey, R. Pinxten, M. Poriau, & F. Vandamme (Eds.), *The cognitive viewpoint. Communication and cognition. CC 77* (pp. 99-113). Ghent: University of Ghent. Retrieved from http://www.discourses.org/download/articles/.

van Dijk, T. (1990). The future of the field. Discourse analysis in the 1990s. *Text, 10*(1/2), 133-156.

van Dijk, T. 1996. Discourse, power and access. In C. R. Caldas-Coulthard & M. Coulthard (Eds.), *Texts and readings in critical discourse analysis* (pp. 84-104). London: Routledge.

van Dijk, T. (1997). The study of discourse. In T. van Dijk (Ed.), *Discourse as structure and process. Discourse studies: A multidisciplinary introduction. Volume 1* (pp. 1-34). London: Sage.

van Eemeren F. H., Grootendorst R., & Snoeck Henkemans, F. (1996). *Fundamentals of argumentation theory: A handbook of historical backgrounds and contemporary developments.* Mahwah, NJ: Lawrence Erlbaum.

van Mulken, M., & van der Meer, W. (2005). Are you being served? A genre analysis of American and Dutch company replies to customer inquiries. *English for Specific Purposes, 24*(1), 93-109.

Vance, S. C. (1983). *Corporate leadership: boards, directors, and strategy.* New York, NY: McGraw-Hill.

Vandermeeren, S. (1999). English as a lingua franca in written corporate communication: Findings from a European survey. In F. Bargiela-Chiappini & C. Nickerson (Eds.), *Writing business: Genre, media and discourses* (pp. 273-291). Essex: Pearson Educational Limited.

Vergaro, C. (2008). Concessive constructions in English business letter discourse. *Text & Talk, 28*(1), 97-118.

Warren, M. (2004). //□ so what have YOU been WORKing on REcently//: Compiling a specialized corpus of spoken business English. In U. Connor & T. A. Upton (Eds.), *Discourse in the professions. Perspectives from corpus linguistics* (pp. 115–40). Amsterdam/Philadelphia: John Benjamins.

Williams, C. C. (2008). Towards a taxonomy of corporate reporting strategies. *The Journal of Business Communication, 45*(3), 232-264.

Wynne, M. (2004, December 9-12). *Annotation of linguistic corpora: Some basic principles.* Paper presented at the Workshop on Tagging, Bergamo, Italy.

Yeung, L. (2007). In search of commonalities: Some linguistic and rhetorical features of business reports as a genre. *English for Specific Purposes, 26*(2), 156-179.

Zhao, J. J. & Alexander, M. W. (2004). The impact of business communication education on students' short- and long-term performances. *Business Communication Quarterly, 67*(1), 24-40.

Zhu, Y. (2000). Structural moves reflected in English and Chinese sales letters. *Discourse Studies, 2*(4), 473-496.

Zhu, Y. (2005). *Written communication across cultures.* Amsterdam/Phildelphia: John Benjamins.

Appendix 1: Keyness scores in the EP corpus

	Semantic domain	Tag code	Keyness score
1.	Money and pay	I1.1	3872.04
2.	Unmatched	Z99	3129.90
3.	Quantities	N5	2365.65
4.	Cause&Effect/Connection	A2.2	2280.21
5.	Size: Big	N3.2+	1821.02
6.	Business: Generally	I2.1	1754.15
7.	Numbers	N1	1654.89
8.	Business: Selling	I2.2	1586.41
9.	Expected	X2.6+	1483.81
10.	Money: Cost and price	I1.3	1132.58
11.	Tough/strong	S1.2.5+	1071.76
12.	Money generally	I1	961.99
13.	Money: Debts	I1.2	900.01
14.	Government	G1.1	756.91
15.	Time: Beginning	T2++	611.03
16.	Comparing: Similar/different	A6.1	607.13
17.	Inclusion	A1.8+	588.25
18.	Information technology and computing	Y2	538.46
19.	Helping	S8+	538.11
20.	Quantities: many/much	N5++	536.46
21.	Important	A11.1+	524.49
22.	Linear order	N4	524.20
23.	Long, tall and wide	N3.7++	514.68
24.	Grammatical bin	Z5	459.79
25.	Reciprocal	S1.1.2+	406.49
26.	Change	A2.1+	401.36
27.	Drama, the theatre and show business	K4	400.90
28.	Measurement: Distance	N3.3	396.81
29.	Measurement: Speed	N3.8	385.69
30.	Time: Period	T1.3	343.58
31.	Quantities: many/much	N5+	338.00
32.	Measurement: Volume	N3.4	331.98
33.	Quantities: little	N5-	296.71
34.	Deciding	X6	267.07
35.	Other proper names	Z3	266.06
36.	Degree: Maximizers	A13.2	254.44
37.	Success	X9.2+	244.49
38.	Degree: Approximators	A13.4	216.06
39.	Attentive	X5.1+	212.68
40.	Time: Ending	T2-	211.10
41.	In power	S7.1+	209.91
42.	No obligation or necessity	S6-	185.24

	Semantic domain	Tag code	Keyness score
43.	Objects generally	O2	162.57
44.	Degree	A13	150.16
45.	Measurement: Length & height	N3.7	148.04
46.	Speech acts	Q2.2	142.41
47.	Danger	A15-	142.32
48.	Open; Finding; Showing	A10+	142.27
49.	Comparing: Varied	A6.3+	129.52
50.	Science and technology in general	Y1	128.35
51.	Power, organizing	S7.1	126.68
52.	Unseen	X3.4-	122.97
53.	Useful	A1.5.2+	117.25
54.	Quantities: little	N5---	117.07
55.	Getting and giving: possession	A9	113.01
56.	Part	N5.1-	107.35
57.	Competitive	S7.3+	106.24
58.	Time: New and young	T3-	105.90
59.	Time: Old, new and young; age	T3	100.06
60.	Belonging to a group	S5+	90.85
61.	Interested/excited/energetic	X5.2+	82.83
62.	Evaluation: Good	A5.1++	82.64
63.	Time: Past	T1.1.1	79.28
64.	Content	E4.2+	74.70
65.	Comparing: Similar	A6.1+	74.22
66.	Light	W2	72.66
67.	Giving	A9-	71.98
68.	Industry	I4	70.30
69.	Exclusion	A1.8-	68.92
70.	Time: Beginning	T2+	68.54
71.	Knowledge	X2.2	66.51
72.	Geographical terms	W3	63.32
73.	Comparing: Usual	A6.2+	62.34
74.	Time: Early	T4+	59.76
75.	Participation	S1.1.3	58.13
76.	Measurement	N3	56.13
77.	Polite	S1.2.4+	52.85
78.	Farming & Horticulture	F4	52.20
79.	Long, tall and wide	N3.7+	51.63
80.	Sound: Quiet	X3.2-	51.55
81.	Long, tall and wide	N3.7+++	51.09
82.	Mathematics	N2	50.38
83.	Important	A11.1+++	50.05
84.	Useless	A1.5.2-	48.66
85.	Paper documents and writing	Q1.2	45.25
86.	Healthy	B2+	44.28
87.	Informal/Friendly	S1.2.1+	44.16

	Semantic domain	Tag code	Keyness score
88.	Exceed; waste	N5.2+	43.10
89.	Medicines and medical treatment	B3	42.34
90.	No constraint	A1.7-	42.30
91.	Personality traits	S1.2	39.50
92.	Cheap	I1.3-	39.13
93.	Investigate, examine, test, search	X2.4	38.99
94.	Participating	S1.1.3+	38.71
95.	Measurement: Size	N3.2	38.64
96.	Tough/strong	S1.2.5++	37.35
97.	Measurement: General	N3.1	37.06
98.	Quantities: little	N5--	35.98
99.	Telecommunications	Q1.3	35.88
100.	Mental actions and processes	X2	34.15

Note: Tag codes followed by plus (+) or minus (-) signs indicates positive or negative values associated with the meanings, which can be further intensified by repeating two or three signs.

Appendix 2: Keyness scores in the ER corpus

	Semantic domain	Tag code	Keyness score
1.	Money and pay	I1.1	2181.65
2.	Quantities	N5	1427.22
3.	Numbers	N1	1397.64
4.	Business: Generally	I2.1	1365.02
5.	Comparing: Similar/different	A6.1	1248.61
6.	Unmatched	Z99	1132.62
7.	Business: Selling	I2.2	1079.13
8.	Cause&Effect/Connection	A2.2	998.84
9.	Money: Cost and price	I1.3	933.16
10.	Money: Debts	I1.2	918.82
11.	Expected	X2.6+	675.68
12.	Long, tall and wide	N3.7++	355.77
13.	Money generally	I1	349.80
14.	Reciprocal	S1.1.2+	318.45
15.	Inclusion	A1.8+	316.17
16.	Degree: Maximizers	A13.2	310.19
17.	Size: Big	N3.2+	300.72
18.	Quantities: many/much	N5+	290.09
19.	Information technology and computing	Y2	267.93
20.	Time: Period	T1.3	258.17
21.	Other proper names	Z3	246.24
22.	Linear order	N4	218.49
23.	Quantities: little	N5-	216.12
24.	Government	G1.1	165.29
25.	Tough/strong	S1.2.5+	143.62
26.	Getting and giving; possession	A9	136.28
27.	Deciding	X6	123.59
28.	Change	A2.1+	118.20
29.	Measurement: Volume	N3.4	117.15
30.	Power, organizing	S7.1	112.05
31.	No obligation or necessity	S6-	106.81
32.	Exclusion	A1.8-	88.60
33.	Objects generally	O2	84.13
34.	Being	A3	81.75
35.	Danger	A15-	67.12
36.	Science and technology in general	Y1	54.48
37.	Paper documents and writing	Q1.2	52.50
38.	Electricity and electrical equipment	O3	51.86
39.	Degree	A13	50.31
40.	Unused	A1.5.1-	48.28
41.	Time: Beginning	T2++	42.94
42.	Light	W2	37.73

	Semantic domain	Tag code	Keyness score
43.	Mental actions and processes	X2	37.48
44.	Informal/Friendly	S1.2.1+	37.22
45.	Measurement: General	N3.1	33.84
46.	Drama, the theatre and show business	K4	33.32
47.	Comparing: Similar	A6.1+++	33.04
48.	Competitive	S7.3+	31.47
49.	Telecommunications	Q1.3	30.77
50.	Tough/strong	S1.2.5++	27.71
51.	Quantities: many/much	N5++	27.50
52.	Concrete/Abstract	A1.6	26.04
53.	Measurement: Speed	N3.8	25.76
54.	Alive	L1+	25.68
55.	Success	X9.2+	23.03
56.	Measurement	N3	22.43
57.	Useless	A1.5.2-	20.98
58.	Helping	S8+	20.03
59.	Time: Ending	T2-	19.24
60.	Able/intelligent	X9.1+	18.13
61.	The Media: TV, Radio and Cinema	Q4.3	17.53
62.	Comparing: Similar	A6.1+	16.32
63.	Useful	A1.5.2+	15.12
64.	Deserving	S1.1.4+	14.82
65.	Degree: Approximators	A13.4	13.67
66.	Evaluation: Good	A5.1++	13.42
67.	Cheap	I1.3-	12.74
68.	Part	N5.1-	12.62
69.	Comparing: Usual	A6.2+	12.32
70.	Quantities: little	N5---	12.05
71.	Evaluation: Good/bad	A5.1	11.94
72.	General actions / making	A1.1.1	10.61
73.	Industry	I4	10.07
74.	Substances and materials: Gas	O1.3	9.83
75.	Time: Old, new and young; age	T3	9.35
76.	Money:	I1.1+++	8.72
77.	Knowledge	X2.2	8.01
78.	Evaluation: Good	A5.1+	7.40
79.	Suitability	A1.2	6.71

Note: Tag codes followed by plus (+) or minus (-) signs indicates positive or negative values associated with the meanings, which can be further intensified by repeating two or three signs.

Appendix 3: Evaluative adjectives in the EP Corpus

Adjective type	N	+/-	Adjective type	N	+/-
1. strong	275	+	43. substantial	7	+
2. good	110	+	44. talented	7	+
3. significant	65	+/-	45. well-positioned	7	+
4. great	57	+	46. comfortable	6	+
5. important	52	+	47. exceptional	6	+
6. key	43	+	48. growing	6	+
7. double-digit	39	+	49. huge	6	+
8. improved	38	+	50. notable	6	+
9. positive	37	+	51. robust	6	+
10. solid	37	+	52. attractive	5	+
11. competitive	28	+/-	53. big	5	+
12. pleased	28	+	54. comprehensive	5	+
13. successful	28	+	55. efficient	5	+
14. flat	25	-	56. extraordinary	5	+
15. favourable	24	+	57. meaningful	5	+
16. major	21	+	58. modest	5	-
17. terrific	18	+	59. remarkable	5	+
18. confident	17	+	60. tremendous	5	+
19. difficult	17	-	61. accelerated	4	+
20. top-line	17	+	62. aggressive	4	+
21. new	15	+	63. disciplined	4	+
22. happy	14	+	64. dramatic	4	+
23. healthy	14	+	65. encouraging	4	+
24. unique	14	+	66. fair	4	+
25. effective	12	+	67. hard	4	-
26. broad-based	11	+	68. high	4	+
27. critical	10	+/-	69. innovative	4	+
28. excellent	10	+	70. interesting	4	+
29. improving	10	+	71. powerful	4	+
30. negative	10	-	72. reasonable	4	+
31. conservative	9	+/-	73. relevant	4	+
32. exciting	9	+	74. amazing	3	+
33. outstanding	9	+	75. bad	3	-
34. premium	9	+	76. blue-chip	3	+
35. consistent	8	+	77. considerable	3	+
36. leading	8	+	78. disappointed	3	-
37. nice	8	+	79. dynamic	3	+
38. tough	8	-	80. excited	3	+
39. accelerating	7	+	81. fortunate	3	+
40. optimistic	7	+	82. heavy	3	-
41. promising	7	+	83. impressive	3	+
42. profitable	7	+	84. popular	3	+

Adjective type	N	+/-	Adjective type	N	+/-
85. proud	3	+	128. ambitious	1	+
86. record	3	+	129. anaemic	1	-
87. relentless	3	+	130. artificial	1	-
88. respectable	3	+	131. average	1	+
89. slow	3	-	132. beneficial	1	+
90. superior	3	+	133. bold	1	+
91. valuable	3	+	134. bright	1	+
92. value-added	3	+	135. broken	1	-
93. weak	3	-	136. bullish	1	+
94. adverse	2	-	137. busy	1	+
95. appropriate	2	+	138. compelling	1	+
96. careful	2	+	139. complex	1	-
97. challenging	2	-	140. customer-centric	1	+
98. convenient	2	+	141. deteriorating	1	+
99. creative	2	+	142. diligent	1	+
100. deep	2	+	143. disproportionate	1	-
101. dependable	2	+	144. double-barrelled	1	+
102. disappointing	2	-	145. easy-to-use	1	+
103. distinctive	2	+	146. elusive	1	-
104. enhanced	2	+	147. enormous	1	+
105. feature-rich	2	+	148. enthusiastic	1	+
106. flexible	2	+	149. fantastic	1	-
107. high-growth	2	+	150. far-flung	1	-
108. minimal	2	-	151. favourite	1	+
109. phenomenal	2	+	152. first-line	1	+
110. pristine	2	+	153. fitting	1	+
111. prudent	2	+	154. formidable	1	+
112. red-hot	2	+	155. fresh	1	+
113. rich	2	+	156. glad	1	+
114. risky	2	-	157. gratifying	1	+
115. satisfied	2	+	158. hard-working	1	+
116. theatrical	2	+	159. heartening	1	+
117. underperforming	2	-	160. high-margin	1	+
118. unfortunate	2	-	161. high-performance	1	+
119. unmatched	2	+	162. high-quality	1	+
120. useful	2	+	163. hopeful	1	+
121. vigorous	2	+	164. inappropriate	1	-
122. well-controlled	2	+	165. inadequate	1	-
123. accurate	1	+	166. keen	1	+
124. across-the-board	1	+	167. lingering	1	-
125. admired	1	+	168. low-margin	1	-
126. advantageous	1	+	169. lucky	1	+
127. affordable	1	+	170. market-leading	1	+

Adjective type	N	+/-	Adjective type	N	+/-
171. misleading	1	-	189. spectacular	1	+
172. muted	1	-	190. stellar	1	+
173. nimble	1	+	191. top-performing	1	+
174. noteworthy	1	+	192. troubled	1	-
175. noticeable	1	+	193. unacceptable	1	-
176. novel	1	+	194. uncertain	1	-
177. opportunistic	1	-	195. unexpected	1	+
178. passionate	1	+	196. unified	1	+
179. patchy	1	-	197. unparalleled	1	+
180. pleasing	1	+	198. unprecedented	1	+
181. poor	1	-	199. value-destroying	1	-
182. proactive	1	+	200. vibrant	1	+
183. record-volume	1	+	201. weakening	1	+
184. resilient	1	+	202. well-capitalized	1	+
185. satisfying	1	+	203. well-defined	1	+
186. simple	1	+	204. well-established	1	+
187. sluggish	1	-	205. world-class	1	+
188. sound	1	+			

Appendix 4: Evaluative adjectives in the ER Corpus

Adjective type	N	+/-	Adjective type	N	+/-
1. strong	89	+	43. inaccurate	2	-
2. double-digit	23	+	44. industry-leading	2	+
3. key	18	+	45. notable	2	+
4. positive	16	+	46. record-breaking	2	+
5. significant	14	+	47. powerful	2	+
6. competitive	15	+/-	48. proven	2	+
7. important	12	+	49. proud	2	+
8. favourable	11	+	50. record	2	+
9. successful	10	+	51. superior	2	+
10. premium	9	+	52. top-end	2	+
11. broad-based	7	+	53. tremendous	2	+
12. excellent	7	+	54. admired	1	+
13. negative	7	-	55. accelerated	1	+
14. outstanding	7	+	56. acceptable	1	+
15. pleased	7	+	57. ambitious	1	+
16. leading	6	+	58. award-winning	1	+
17. robust	5	+	59. best-in-class	1	+
18. weak	5	-	60. business-building	1	+
19. new	4	+	61. clear	1	+
20. improving	4	+	62. compelling	1	+
21. improved	4	+	63. confident	1	+
22. difficult	4	-	64. creative	1	+
23. efficient	4	+	65. customer-centric	1	+
24. flat	4	-	66. disappointed	1	-
25. growing	4	+	67. disciplined	1	+
26. healthy	4	+	68. distinctive	1	+
27. innovative	4	+	69. dynamic	1	+
28. major	4	+	70. eminent	1	+
29. reasonable	4	+	71. encouraging	1	+
30. top-line	4	+	72. enhanced	1	+
31. unique	4	+	73. ever-growing	1	+
32. adverse	3	-	74. exciting	1	+
33. consistent	3	+	75. extraordinary	1	+
34. exceptional	3	+	76. faltering	1	-
35. high-quality	3	+	77. fast-growing	1	+
36. solid	3	+	78. first-in-class	1	+
37. aggressive	2	+	79. flexible	1	+
38. depressed	2	+	80. great	1	+
39. effective	2	+	81. huge	1	+
40. good	2	+	82. high	1	+
41. high-performance	2	+	83. higher-value	1	+
42. impressive	2	+	84. incorrect	1	-

Adjective type	N	+/-	Adjective type	N	+/-
85. innovation-driven	1	+	98. top	1	+
86. lean	1	+	99. trusted	1	+
87. market-making	1	+	100. unmatched	1	+
88. meaningful	1	+	101. unparalleled	1	+
89. noteworthy	1	+	102. unprecedented	1	+
90. optimistic	1	+	103. unprofitable	1	-
91. passionate	1	+	104. useful	1	+
92. poor	1	-	105. value-added	1	+
93. promising	1	+	106. well-capitalized	1	+
94. profitable	1	+	107. well-controlled	1	+
95. revenue-producing	1	+	108. well-positioned	1	+
96. relentless	1	+	109. winning	1	+
97. terrific	1	+	110. whopping	1	+

Name Index

Subject index

Printed in the United States
By Bookmasters